"Public Misinformation About NCLB Ends on Page One of This Book"

We are engaged in an unprecedented war against children, teachers and schools. The contributors to *Saving Our Schools* are among the few who understand and know what to do about it. *Saving Our Schools* exposes what may be the most damaging action taken by the Bush administration: The war against children, teachers, and schools. Bush's No Child Left Behind is not merely "underfunded." It is all wrong. It has the potential of ruining millions of lives and destroying the public education system. The contributors to *Saving Our Schools* are among the most distinguished scholars in the field of education in the world. They understand the dangers and know what to do about them.

—*Stephen Krashen, Professor Emeritus*
Rossier School of Education
University of Southern California

Public misinformation about NCLB ends on page one of this book. This informative and incisive account of how NCLB came to be and why we must get rid of it will be the cornerstone of the resistance.

—*Susan Ohanian, author of*
Why is Corporate America Bashing Our Public Schools?

Saving Our Schools

THE CASE FOR PUBLIC EDUCATION
SAYING NO TO "NO CHILD LEFT BEHIND"

Edited by
KEN GOODMAN
PATRICK SHANNON
YETTA GOODMAN
ROGER RAPOPORT

RDR Books
Berkeley, California

Saving Our Schools

RDR Books
2415 Woolsey
Berkeley, CA 94705
Phone: (510) 595-0595
Fax: (510) 238-0300
E-mail: read@rdrbooks.com
Website: www.rdrbooks.com
www.savingourschools.info

ISBN 1-57143-102-0

Library of Congress Control Number 2003094931

Associate Editors: Wendy Goodman and Joanna Pearlman
Book Design and Typography: Richard Harris
Cartoonist: Georgia Hedrick
Indexer: Nora Harris

Distributed in Canada by
Jaguar Book Group c/o Fraser Direct, 100 Armstrong Way,
Georgetown, ON L7G 5S4

Distributed in the United Kingdom and Europe by
Roundhouse Publishing, Ltd., Millstone, Limers Lane, Northam,
North Deven EX39 2RG, United Kingdom

Printed in Canada by Transcontinental Printing

for Shirley Rapoport
who often said the world is getting
curiouser and curiouser

ACKNOWLEDGMENTS

There are so many to thank who were involved in bringing together this book.

We want to thank Wendy Goodman, who helped with editing, rewriting and other important tasks. Thanks also to the authors in this book and other diligent professionals who sent us information, news items and stories. Thanks particularly to brave professionals who have had the courage to speak out and expose that the emperor is wearing no clothes. We name a few: Gerald Bracy, Steve Krashen, Susan Ohanian, Joanne Yatvin, Margaret Moustafa, Ardith Cole, Georgia Hedrick, Gerry Coles, Brian Cambourne, Susan Harmon, Sharon Zinke, Bess Altwerger, Elaine Garan, Denny Taylor, Steve Strauss, Alfie Kohn, Regie Routman. To those we missed, please forgive our oversight.

We owe the most to the classroom teachers and schools administrators who are fighting every day for their students and for decency in education. And thanks to the growing number of journalists who have seen through the slick PR and are reporting the truth.

CONTENTS

SECTION ONE

No Child Left Behind:
A Reality Check

SAVE OUR NEIGHBORHOOD SCHOOLS

Ken and Yetta Goodman

Around the world there are countries trying to achieve what America has created, a universal system of free, public, inclusive, neighborhood elementary and secondary schools. These public schools are counted on to provide the education needed for full productive participation in a democratic society.

In developing countries children of the well-to-do are sent to private schools of varying quality. The public schools, meagerly funded by local and/or central governments, serve the children of the working poor. Large numbers of even poorer rural and urban children either don't go to school or leave within the first few years.

We have worked extensively with schools and education authorities in Central and South America and the Caribbean, in Asia, Oceania, and Africa. We have seen heroic teachers working with 40 to 50 children in tiny, dimly lit rooms. And we've met taxicab teachers in private and public schools in Mexico, Peru, and Argentina. They teach in the morning in one school and jump in a taxi to teach in another school in the afternoon. Every economic downturn drives families of even moderate means to take their children out of costly private schools. Even in developed nations only a fraction of those who make it through secondary schools go on to some form of higher education.

In this book we want to help parents understand that the NCLB (No Child Left Behind) law does not have good intentions. It is a major part of a sustained campaign being waged to transform American education from one in which almost all our children and young people attend common, neighborhood schools administered by an elected community board of concerned citizens governed by state laws, into a system which more closely matches that of third-world nations. This book is about an all-out attack on our neighborhood schools which is disguised under the slogan "No Child Left Behind." This is not a professional or academic book. It is aimed at informing parents, teachers and all those in American society who care deeply about the future of our nation's young people that there is an imminent danger to our democratic education system.

The law established under NCLB is very complex and hundreds of pages long, with its enforcement and implementation changing from day to day. Congressman John Boehner, who was a major force behind passage of NCLB, admits there is "confusion that exists in virtually every state about what the real facts of the law are." According to *Education Week,* Boehner told a panel sponsored by the Business Roundtable, made up of CEOs from most of the country's largest corporations, that some of the confusion was "propagated by critics who doubted the law's merits from the beginning."

Former Arizona Education Superintendent Lisa Graham Keegan told the same panel, "Among people from all over the political spectrum you'd be hard pressed to find people who say this is not the right thing to do." Keegan now heads the Education Leaders Council, a major group formed to support NCLB when the Council of Chief State School Officers began to express concerns. (Cavanagh, *Education Week,* 12/10/03)

The editors of this book have doubted the law's merits and its intentions long before the bill became law. We believe it is not the right thing to do. As the law is being implemented we see American public education being transformed into a third-world system. And we are not alone in our concern. The terrible intentions of this law are becoming clearer to many educators, parents, and even a few politicians. Each day there are new horror stories of the impact on teachers and students. A recent study by Public Agenda found a third of school superintendents believing that NCLB is an attack on public education. Another 20 percent said it was politically motivated.

If there is confusion about the law, it is being created deliberately by the faceless—often nameless—bureaucrats interpreting the law. They make different demands on different states and say different things to different audiences.

According to a survey conducted by Results for America, most parents tend to think NCLB has good intentions, but a third see the law as punishing failure instead of rewarding success. Some 25 percent of parents view it as limiting learning and only 46 percent associate the law with improving learning. Almost 75 percent would not support withholding funds from their neighborhood school for failing NCLB.

The campaign to bring this third-world market system to American education is already taking its toll. An increasing number of our teens are being pushed out of school into a dismal job market. It's no accident that a provision of NCLB requires districts to provide the Department of Defense with names and addresses of dropouts so that they may be recruited into the armed forces to become expendable in Iraq, Afghanistan, and elsewhere.

This conservative movement to privatize American education presents itself as a reform movement. Its leaders understand that they cannot directly attack the ideals of public education. They understand the American belief that public education is the great leveler in a democracy that gives every child the possibility of growing up to be president even if his father doesn't have friends on the Supreme Court. They know how much the neighborhood schools mean to each community.

So instead of a frontal attack on public education they relentlessly spread the view that our public schools are a failed social experiment. They exaggerate the weaknesses of the system into a crisis and divert attention away from the real school problems that stem from unequal and inadequate funding. They manufacture a crisis, claiming schools are so bad they can't even teach kids to read and write, add and subtract. They impose by state and federal laws and edicts a system of unachievable test-based goals so that even the most successful schools will appear to be failing. And they impose punishments on the schools, and the pupils and hard-working teachers in them, for the failures. NCLB is a very negative and highly punitive law.

The movement cleverly also has taken over the slogans and phrases that were used by those who fought to achieve universal access to free local schools. Leave No Child Behind itself is stolen from the movement to serve the neglected children living below the poverty line in this, the richest country in the world. Differential success rates of our ethnic minorities and rural and urban poor children are a real problem in American schools. But NCLB gives them a one-size-fits-all curriculum and methodology and a law which punishes the schools if any one group falls below an increasingly unobtainable test score. They all, under NCLB, have an equal right to fail. If a group of severely handicapped children or non-English speakers or a particular minority falls short on one test then the whole district is a failure. If even 5 percent of any one group of parents choose to keep their children home at test time to spare their children the pressures of the test then the school fails.

In this book we will lay out the ways in which NCLB is already damaging every neighborhood school. One provision of the law is not confusing; it clearly states that schools failing to make acceptable yearly progress will be closed, taken over by the state, or turned over to private business. Who would want to do this and why? Certainly not people whose goal is to improve our public schools. Rather, they are those who have shown in many aspects of American life that they have the money and power to use the institutions of democracy to subvert democracy for their own self-interests.

Reference

Sean Cavanaugh, *Education Week,* 12/10/03 pp. 22, 25

TEN ALARMING FACTS ABOUT *NO CHILD LEFT BEHIND*
Ken Goodman

1. The long- and short-term effects of NCLB will be devastating for American education.
NCLB is a law that is both negative and punitive: It is designed to force conformity and achievement of impossible goals through a system of punishments of local and state authorities, administrators, teachers, students, and parents.

During a period that extends from the present until 2014, NCLB will close or drastically change most neighborhood schools.

Schools labeled as failing (needing improvement) would be closed, taken over by the state, or turned over to private, profit-making interests. Could the state take over the schools? That's already happened in several big cities—Detroit, Philadelphia, and Newark among them—and no problems have been solved. The ultimate goal is to privatize American education. Will American parents let their neighborhood schools be taken over?

2. NCLB is the climax of a long-term campaign to privatize American education.
Within a neoconservative movement to privatize all aspects of American society, a heavily funded and well-organized campaign has created NCLB to discredit and destroy public eduation. There is no other explanation for the impossible, destructive conditions it imposes on the nation's schools. Its enactment and implementation will wipe out a century and a half of progress in which American public education has evolved, with all its deficiencies, into the most successful and inclusive system the world had yet known.

3. NCLB is driving both students and teachers out of education.
There is already a dramatic increase in dropouts and pushouts from high schools due to increased high-stakes testing, the nar-

rowing of curriculum, and controls on how and what teachers may teach. Many students are being driven out of high schools because they can't pass the tests, get promoted from ninth to tenth grade, or earn a diploma. And many schools and school systems are hiding the data on the dropouts. This dropout rate will increase as NCLB reaches more punitive phases. In fact, the law sets up conditions in which it is to the advantage of schools to drive out low achievers. NCLB requirements lead to massive numbers of failing learners. Research shows that children who fail a grade are very likely to drop out of school before finishing high school.

Many highly professional teachers are leaving teaching or taking early retirement to escape being required to conform to aspects of the law that they believe make it impossible to teach in the best interests of their pupils. In addition, the requirements of academic majors in each subject they teach is causing certified secondary teachers to lose their certification and be labeled as unqualified. This is a particular problem in middle schools and in smaller rural secondary schools where teachers often are needed to teach multiple subjects.

4. NCLB centralizes control of every aspect of American education, including policy, methodology, curriculum, choice of text books, evaluation, and staffing, shifting power from local districts and states to a Washington bureaucracy.
NCLB establishes a national curriculum and methodology in reading and mathematics and other fields. Faceless bureaucrats in Washington are telling local schools which commercial programs and tests they may and may not use. The teaching of reading and math has been turned upside down with tired discredited methods and curricula being anointed as scientific, while the most effective methods and materials based on the years of research in and out of classrooms are marginalized and forbidden. This has produced an opposition to NCLB composed of states rights conservatives and academic freedom liberals.

5. NCLB defines what is and isn't science.

Through a series of panels, laws, and mandates, the federal government has defined what is science so narrowly, that 95 percent of scientific study in education has been swept aside as unscientific and decades of research has been wiped off federal websites such as ERIC. NCLB and the antecedent Reading Excellence Act contain literally hundreds of redundant references in the law requiring conformity to that definition of scientific research as a condition of participation. Text materials, teacher certification, tutors, staff development, and curriculum must all be based on the same narrowly defined "science."

6. NCLB makes scores on mandatory tests the basis of all major decision-making in the schools, including which schools are failing.

The fight for civil rights of the 1960s made it illegal to segregate pupils by race, color, sex, or creed. Testing remains the only legal way to discriminate in American schools. NCLB mandates testing of all pupils for all schools in all states from 3rd to 8th grade and at least once in high school.

NCLB requires schools to be labeled as "needing improvement" (that is, failing) on the basis of "adequate yearly progress" on test scores by each subgroup, including handicapped and second-language learners. If one subgroup falls short in any one area, the school fails. Furthermore, the bar is raised until in a dozen years *all* pupils in *all* subgroups must reach the "proficient level," a term now used to describe the score achieved by less than 20 percent of all pupils. The National School Boards Association says that within a dozen years the vast majority of all schools in all states will be labeled as failing to improve.

Parents are denied their rights to withhold their children from testing; 95 percent of each subgroup must be tested or the whole school is labeled failing.

Costs to states and LEAs are far more than they receive.

Several states, districts, and schools have opted not to participate. All states are also mandated to participate in the National Assessment of Educational Progress. Test companies and test-scoring companies are making huge profits while providing bad tests and error-ridden scoring. Many states are desperately trying to massage the testing and their passing criteria to produce a higher success rate. But the feds have already put states on notice that they won't let them ease the passing criteria and the law will eventually require achievements no state can finesse.

7. The law requires busing of pupils, at district expense, from non-improved schools to other schools.

Receiving schools must accept "NCLBs" regardless of space. In New York, a middle school has been forced to add more than 200 "NCLB" kids to their already full classrooms. Where is there a nearby school in Alaska or rural Arizona to send kids to? Even Mayor Daley in Chicago is complaining about moving hundreds of kids from failing school to failing school.

8. NCLB controls who may teach and not teach and how they will be certified.

Federal standards are established which take control away from states in the name of assuring qualified teachers in every class. Requirements for teacher aides effectively close down heritage language programs. In Florida and certain other states, the state has called in teaching certificates and refused to reissue them. On the other hand, the federal government has funded a national board, which will certify people who can pass tests without any professional education.

9. Enforcement of NCLB employs blacklists.

A list of who and what conforms and does not conform to NCLB criteria is being used to blacklist people, institutions, methods, and materials. Mostly this is accomplished without direct confrontation through "scientific criteria" in funding reviews, but it is widely known whose names disqualify a proposal and which terms and programs are to be avoided. Conflicts of interest are the rule rather than the exception.

For example, to be a literacy trainer in Arizona, one must pass a test where newly-banned terms such as miscue analysis and print awareness are wrong answers.

10. NCLB, the federal law, is unconstitutional, as it violates the Constitution, which leaves education to the states.
NCLB affects every child and teacher in every school in the United States. It establishes a national curriculum and methodology in reading and math.

What's the Problem for which
No Child Left Behind is the Solution?
Patrick Shannon

The No Child Left Behind (NCLB) law of 2002 has been described as the most important education legislation since the passage of the Elementary and Secondary Education Act of 1965. Actually, the two are the same law. NCLB is simply the latest iteration in the continuing seven-year cycle of reauthorization of the Elementary and Secondary Education Act (ESEA). All of the tenets of NCLB (but not the way it is being implemented) were proposed or enacted in prior reauthorizations. Why then does NCLB warrant such notoriety? In a word, fear.

NCLB passed four months after the terrorist attacks called 9/11, a period when federal legislators found ways to overcome previous partisan concerns. The product of years of political negotiation, NCLB includes something to placate the concerns of all political groups, while not necessarily guaranteeing that any group will be completely satisfied with the process or outcome. For example, NCLB proposes to bring all American students to proficiency on world-class state standards by 2014 (a neoliberal position) with state governments in control (a conservative goal), teachers accountable for student learning (a neoconservative aim), and more funding for minority and poor students who lacked opportunities to succeed (a liberal objective).

Driving the political negotiations surrounding the bill was the notion that America is increasingly vulnerable to global economic, political, and social threats. Advocates of NCLB reasoned that our vulnerabilities could be at least partially assuaged by preparing the nation's children and youth for the intellectual, moral, and technological challenges now at hand. Without a greatly improved educational system, they argued, America would fail to continue to lead the world economically, and Americans' standards of living would sharply decline. The horror of 9/11 gave the crisis rhetoric greater gravity.

What Is the ESEA?

While scrambling for votes during the 1960 presidential election, John Kennedy positioned Richard Nixon as being against public schooling and schoolteachers. To support his claim, Kennedy hit on Nixon's tie-breaking vote in the Senate against federal funding for teachers' salaries. Fearing federal interference in a state's right (a Republican standard), Nixon declined to defend his decision. Kennedy's election ploy (and Nixon's mistake) made education a Democrats' issue (for the next 40 years), and arguably, won the 1960 election. Kennedy, and then Lyndon Johnson, repaid teachers by making education a priority during their administrations, proposing greater federal funding for public schooling.

The Kennedy/Johnson educational policies were rooted in economic conditions as well as political issues. Michael Harrington's book *The Other America* found 50 million Americans living in poverty, sharply contradicting the widely held assumption that America was an affluent society for all. The Civil Rights Act of 1964 culminated 10 years of systematic struggle for racial justice in America and extended federal regulation over state laws in areas of voting rights, public accommodations, education, and employment. Title VI of the Civil Rights Act gave the government the right to withhold funds from any state or school district that would not comply with these federal regulations. In his 1964 State of the Union Address, Johnson declared, "This Administration, here and now, declares unconditional war on poverty in America."

Much of the rationale for the eventual ESEA, the educational campaign in the "war," was captured in Walter Heller's essay "The Problem of Poverty in America" within the 1964 Annual Report of the Council of Economic Advisors.

"Equality of opportunity is the American dream, and universal education our noblest pledge to realize it. But for children of the poor, education is a handicap race; many are too ill-motivated at home to learn at school. It is difficult for children to find and follow avenues leading out of poverty in environments where education is deprecated and hope is smothered. This often means that schooling must start on a preschool basis and include a broad range of more intensive services and schools must play a larger role in the development of poor youngsters if they are to have, in fact, equal opportunity."

Heller's statement implied a dramatic shift in the official understanding of the causes of American poverty. Rather than blaming individuals' faulty choices or flawed moral characters for poverty, the Kennedy/Johnson officials recognized that the poor and minority groups were systematically denied equal opportunity to develop themselves to their fullest potential. Accordingly, the War on Poverty would need to be fought on many fronts: hunger (food stamps), income maintenance (welfare), housing (public projects), employment (Job Corps), health care (Medicaid and Medicare), justice (legal aid), participation (Community Action Programs) as well as education (Head Start and Title I of ESEA). The operating metaphor for the war was that all the poor needed was a hand up (not a handout) to compete for the American Dream.

The Head Start preschool educational program for 4- and 5-year-olds began as part of the Economic Opportunity Act of 1964. EOA's centerpiece was the authorization of community-action programs to encourage local communities to develop their own plans to overcome poverty. According to historian Lawrence Cremin, "the single most popular creation of community action across the country was Head Start, a collection of programs for preschool children from poor families." The first Head Start programs were introduced during the summer of 1965 with 500,000 children participating. Although programs varied in philosophy and application among sites, they all sought to prepare poor children to enter school on equal footing with children from more affluent backgrounds. All Head Start curricula included strategies and activities that researchers had determined were undertaken as a matter of course in middle-class homes (e.g., parents reading to children, conversing with them, and playing games with them). In 1967, the Head Start program added a home component through Parent and Child Centers, which offered entire families strategies to overcome these academic deficiencies.

Some of the alternatives were academically focused on letters, counting, and speaking, while others were more concerned with social issues of play, nutrition and hygiene, and schedules. Academic advantages among programs as measured by standardized tests disappeared as Head Start graduates worked their ways through primary grades. However, all programs improved the nutrition and health of participants and maintained the academic advantage of this group over nonparticipating poor children. However successful, Head Start was and still is not funded sufficiently to accommodate more than half of the eligible American children.

Title I of ESEA was designed to provide additional academic support in reading and mathematics for poor students who were falling behind their peers. The federal government would pay for new teachers, supplies, and space in order to provide these additional services beyond regular classroom instruction. When the ESEA bill was signed into law on April 11, 1965, Commissioner of Education Francis Keppel declared, "Archimedes told us many centuries ago: 'Give me a lever long enough and a fulcrum strong enough and I can move the world.' Today at last, we have a prospect of a lever long enough and supported strongly enough to do something for our children of poverty. The lever is education, and the fulcrum is federal assistance." According to the law, states and local school districts would develop and implement the provisions of Title I, while the federal government monitored their efforts from afar.

Because officials from the Bureau of the Budget doubted the competence of state and school district bureaucracies, they provided detailed guidelines regulating how the federal dollars could and could not be spent and conducted periodic audits to see that guidelines were followed. Moreover, because some liberal senators doubted some state and local officials' commitment to equal opportunity of education for the poor, participating districts were required to test each Title I student annually and make the scores known to parents. As New York Senator Robert F. Kennedy put it, "We really ought to have some evaluation in there, and some measurement as to whether any good is happening." Professor Ernest House of the University of Illinois argues that Kennedy's concern for accountability is the beginning of standardized testing as the official measure of successful programs in public schools.

The motives for the ESEA and the War on Poverty were not completely altruistic. Competing world powers pointed at America's poor and minority populations as demonstrations that American economic and political systems could not serve as effective models for other nations. Generals in the War on Poverty feared that America could not compete for the allegiance of developing and industrialized nations, if it systematically denied the pursuit of happiness to any segment of the population. One of the original rationales of ESEA, then, was to demonstrate to the world that the government could provide equal opportunities for poor children to learn at school. It was generally assumed that higher achievement in school would translate directly into greater opportunities in life after school.

Architects of Title I believed that given sufficient support teachers would develop appropriate curricula and instructional strategies to raise the academic achievement of newly well-fed, economically secure, warmly housed, healthy students whose parents were now gainfully employed. Teachers were expected only to coordinate their efforts with other civil workers in order to conquer poverty in America. In 1964, federal officials, school personnel, and citizens seemed optimistic that this war on poverty could be won. However, Johnson's, and then Nixon's, war on the Vietnamese soon quelled this optimism and diverted funding away from this domestic front.

Since that time, the official assumptions about the causes of poverty have become more conservative, suggesting that individuals, and not circumstances and opportunities, are responsible for America's wealth and poverty. Reagan administrators argued that governmental social programs actually created a culture of dependency among the poor and minorities, ensuring that they will never learn to fit productively into the American economy. Then Secretary of Education William Bennett called for a return to a moral curriculum that would reclaim this underclass. Later, Harvard psychologist Richard Herrnstein and Heritage Foundation researcher Charles Murray reported that the poor and minorities lacked sufficient intelligence to take advantage of the opportunities available to them in order to work their ways toward economic success. They wrote, "For many people, there is nothing they can learn that will repay the cost of the teaching."

Over the last 30 years, succeeding administrations have employed conservative solutions to social problems, significantly reducing federal programs to provide equal opportunities for the poor and minorities. Federal officials have redefined and curtailed assistance to combat hunger, insufficient income, poor housing, unemployment, and poor health care, leaving teachers as the only public workers charged with the responsibility to help Americans (regardless of their backgrounds) prepare themselves morally and mentally to compete in the world.

What Is NCLB?

During the 2000 campaign for president, George W. Bush presented himself as a "Compassionate Conservative" who was responsible for the "Texas Miracle." "I call my philosophy and approach compassionate conservatism. It is compassionate to actively help our fellow citizens in need. It is conservative to insist on responsibility and results. And with this hopeful approach, we will make a real difference in people's lives." As evidence of the effectiveness of his philosophy, Bush pointed toward his record as Governor of Texas and the improving state statistics representing decreasing dropout rates and increasing academic test scores in reading and math. He considered this Texas miracle compassionate because it required schools to help all Texas students and conservative because it held teachers and principals responsible for students' learning and required that students pass state exams to progress through the grades and to graduate from high school.

If elected, Bush argued, he would bring a similar system and comparable results to the nation's schools. His opponent, Vice President Albert Gore, had no record in education beyond his failed attempt to move President Clinton's second reauthorization of ESEA through the Senate. With his proposal to perform a national educational miracle, Bush stole education from the Democrats as a campaign issue.

Upon being appointed president by the Supreme Court during a voting fraud investigation in Florida, Bush began the policy process which led to the reauthorization of the ESEA under the title "No Child Left Behind" (NCLB). According to the law, schools would continue to receive federal funds only if all students make adequate yearly progress toward proficiency on state-designed world-class academic standards as measured by state tests. Moreover, school district officials must publish the results of these tests separated into demographic categories: economic class, race, ableness, and English language learners.

If any group fails to make adequate yearly progress (as determined by state officials), then the school is designated as "in need of improvement." Repeated failures bring penalties against schools: parents are allowed choice among schools within the district with travel cost provided by the district, parents may choose private tutoring services at district cost, and, finally, the state can reconstitute the school, changing its curriculum, faculty, and administration, turning it over to private business, or closing it. All students regardless of category are to be proficient in reading and math on all tests by the second reauthorization of NCLB (2014). In return for participation in the federal program, states and schools are allowed greater discretion over how ESEA/No Child Left Behind funds are spent. These funds constitute about 8 percent of school budgets.

The basic tenets of NCLB are a collection of proposals from previous ESEA reauthorizations, and they have little to do with the Texas Miracle. First, the change in priorities from poor students to all students began in response to the "A Nation at Risk" report during the Reagan Administration. In the best Cold War language, that report charged that America's public schools were so inadequate that the country was in danger economically. It claimed that American workers were less productive than international counterparts because students could not compete academically with their international peers. Reagan officials, and later President Clinton's authorities, called for high academic standards, high-stakes testing, and parental choice.

Differing political philosophies between Reagan and Clinton meant differing spins on these proposals. Reagan couched his educational proposals in the conservative language of parental prerogatives, prayer in schools, and a return to traditional standards. Clinton argued a neoliberal position that traditional standards were inadequate to meet America's current challenges and that only a complete reorganization of schools would prepare students to keep the country strong in a global economy. Rather than Reagan's call for a return to past glories, Clinton sought high standards and high-stakes testing in order to prepare American youth for high-skill/high-wage jobs, which he claimed were awaiting all qualified graduates.

Within Clinton's proposals for the expected 1999 reauthorization of ESEA, state standards were set, state tests were written, a 10-year deadline for proficiency was proposed, reporting by categories would be required, annual yearly progress and the penalties were to follow in case of failure. Clinton included a block-grant system, which allowed state officials more control of federal education funding.

Bush invented none of the components of No Child Left Behind. He did, however, pattern its implementation after his Texas Miracle. The story of the miracle is based on Texas Department of Education figures which suggested that a tight centralized system of curricular and instructional standardization enforced by strict school, teacher, and student accountability procedures drastically lowered school dropout rates, improved student scores on state tests of reading and math, and narrowed the achievement gap between poor and middle- and upper-class students and minority and white students. The tight system required teachers to follow scripted lessons in commercially prepared guidebooks during reading and math instruction, to devote twice the instructional time to these subjects (limiting science, social studies, and the arts in the elementary school curriculum), and to prepare students to take yearly state examinations. Teachers' and administrators' competencies were tested by paper and pencil examination. School funding and continued employment were contingent on Texas students' from second grade through high school improving their scores on state tests.

Bush appointed Rod Paige, the former Superintendent of the Houston City School District, as Secretary of Education, to replicate the Texas system on a national scale. Just as in Texas, the new NCLB single system relies heavily on the tight articulation of a small number of approved commercial instructional materials, curricula focused on state examinations in reading and math, and financial incentives. Federal officials must approve all state standards, state tests, and implementation procedures before federal funds are released to the state and channeled to school districts. The NCLB implementation plan is the Texas Miracle system magnified.

The problem with this design is that the Texas Miracle was/is a fantasy. Professor Walter Haney of Boston College, who conducted a detailed study of public education in Texas stated, "What is happening in Texas seems to me to be not just an illusion, but from an educational point of view an outright fraud." Rather than the reported low dropout rate, 30 percent of Texas ninth-grade students leave high school before graduation. For minority students, fewer than 50 percent of the ninth-graders ever receive a diploma. In order to achieve the Texas Miracle, high school administrators reclassified the adolescents who stopped attending high school as transient students because they could re-enroll in the future. Few make this choice, however. The Texas Miracle for high school completion is simply a rhetorical trick. Texas high school completion rates rank toward the bottom of the fifty states.

Education Trust, a private research group, reported that several states have adopted the Texas model when required by NCLB to publish high school dropout rates. According to Education Trust, "Many states seem to have taken advantage of the department's lax oversight to choose calculation methods that portray a rosier picture than external evidence suggests, adopting definitions and methodologies that significantly understate the problems that their schools and students are facing in high school graduation."

The Texas Miracle for test scores appears to be an illusion also. Students' increased scores on the Texas examinations have not translated into improved scores on national tests. Texas students still rank in the lower third among states for measures of achievement. Texas student scores on the National Assessment of Educational Progress remain stable for reading, and have actually declined for math. Poor and minority student achievement scores are no closer to those of their white, more well-to-do peers on these tests. Student scores on the Standard Achievement Tests (SAT), which most college-bound students take, were unchanged during the 1990s, and a full 30 percent of Texas students continued to begin their college studies needing remedial programs.

Rather than a miracle caused by a model system, students' increased scores on Texas tests were achieved by setting low state standards in reading and math, and then teaching to those standards according to the format of the tests to follow each spring. The results present the illusion that students are learning without much substantial improvement in student knowledge or skills. What Haney calls the Texas "chains and whips" accountability system has not accomplished a miracle at all—nor has it approached its public goals. Without empirical or historical evidence that it works, why, then, does it serve as the model for NCLB?

"The Damn Law is Ludicrous?"
By the 2004 Presidential campaign, the original political consensus has crumbled around NCLB. Liberals lamented Bush's insufficient funding for the law. Massachusetts' Senator Edward Kennedy stated in a January 2004 press release, "President Bush thinks he is providing enough for schools. Parents, teachers, and I don't. When President Bush's inadequate education budget is debated in Congress, Democrats will fight for the resources originally promised to reform and improve schools. Funding only 65 percent of the No Child Left Behind Act, as President Bush would, in my book is a D-minus grade." Joel Packer of the National Education Association charged that Bush proposed cuts in NCLB funding during 2002 and 2003. Democratic presidential candidate John Kerry declared, "There is nothing in the No Child Left Behind Act that requires it to be implemented the way this

[Bush] administration is doing it." Clearly NCLB will not solve the problem of dramatic inequalities in school funding across income and racial lines.

Conservatives also seem increasingly unhappy with NCLB. Most hoped that the law would reemphasize state and local control of education within the national efforts to improve individuals' chances to lead good and productive lives. Yet, the restrictions of the law make public schooling a federal program to be funded and implemented by states and local communities. Several Republican-dominated state legislatures have challenged the single system implementation of NCLB. Utah, North Dakota, Indiana, Virginia, and Ohio have required cost/benefit studies of compliance with the federal law's testing and reporting requirements. Utah House Speaker Martin Stephens has been quoted as saying that he cannot recommend a national educational program to the citizens of Utah. "No Child Left Behind is a great rallying cry but, at the same time, not every student is going to meet the standards with a one-size-fits-all education. I cannot recommend to the people of Utah that we follow this federal program." The Republican-controlled Virginia House of Delegates passed a resolution unanimously calling on the U. S. Congress to exempt Virginia from the law. House Education Committee Chairman James H. Dillard II told the *Washington Post,* "The damn law is ludicrous."

Although some neoliberals may bristle that Bush's implementation system restricts local innovation, most recognize that NCLB opens public schools to market and business forces. Market principles require that any enterprise justify its funding by becoming more productive for less cost, continually remaking itself in order to maximize profits. Although schools have been encouraged to change for two decades, NCLB focuses public school's mission—to produce students who meet world-class standards—by tying its continued funding to its tightly defined productivity. As President Bush explained simply, "When the federal government spends tax dollars, we must insist on results."

Although success means that schools enjoy continued federal funding at decreasing rates, failure means that more and more of the public investment in education moves through schools toward private educational firms. As June Kronholz reported in the *Wall Street Journal,* businesses already recognize the new markets created by NCLB.

> Companies that sell to the schools—from test publishers to tutoring services to teacher-training outfits—say business is booming as troubled districts turn to them for help. There's a burgeoning sense of consumerism in public education as parents learn about the law and begin demanding services, says Jeffrey Cohen, president of Sylvan Education Solutions, a unit of closely-held Educate, Inc. His company says it expects to tutor 20,000 youngsters in struggling schools this year, with No Child Left Behind requiring schools to pick up the $40- to $80-an-hour-per-child tab.

In this public to private cash flow, the problem for which NCLB is the solution becomes most visible. How can the cost of public schooling be significantly reduced, while creating markets for new businesses? Lower costs for public institutions means lower taxes and smaller government, and new markets encourage business solutions to social problems. The irony of Mr. Cohen's statement, however, should not be lost in the glare of the identification of a real intent of NCLB. If schools were funded at even $40 per hour per student—the low end of tutoring—then a public school teacher with 25 students in her class (a lucky teacher in most school districts) would make over $1000 per hour.

University of Colorado Professor Robert Linn demonstrates that NCLB requirements and implementation system doom most schools to be failures. "The goals that NCLB sets for student achievement would be wonderful if they could be reached, but unfortunately, they are quite unrealistic, so much so, that they are apt to do more to demoralize educators than to inspire them." Therefore, a second problem for which NCLB is a solution is to demoralize and deskill public school teachers. This seems to be a purely political goal—getting even with the largest organized block of Democratic voters in the United States. As on many other issues, neoconservative advocates of NCLB have adopted and adapted the liberal rhetoric for increased funding for public schooling in order to hold teachers accountable that all students succeed at school. Teachers are to succeed, however, without the benefit of other social programs to ensure that all are fed, financially secure, and healthy. If Texas supplies the model for national social programs, the American children are headed for a tough time. Texas ranks at the bottom of the states in providing these types of support for children.

NCLB seeks to solve two problems—1. To reduce the costs of public schooling, and 2. To demoralize and deskill teachers in order to discredit the public schools in which they teach. Both are to be accomplished by enforcing a rigid system that combines unattainable goals with punitive measures for failure. This system reduces public schools to the equivalent of middlemen delivering tax dollars to private companies established to profit from children's schooling and opens the door to private schools to replace public schools. According to journalist Stephen Metcalf, this was the pattern in Texas when Bush was governor, and it is repeating itself nationally now that he is president. Educational publishers, particularly the big three—McGraw-Hill, Houghton Mifflin, and Harcourt Brace—are identified as Bush stocks on Wall Street, paying record dividends since 2000. NCLB makes a bull market for business, but a bear market for public schools.

Without the likelihood of success in a rigged system, NCLB will continuously erode public schools' social value over the next 14 years. With each school being classified as in need of improvement, public school teachers will lose more of their capacity to act collectively in order to continue and enlarge the public sphere of governmental responsibility. Remember public schools were once expected to fashion a common national culture and prepare young people to be reflective and critical citizens in our Republic. The result of NCLB is that education will become a private matter in which individuals choose their futures, rather than a public responsibility of all citizens to each citizen. Advocates of NCLB will shout that because each individual is afforded this private educational choice, all American children enjoy equal opportunity to pursue the American Dream. Yet, as the hoax of the "Texas Miracle" clearly demonstrated, NCLB sacrifices our dreams to achieve lower taxes, political advantage, and business profits. Unless significant changes are made in the tenets and system of NCLB, the next decade will be a sad end to the most ambitious American experiment—universal free public education.

THE FAULTY LOGIC OF NCLB

Patrick Shannon

No Child Left Behind does not trust teachers to teach and evaluate their students. Rather, the NCLB accountability system substitutes technology (scripted lessons and paper and pencil machine-scored tests) for teacher judgments on these matters. Although it is part of a century-long effort to discover the one best method to teach all children, this substitution obscures the human decisions behind the legislation and devalues the people involved in public education.

The search for the one best method would render the effects of schooling more predictable, enabling precise planning and allocation of resources within schools and eventually society. Calculating students' trajectories through their schooling is simply a precursor to charting their paths through later work and life. To work toward predictable schooling, NCLB designed what it considers to be a completely rational scheme:

1. States set goals for all students in all important subject areas and distribute those goals across grade levels.
2. Educational scientists discover through experimentation the optimal route to meeting those goals.
3. Educational businesses produce teacher-proof technology (i.e., textbooks with scripted teachers' manuals, workbooks, computer programs, tests, etc.) to map that route for teachers and students to follow.
4. States compose or acquire tests that will measure students' progress toward established goals.
5. Federal officials provide financial incentives for states to employ their scheme, for educational scientists to discover the optimal route, and for educational businesses to produce these commodities. And federal officials inflict penalties to states that do not follow their instructions.

NCLB legitimizes its scheme by relying on the social authority of science and business and the political authority of the federal government. Most of the accomplishments of the 20th century—our standard of living, our quality of life, and our position in the world—are attributed to science and industry aided by a not-always-steady hand of the federal government. Think about the physics and chemistry of transportation, and the jobs and benefits that accrued. Consider the biology, chemistry, and physics of medicine and the ways that our lives have been enriched.

In this context, NCLB's scheme for education appears to be a natural, and therefore, a prudent course of action. Of course, schools should have standards, use scientifically based methods, reduce human error, and test students objectively. Of course, the federal government should require a return for its investment in public education and should dissuade schools from developing alternatives to the one best method. Of course, technology and objectivity are the solutions to all social problems.

But as we have learned with transportation and medicine, science and business do not always account for all the consequences of discoveries and actions. The benefits come at personal and social costs, and human beings make the decisions about which discoveries are considered important and how they shall be allowed to influence our lives for better or worse. Think about the ozone layer and fossil fuels, the recent wars in Iraq, and the prices of health care. Neither the science nor the business is a natural occurrence. Rather, people create them with their heads, hands and hearts, and the government officials regulate them according to their ideas about what will improve and protect Americans' life, liberty, and pursuit of happiness.

The NCLB cannot escape the human essence of learning, teaching, and valuing regardless of how tightly it organizes our educational system. Each step in the NCLB scheme is based on people's beliefs and decisions about what should happen, why it should happen, and who may make it happen. The goals are set by select experts in the state departments of education or by groups of select experts in the subject areas or by select experts in an educational think tank or commercial enterprise. These small groups may consult larger groups to reach some consensus on the goals' viability, but agreement upon their value doesn't make the goals any less artificial (made by people).

State and federal authorities can't elevate the goals beyond human opinion simply by writing laws about them and enforcing them. Not only do people set the goals, they decide on how many goals should be met by whom and at what point in their education. The goals, the audience, and the sequence are human choices, subject to change with a change of the group in power or social priorities. For example while all the components of NCLB were in place or proposed before it became law, its organization and means of enforcement are unique to the Bush Administration.

The authors of NCLB don't value school personnel's judgments about student knowledge and learning or their creative interactions with children and youth. If this were not true, then teacher judgment would figure prominently in the NCLB accountability system. But it does not.

In fact, NCLB emphasizes technological solutions which limit teacher and administrator, and ultimately, even state input in schooling. For example, federal officials recommend scripted lessons which direct teachers' statements and actions as they lead students systematically through commercially-prepared materials toward standardized assessments of students' reading. The rationale for this recommendation is that the scripts enable teachers to be more efficient, less prone to error or bias, and uniform in their instructional efforts. The state standard tests afford objective evidence of reading progress, and the National Assessment of Educational Progress monitors state-level decisions. However, it is only the teacher and other school personnel who are being so directed. The rest of the people involved have much more freedom to make decisions and pass judgments that count.

The scripts, materials, and even tests are commercially prepared. They are subject to both scientific and market forces. The writers work according to their interpretations of parameters set by educational scientists who have systematically observed effective teachers (who apparently weren't working according to someone else's script at the time) and market analysts who determine what might sell. Although constrained, these writers, scientists, and business people are encouraged to be creative. It's only the teachers who must follow someone else's scripts, manage someone else's materials, and administer (but not score or interpret) someone else's tests.

Early results on NCLB's technological logic are not encouraging. Although about 60 percent of American schools are "making adequate progress," no scripted program has yet demonstrated that it will produce 100 percent student mastery of any state's standards. This conclusion should be alarming because if the scripts worked as planned, then mastery would already appear where the scripts have been in place for years. But no school following the scripts has attained that promised outcome. Even against such disturbing evidence, the NCLB presses its logic. The official NCLB responses to this failure are calls for more technology because: 1) teachers are not following the scripts precisely; 2) schools do not devote enough time to targeted subjects (instead, wasting time on non-tested subjects); and 3) some scripts are not sufficiently scientific.

According to NCLB criteria, 40 percent of American schools have been designated as in need of improvement. This result flies in the face of national survey results. More than 80 percent of Americans think their local schools are doing well, and over 90 percent believe that their schooling serves them well in their current jobs and does not limit their future employment prospects. These positive results cut across demographic lines with citizens in rich and poor neighborhoods backing their local schools and with only adult Hispanics acknowledging trouble with English literacy. However, self-reports based on everyday experiences carry little weight in the deliberations of NCLB. According to the federal government, teachers', students', even the public's opinions matter little in making decisions about the status of American schools and how they might be improved. Only students' results on standardized paper and pencil tests matter.

Yet, as the National Academy of Science reported, "The strength of a standardized reading test is not that it can provide a deep assessment of reading proficiency, but rather that it can provide a fairly reliable, partial assessment cheaply and quickly." In the logic of NCLB, these cheap and quick assessments provide the foundation for any decision concerning whether or not students know something of value and teachers teach effectively. Even when the test results conflict with the perceptions of all involved and the day-to-day performance-based assessments in classrooms, the NCLB considers the scores on paper and pencil, one-shot tests to be more credible. According to NCLB logic, the tests' scores cancel the value of the everyday judgments of the people involved. No one is expected to trust those people—not even the people themselves. Rather, everyone should believe in the illusion of the objectivity of the NCLB accountability scheme.

But should we believe in a scheme when it doesn't work and it leads us away from the legal and moral goal of integrated schools? NCLB logic punishes communities which strive to meet the national goal of racial and economic integration across America. Schools serving more ethnically, racially, and economically diverse populations are statistically more likely to be designated as in need of improvement than more homogeneous schools. (This is true even when they have similar and acceptable average scores.) Greater diversity means that the school must hit more target goals because NCLB requires test results to be reported for each demographic group. Even the casual gambler knows that more options increase the chances of failure. While NCLB federal officials acknowledge this statistical fact, they maintain that all schools must account for the learning of all children within the parameters of its scheme.

But the system and its logic do not work as planned. For all the talk of science and objectivity surrounding NCLB, there is no scientific evidence to demonstrate that any part of the scheme (state standards, optimal routes, technological solutions, paper and pencil knowledge tests, or federal mandates and punishments) will increase all students learning to proficiency in the future. Rather than avoiding subjectivity, the entire NCLB system boils down to the logic of some well-financed, self-serving groups who have the power to allocate resources according to their beliefs and values. This is not science; it is politics.

Although NCLB logic might look good on paper and may work in some schools: there is not clear evidence that it is needed or will work; it devalues the work and thoughts of all involved in schools and encourages us to mistrust them; it continues the cheap and quick, but not necessarily accurate, assessment of students' learning; and it precludes all alternatives in school reform.

Where's the logic in that?

ADEQUATE YEARLY PROGRESS?

Patrick Shannon

No Child Left Behind requires each state to develop an accountability system to ensure that every American student is proficient
on all state academic standards for reading, language arts, mathematics, and science. By 2014, every American student should
pass every state exam. NCLB appears to be that simple. In order
to monitor states' progress between now and then, each school
must report student test scores to parents, the state, and the federal government annually. All students must make adequate
yearly progress in order to demonstrate that their school is working. If they do not, the state will punish the school: close it, reconstitute the schools of failing students by replacing unsuccessful
administrators, curricula, and teachers, or turn the schools over to
a for-profit private company. Despite the rhetorical appeal of adequate yearly progress, it is a dubious concept which only schools
are expected to apply.

Adequate Yearly Progress as a Concept

The following is a text quote from State Plans, Section 1111:

> (B) ADEQUATE YEARLY PROGRESS—Each State plan shall
> demonstrate what constitutes adequate yearly progress of the
> State, and all public elementary schools, secondary schools,
> and local educational agencies in the State, toward enabling
> all public elementary schools and secondary schools to meet
> the State's student academic achievement standards, while
> working toward the goal of narrowing the achievement gaps
> in the State, local education agencies, and schools.
> (C) DEFINITION—Adequate yearly progress shall be defined
> by the State in a manner that applies the same high standards
> of academic achievement to all students in the State; is statis-

tically valid and reliable; results in continuous and substantial academic improvement for all students; measures the progress of public schools; includes separate measurable annual objectives for continuous and substantial improvement for the achievement of all public school students including economically disadvantaged students, students from major racial and ethnic groups, students with disabilities, and students with limited English proficiency. (Section 1111. State Plans)

Adequate Yearly Progress (AYP) is the engine of the NCLB's commitment to school improvement. It requires steady, annual improvement in students' test scores until the final goal is accomplished. Previous reauthorizations of the federal Elementary and Secondary School Act called for world-class academic standards, but left states to determine the rates at which those standards would be met. Moreover, earlier iterations of the act did not require schools to account separately for the achievement of all groups of students. Historically, children of the poor, minority groups, English-language learners as well as children with diagnosed learning disabilities, have scored lower on standardized tests than their white, able, English speaking, middle- and upper-middle-class peers.

Although FairTest and others interpret these gaps as evidence of cultural bias in the logic of testing and the test themselves, the authors of NCLB assume that the tests measure valued learning and that lower teacher expectations, poor instruction, and lack of teacher and student effort cause the gaps. Most teachers recognize that the gaps in achievement mirror the inequalities in society and question the lack of coordination among social services for children. All children do not enter school on equal footing; they are not supported equally as they grow; and they do not have the same opportunities available to them upon graduation. Some of these teachers question the fairness of requiring all students to meet the same standards at the same pace when no other aspect of their lives treats them equally. Regardless of these concerns, AYP mandates that schools separate the achievement levels for each group and make those levels known to the public.

From its inception in 1993, AYP has been a controversial issue. Governors pressured first the Clinton, and then, the Bush administrations to weaken AYP requirements in order to allow schools time to invent new ways of teaching needed to completely close the achievement gaps. Although many schools have made progress in narrowing the gaps, none show complete proficiency for each group in all tested areas at each level. That's right, *none!*

The final wording for AYP reflects a political compromise to accommodate conservatives' concerns against a national education system and governors' belief that AYP would yield between 20 and 80 percent school failure. The compromise gives states control of academic standards, test design, and definitions of expected progress, and offers some statistical wiggle room for schools which do not reach proficiency targets, but do make progress. Consequently, fifty different sets of standards, fifty different tests, and fifty different definitions of progress have been implemented across the country. To monitor this variability, however, the federal government named the subjects to be tested, established a testing schedule, and required states to submit their plans for approval. These acts demonstrate federal impatience with states' previous efforts toward school improvement over the last two decades. The fact that all states, the District of Columbia, and Puerto Rico were reported to have met the January 31, 2003 deadline to submit plans suggests that states do take NCLB seriously.

Approximating AYP

AYP assumes that learning is predictable, regular, and easily mapped across grade levels. In this way, AYP treats learning as a mechanical process of assembly, attaching new knowledge to old at a regular pace. Like the instructions for assembly of furniture, state standards provide the blueprint of the proficient learner, the inventory of necessary parts, and the general order in which they will be learned. These plans promise a standard unit, which is the academic equivalent of a couch in one style, fabric, and size. Unlike those instructions, however, the standards, tests, and predictions do not and cannot specify exact steps that will ensure the correct assembly of all proficient learners. Neither federal nor states' officials have empirical evidence or practical experience which demonstrates how teachers can help all students to become proficient on all the arbitrary, but world-class, standards in the designated subjects during a specified time frame. This is new territory.

AYP's assumption that learning is mechanical and NCLB's insistence that all schools accomplish what no school has done before create considerable problems for states and schools. How do they reinvent the American educational system at a prescribed rate without increased funds for innovations? Moreover, how do they avoid casting minorities, the poor, English language learners and learning disabled students as drains on school resources. If each group does not reach those targets, then the schools must offer them budget-busting alternative programs, while suffering the embarrassment of being labeled as "in need of improvement" despite everyone's best effort. According to Professor Robert Linn of the University of Colorado, "The goals that NCLB sets for student achievement would be wonderful if they could be reached, but, unfortunately, they are quite unrealistic, so much so, that they are apt to do more to demoralize educators than to inspire them."

States have been creative to position themselves to avoid the appearance of failure. For example, Colorado changed the scoring system of its state tests. Previously, students' scores were partitioned in four levels ranging from failure to mastery. By collapsing its middle two categories into one level and calling it proficient, Colorado nearly doubled its success rate without making any instructional changes. Massachusetts has converted its four levels into a 100-point index, awarding 100 points for proficiency or advanced levels and assigning fewer points depending on how far students' scores differ from the proficiency cutoff score. This partial credit system for approaching proficiency raises group average scores. Ohio took still another tack. Instead of adequate yearly progress, it will measure students on a three-year cycle. This move buys Ohio schools more time to find a success formula.

Such statistical maneuvering might seem devious to some. Indeed, most contributors to Brookings Institution's 2003 report on NCLB believe that such variability among states renders the NCLB accountability system moot. Without a clear model of success, however, states' plans might better be understood as attempts to play by the AYP rules when they recognize that AYP's assumption about learning does not make practical sense. At some level, each of these examples shows a lack of faith in AYP, if not NCLB. Colorado and Massachusetts play with the concept of proficiency, seeking the appearance of initial success or steady progress without much effort. Ohio challenges the assumption of linear learning, trading early relief for later panic.

In its own wy each example doubts the possibility of measured predictable learning, and all appear to be hoping that Congress will modify AYP or the timetable for universal proficiency on world-class standards. None reject the notion that given time and opportunity, all learners can make meaningful progress while in school.

AYP as a Tool

If the Bush administration and Congress are enthusiastic about adequate yearly progress as an engine for institutional and social improvement, then they might consider including it in their legislation on access to food, housing, health care, and income security for all groups of American children. Such a commitment would require states to establish world-class standards for children to be well-fed, well-housed, well-cared-for, and secure in this standard of living. According to the Children's Defense Fund, the United States does not rank high among industrialized nations on these basic needs. Under AYP, each year the states would report on their success in feeding more children who were hungry, finding good permanent shelter for more homeless and dangerously housed children, providing health care for all children who need it, and raising more children out of poverty to a livable secure income.

Until the President and Congress are willing to make these commitments, AYP will remain a tool to discredit schools and to demoralize educators, not a tool to provide equal opportunity for all American children.

NCLB's Pedagogy of the Absurd
Ken Goodman

We have reached a point where truth is marginalized and absurdity is treated as truth. I am convinced that this period will be known in the not-too-distant future as the period of the Pedagogy of the Absurd. Several years ago I began publishing a monthly Absurdity award on the internet. Since then, examples have become increasingly absurd, centered around the absurd claim that the science of reading can be reduced to a small number of phonics-based commercial reading programs and assessments.

Enforcement of the Absurd

The campaign to impose the Pedagogy of the Absurd on American teachers and students is leaving no aspect of education untouched. Foremost is the way the Reading First aspect of NCLB law is being enforced. Bush's Secretary of Education Rod Paige sums up this enforcement:

> In response to the new federal law (NCLB), nearly every state has recognized the absolute reality that thousands of schools are in need of improvement and that millions of children are not learning. In fact, some states have taken a bold stand and listed hundreds, even thousands, of schools "in need of improvement" in an effort to get those schools the help they need . . .
>
> Simply put, a school identified as "in need of improvement" is a school that the president, the leaders in Congress, and the American people believe can improve.
>
> Unfortunately, some states have lowered the bar of expectations to hide the low performance of their schools. And a few others are discussing how they can ratchet down their standards in order to remove schools from their

lists of low performers. Sadly, a small number of persons have suggested reducing standards for defining "proficiency" in order to artificially present the facts.

The good news is that we know what works: scientifically proven methods, aligned standards, assessments, and instruction, school and district leadership focused on student learning, accountability for results, and highly qualified teachers will improve achievement and bring success. By providing for alternative routes to the classroom, our schools can supplement their faculties with engineers and programmers, nurses and researchers, soldiers and scientists, who are willing to step forward to help children learn. Although some critics continue to attack aspects of the law and some naysayers have even convinced themselves that some children are too poor or too different-looking to learn, we know they are wrong.

In the beginning it was sufficient to blame and blacklist whole language, a popular pedagogy among innovative teachers and teacher educators. But having declared the reading wars of phonics vs. whole language over, it became necessary to marginalize the entire educational establishment.

Susan Neuman was the chief enforcer as Assistant Secretary of Education up until her abrupt departure from federal office. She bragged that NCLB "if implemented the right way, will put an end to creative and experimental teaching methods in the nation's classrooms. It will stifle, and hopefully it will kill (them), Our children are not laboratory rats."

The law also imposes controls on who may teach and how they may be educated, preservice and in-service. And it will eventually close schools that fail to meet the standards of the new "science."

Extension of the Absurd

Also underway is the overhauling of National Assessment of Educational Progress (NAEP) to bring it in line with the new "science." The governing board hired a contractor to develop the NAEP reading framework that will serve as a guide for the test, beginning with its 2007 administration. For the first time, the contract does not require that future tests yield results comparable with those on previous NAEP exams. That flexibility could lead to changes that reflect what are deemed "scientifically proven" teaching methods, which are being promoted under the No Child Left Behind Act of 2001. Those methods, which have been guiding many state and local reading policies and practices in recent years, have led to a greater emphasis on the teaching of phonics and other basic skills in the early grades.

There is an effort to revise the NAEP reading tests. Going a step further, the president himself has a new initiative to bring the blessing of scientific reading to Latin America. Three centers will be set up in the Caribbean, Central America, and South America to further this missionary effort. (Today the U.S.; tomorrow the world; "science" uber allus.)

Also underway is a panel to do unto Bilingual Education what was done unto reading, that is bring it in line with the new "science" Tim Shanahan (another member of the NRP) has a leading role in that effort. Robert Holland and Don Soifer of the Lexington Institute describe it this way:

> One of the boldest education reforms advanced by No Child Left Behind (NCLB) can be summarized in three words: Teach them English. NCLB replaced a $300 million federal grant program supporting bilingual education programs that trap limited-English-proficient (LEP) children in segregated classes taught exclusively for many years in the children's non-English native languages. Instead, it set up block grants for states on condition that

they promptly demonstrate results teaching children English.

Preschoolers are not spared the rod. An effort under the direction of Reid Lyon, George Bush's chief reading advisor, is underway to bring the blessing of "science" to the very young, starting with preschool testing. Freelance education writer Alexander Russo recounts early childhood absurdities in Chicago.

> . . . two years ago, federal officials told Head Start programs that they had to administer one of three commercially developed tests used throughout the country . . . so that results could be validated broadly and programs could be more easily compared.
>   . . . This fall, Head Start started requiring an additional assessment that focuses mostly on academic questions such as colors, numbers, and letters. It must be given at the beginning and the end of the school year.

Perhaps the data gathered from these assessments could be useful for individual early child instructors however, " . . . officials who collect the data and pass them along to the state or the federal government don't report them back to the centers."

In perhaps the boldest stroke of the campaign, HR3801 replaces OERI in the Department of Education with a new Institute of Education Science. To quote Rep. Boehner, a key Congressional sponsor, the bill:

> . . . requires Scientifically Based Research [caps his]— Research that can't or won't meet these standards will be ineligible for federal funds. This means scientific experiments will help ensure that schools do not waste scarce resources on ineffective programs and methods of instruction.

If Neuman's rejection of experiments and Boehner's promise to blacklist all non-experimental research seem contradictory, remember this is the era of the Pedagogy of the Absurd.

Retroactive Censorship
It is not sufficient for the new federal education bureaucracy to censor and control current and future belief and practice. They are in the process of rewriting history and wiping off the books decades of research: The federal bureaucracy has announced its intentions to eliminate the ERIC system and wipe the pages of research history clean so they will no longer be accessible to future scholars and researchers.

Bureaucrats have been busy culling ERIC documents which do not support the administration education policies. Their new plan:

- Closes All 16 ERIC Clearinghouses
- Eliminates personalized reference and referral services
- Terminates Ask ERIC and clearinghouse question-answering services
- Ends all networking and outreach activities, including ERIC-sponsored Listservs
- Shuts down Clearinghouse Web sites currently visited by 22.5 million unique visitors a year
- Eliminates ERIC Digests, books, and other synthesis publications
- Reduces coverage of the journal literature from 1100 journals to an estimated 400
- Restricts consumer access to information, limiting ERIC database coverage to "approved lists" of journals and document contributors

Taking Control of Teacher Education
In March of 2004, $1.5 million was appropriated in an unrelated bill without any public discussion, to study how reading and

math are taught in teacher education programs and the degree to which programs are aligned with scientific evidence on the subjects according to Grover J. "Russ" Whitehurst, the director of the Federal Institute of Education Sciences. G. Reid Lyon helped spearhead the concept of the teacher-preparation study *Education Week* reported.

This is the latest attempt by the campaign against public education to deprofessionalize teaching and blame teachers' colleges for the failure of the "scientific" reading and math programs. There is little doubt that the "data" will be used for political purposes. *Education Week* quotes Karen Zumwaldt, a professor of education at Teachers College, Columbia University. "That's a hornet's nest. What is 'scientific evidence' and how is it applied?"

Education Week reports:

Some, in fact, point to Mr. Lyon's role in shaping the study as an indication that the information gathered will be used to quash colleges of education. Those critics, who do not wish to be identified for fear of political retaliation, go so far as to contend that Mr. Lyon used his influence to place the study in the catchall spending bill enacted in January, rather than make it part of the Higher Education Act. The HEA is up for renewal this year and will likely be the subject of public hearings.

Mr. Lyon, an outspoken critic of traditional teacher preparation, said such theories "sound pretty Machiavellian" and hold no truth.

Let's see: Lyon, a federal bureaucrat, gets Congress to smuggle a study of whether teachers' colleges conform to science according to his federal agency into an unrelated appropriations bill thus avoiding open hearings. That sounds pretty Machiavellian: absurdly Machiavellian.

Limiting Science by Law and Fiat

The absurdity of claiming to solve the problems of teaching children to read by defining what is and isn't "scientific" research and how the findings of sanctioned research must be applied in classroom reading instruction is illustrated by a case of teachers in one school district being told to stop sustained silent reading because the federal government says there is no research to support it. Edmonson and Shannon in "Politics of Reading" column in the *Reading Teacher* (2/02) cites Tim Shanahan in *EDWeek*, "If it isn't proven through research, you can't count it toward reading instruction"

Since the time of Galileo, there have been attempts to use authority, both religious and political, to limit what counts as science, what methodologies may be used, and how the results of research may be reported and applied. Copernicus waited until he was dying to publish his research and theory for fear of the consequences. And Decartes postponed his own publication when he saw what Galileo was made to suffer for his heresy of supporting, with research evidence, the Copernican view that the sun was the center of the solar system. Now federal and state law is being used to define what is and isn't literacy research and educational research in general, which materials can claim a basis in research and precisely what teachers may and may not do. And the National Reading Panel among other federally funded efforts is being used to excommunicate and brand as heretical, researchers, their methodologies and their findings.

Whole language is now the catch-all term for anything not supported by sanctioned research and is a heresy to be eliminated on penalty of law. The motivation is political as it always has been: 1) to settle by law what cannot be settled by scholarly argument; 2) to secure the power for those whose power is challenged by the findings of research; 3) to marginalize those who persist in conducting and publishing the results of research which threaten dominant theory; and 4) to protect believers from new ideas.

In 1633, his friend Bishop Piccolomini wrote to Galileo:

> ... I will say you deserve this and worse, for you have been disarming by steps those who have control of the sciences and they have nothing left but to run back to holy ground.

Science cannot be advanced by legal limitations and definitions which restrict its questions, methods, or findings. Nor can the problems of society be solved by restricting access to knowledge and limiting innovation. I console myself that the attempts in Galileo's day to limit science failed and few remember who his prosecutors were. But in the meantime a covert blacklist is being applied to research, to researchers, to methods, instructional materials, and to ideas. Truth is being defined by federal law and mandate and imposed by a federal bureaucracy through funding on every state, district, school, classroom, teacher, and pupil. And it is being done in the name of improving education.

References

Holland, Robert and Soifer, Don "Education's Vested Interests Seek to Roll Back Reform of Bilingual Education" Issue brief Lexington Institute August 2003 http://www.lexington institute.org/education/030805.pdf

Russo, Alexander. "Test glut a burden to preschools: But programs don't get data that would help improve teaching, learning." *Catalyst:* Independent coverage of Chicago school reform since 1989. February 2004

Blair, Julie. *Education Week* March 3, 2004, "Congress Orders Thorough Study of Teacher Education Programs"

INFLEXIBLE FLEXIBILITY
Ken Goodman

Secretary of Education Paige and the Bush Administration after months of scolding state and local education officials for whining and trying to sabotage the No Child Left Behind Law began in the Spring of 2004 to make some minor changes in the enforcement of the law without changing the law itself.

According to the *New York Times* (March 14, 2004), Paige told state legislatures the administration will fight against any attempt to rewrite the law. But his staff and the White House are trying to "wring every ounce of flexibility out of the existing language" to make it workable for local educators.

The *Times* estimated about 28 percent of 93,000 American schools were on probation, with most other schools likely to be classed as needing improvement in the next few years.

Sam Dillon reported in the *Times:*

President Bush is seeking to use the law as a centerpiece of his reelection campaign. Some experts said the administration's emphasis on flexibility was a new posture contrasting sharply with its stance last year, when officials in many states reported that federal officials were brushing aside complaints that some provisions were unreasonable.

Dillon reports that Jack Jennings, executive director of the Center on Education Policy said "The department has been dragged into giving new flexibility because of the uproar over the rigid way officials have been interpreting the law. " But Jennings thinks the proposed changes are only 10 percent of those thousands of school districts want.

Bruce Hunter, a lobbyist for the American Association of School Administrators, is quoted: "I agree with Secretary Paige that the rule revisions have created more flexibility, but the law is still an attempt to throw out one blanket over every American school . . . The changes have given schools tools to manage problems created by the law. But the department is still saying, 'You've got to play by our rules, even if they don't make sense.'"

SECTION TWO

The Cast of Characters

NCLB: A TOOL IN THE NEOCONSERVATIVE MOVEMENT TO PRIVATIZE AMERICAN EDUCATION

Ken Goodman

I've always thought of myself as politically aware. But over the past dozen years I found myself at the vortex of the "Reading Wars" and I tried to understand where the attacks in the media were coming from. It took me a while to recognize that what was happening was not the vast conservative conspiracy that Bill and Hillary Clinton complained about. It was even worse, an example of what the right wing think tanks call "movement conservatism."

My awareness that some powerful forces were at work came on Halloween weekend in 1997. Early in the Spring of 1997, Jim Collins of *Time* magazine came to Tucson and spent two days interviewing me and my wife, Yetta Goodman. He wanted to do an article, he said, on whole language. It was an amicable interview. He thought that his article might appear in May or June as school ended that year. When it didn't he told me by email that he thought they would hold it for the opening of school in the Fall. It didn't come out then either.

Meanwhile, the Reading Excellence Act, predecessor to NCLB's Reading First mandates was quietly moving through the legislative process in the U.S. House of Representatives. I say quietly because there was almost no coverage in the press of this major law that proposed to establish a national reading methodology as well as a national definition of reading research. At the end of October, the House Committee, considering the bill, sent it to the floor of the House with a "do-pass" recommendation.

Imagine my surprise when, the very weekend that H2614, The Reading Excellence Act went to the floor of Congress, Collins article was the cover story for *Time* (Collins, 10/27/97).

Here is the conclusion of his article.

> After reviewing the arguments by the phonics and whole-
> language proponents, can we make a judgement who is
> right? Yes. The value of explicit systematic phonics instruc-
> tion has been established. (Collins, 10/27/97 *Time* p81)

It was a mild shock that the article took such a strong position on
behalf of this powerful news magazine. But that was nothing
compared to my surprise when I discovered that that very same
weekend *Newsweek* (Wingert and Kantrowicz, 10/27/97), *U.S.
News & World Report* (Toch, 10/27/97), *Atlantic Monthly* (Lemann
11/97), and *Policy Review* (Palmaffy, Nov-Dec 1997) all published
articles on the "Reading Wars" that came out squarely for phonics. The *Baltimore Sun* and the *Washington Post* also published
major articles in their Sunday editions. None of these "coinciden-
tal" articles mentioned H2614, but all slammed whole language
and promoted phonics. And all carried the same essential theme:

> The evidence is overwhelming that kids with reading
> problems need phonics-based instruction. Why aren't edu-
> cators getting the message? (Palmaffy, *Policy Review*
> November-December 1997 p 32)

It would have been impossible for any member of Congress to
avoid getting the message as the Reading Excellence Act hit his
desk. That's when I became aware that there was a campaign
being conducted by a group so powerful that they could pull off
this unprecedented media blitz. But who had such powerful connections, not just to get these stories out with the same message
at exactly the same time?

Movement Conservatism
I'm calling this a campaign and not a conspiracy because I believe
that none of the reporters themselves were aware of the role their
articles were playing. The decision to publish articles at the same

time on the same topic with the same conclusion had to involve someone getting to the owners or publishers who gave the reporters the assignments and made the timing decisions. But that doesn't mean that they are co-conspirators. They didn't meet in a smoke-filled room and mutually plot this media blitz.

They are part of what Robert Kuttner has called "Movement Conservatism." In this movement the goal is privatizing all aspects of American society including its schools.

NCLB and its predecessor, the Reading Excellence Act, are major landmarks in a conservative movement (a political campaign in every sense of that term) to privatize America's schools. As in all modern American political campaigns the stated purposes often mask an underlying political agenda. NCLB says its goals are raising achievement, increasing literacy, and eliminating disadvantages for minorities. But why then does it provide so many ways for schools to be labeled failing and so many punishments including closing, reorganizing, or turning schools over to private profit-making companies?

The answer is that its intent is not to help schools succeed but to make them appear to be failures. Universal free public schools is an idea so strongly supported by the American people that no campaign could succeed in privatizing them unless the public lost faith in public education. So NCLB is carefully constructed to gradually, over 14 years, turn the majority of schools into failures. Groups such as the National School Boards Association have predicted that the implementation of NCLB will result in most schools in every state being labeled as failing.

The euphemism for failing in the law is "needs improvement" but as Ken Meyer, a spokesman for NCLB said to an audience in Utah, "I like to quote the President, 'There's not a school in this country that doesn't need improvement.'" (Dillon, *NYTimes* 2/22/2004)

Free public schools did not come to America without a fight. It took child labor laws to get children out of the factories and fields and into school. And compulsory education laws were fought for state by state. Free common secondary schools are less than a century old. Through these battles Americans came to believe that schools provide access for every child to a good and self-sufficient life. At the same time, there have always been those who resented paying taxes for schools for other people's children. And big business dislikes the taxes they must pay that reduce their profits. Besides, too much education makes workers less willing to work for low wages. These forces have come together in an organized and well-financed political campaign to label the American public school as a failed experiment.

It is important to understand that it was a carefully coordinated campaign within a neoconservative movement which brought about NCLB, not a conspiracy. In a conspiracy the participants (at least the major ones) are all engaged together in planning and executing some series of actions for a common purpose. Rather, NCLB is a tool in a political campaign with all the aspects of such a campaign includes and the same low level of morality. In such a campaign what you say has little to do with your underlying objectives; in political campaigns "spin doctors" develop "spins" to conceal what they really advocate. For example, they profess the desire to further the rights of all for equal opportunity while repealing laws passed to achieve equal opportunity. They profess to want every child reading by third grade but then define reading as a score on a test as "basic" which makes 40 percent of all pupils look like they are reading below a basic level. And schools are required over time to have all pupils achieve the score labeled proficient which was set to equal what only 20 percent are now achieving. Even in Garrison Keillor's Lake Wobegon, where "all the children are above average," they would not all be able to be above the 80th percentile. In fact, a Minnesota legislative report projects that in that high-scoring state 80 percent of all public schools will be labeled by NCLB as failures by 2014.

NCLB requires that every classroom will have a qualified

teacher but then defines a qualified teacher as one who has an academic degree in the field being taught. Thus a small town high school is required to report to parents that most of their highly experienced teachers are unqualified because, for example, the chemistry teacher has a degree in biology.

Teacher aides under NCLB are required to earn AA degrees from a community college, which seems laudable. But that requirement effectively wipes out heritage language programs since they have been maintained with the use of aides from the heritage community who speak the community language but have little academic education (generally as a direct result of past federal education policies).

A key tactic of recent political campaigns is to take the goals of your opponents, offer your own simple direct path to those goals, and then marginalize the opponents as opposing reform and change.

To run such a campaign you don't need large numbers of people planning and executing the campaign—in fact a small close-knit group is best. According to Richard Feulner, head of the Heritage Foundation, what a conservative movement needs are the four M's: Mission, Money, Management, and Marketing. (Kuttner, 7/15/2002)

Here is my reconstruction of how these four M's work in the campaign to privatize education in which NCLB plays a key role:

Mission and Management
The mission of the campaign to privatize education is part of a more general conservative movement to privatize every aspect of American society, the result of what Kuttner calls "the 25-year strategic alliance between organized business, ideological conservatism, advocacy research, and the Republican party."

But Christopher DeMuth, head of American Enterprise Institute, says, "All fundamental changes are bipartisan when they happen." It was the Democratic state legislature in California that wrote much of the movement's agenda into state law. Ted Kennedy, among other liberal Democrats, strongly backed NCLB, and Diane Feinstein, a moderate senator from California, announced her support for vouchers, a major tool of the campaign. Senator Joseph Lieberman is a long-term supporter of vouchers as a way of giving public support to private schools.

The Manhattan Institute, according to Kuttner, is "especially nimble at co-opting liberals". That may explain the role that the American Federation of Teachers has played in promoting the agenda that produced NCLB.

Formulating the mission is the job of neoconservative think tanks. Those most visible in the campaign which produced NCLB are the Heritage Foundation, the American Enterprise Institute, the Thomas B. Fordham Foundation, the Cato Institute, and the Manhattan Institute.

They provide the brains for planning and managing the campaign that serves the mission. I have no doubt that within one or more of these think tanks a small group of very smart and well-paid people have produced a strategic management plan which over time is designed to bring about the privatization. These are the people who decided that attacking reading methodology (and to a lesser degree writing and arithmetic) is a key way of making public education appear to be failing. They are the ones responsible for the emphasis on testing, the labeling of schools, and the punishments designed to lead to their privatization. Each of these is not an end in itself but a device to advance the campaign.

They've carefully cultivated the mistrust of poor and minority parents, who believe the schools don't care about them and don't demand enough of their kids. And they've exploited the concerns of those who fear the public schools are undermining the religious and moral values of the home.

Marketing the message of the campaign exploits the willingness of the press to print negative stories about the public schools. They've also built on the public confusion between science and technology, promoting mass high-stakes tests as the only sure way to hold the schools and teachers accountable, and promoting rehashed phonics as the new research-based sure-cure for what ails the schools.

Money

The campaign has no shortage of available funding from wealthy right wing "nonprofit" foundations, which have convinced the Internal Revenue Service that their support of these political campaigns is charitable and not political. Kuttner sees the $70 million or so a year that these neoconservative think tanks cost their benefactors as "chump change" considering what they deliver in return.

The moneyed foundations often aid directly in the marketing of the campaign's mission as the Packard Foundation has done with several major districts in California underwriting the costs of the McGraw-Hill's Open Court policing of their program if the districts bought Open Court materials with state funds.

The National Business Roundtable and the various State Business Councils not only provide funding to the campaign directly, but also serve the mission through their contributions to the political campaigns at national, state, and local levels. That gives the campaign direct access to key office holders and strong leverage on schools and universities. They include in their ranks the executives and chief editors of major news magazines, newspapers, electronic media, and textbook companies. That's how the campaign managers were able to coordinate their spectacular blitz that Halloween weekend in 1997.

As the agenda of the campaign is written into law, money becomes the main vehicle for forcing state and local education agencies to follow the mandates of the campaign. Chester Finn of the Fordham Foundation likes to remind school officials that they don't have to accept the money that NCLB provides. In addition, right-wing think tanks and the subsidiaries they set up receive grants from government agencies to carry out parts of their campaign.

Insight into how this works was gained in a fallout between two players in the campaign.

Lisa Graham Keegan, former Arizona State School Superintendent, heads Education Leaders Council (ELC), which was formed just after the 2000 election to rival and eventually replace the Council of Chief State School Officers (which the campaign found it could not easily control). Keegan brought with her two former assistants. All three drew salaries of over $200,000 but kept their residences in Arizona.

Almost all Chief School Officers stayed with the older group. But the new organization got some immediate substantial federal grants and the salaries of the "Arizona Three" were paid as consultants on these grants.

In fact, the *Washington Times* reported (2/17/04) "the Council's auditor concluded . . . that the amount of time the executives spent on the federal projects was not commensurate with their salaries."

Chester Finn, head of the Thomas B. Fordham Foundation, became impatient with Keegan. He issued a memo saying that "ELC is not currently a visible or audible influence on federal education policy." In other words, they weren't carrying out their assignments in the campaign.

Keegan retaliated by cancelling a subcontract her council had awarded to the Fordham Foundation for an independent evaluation of a federally funded school instructional project.

This illustrates a general problem with campaigns. Sometimes the managers have difficulty controlling all the players and their personal agendas.

Marketing

The Heritage Foundation, besides subsidizing newspaper columnists in small and medium-sized towns, places hundreds of op-eds (opinion essays) in newspapers. These essays are devoted to reinforcing the message of the foundation's campaigns.

Kuttner reports that Larry Mone of the Manhattan Institute emphasizes the importance of targeting opinion elites. In the campaign that produced NCLB and similar state laws, legislators and schoolboard members were literally bombarded with opinion pieces, "research" reports, summaries, and other propaganda designed to keep the message in front of them and give the impression of widespread public support. (Molly Ivins has dubbed this an astro-turf movement with artificial grassroots.)

The marketing plan also uses professional public relations (PR) firms such as the Widemeyer Baker Group, which was hired to publicize the report of the National Reading Panel. Before the panel had completed its thick, wordy report, the PR company had a slick-paper, brightly illustrated summary for distribution to the public and the press. This summary misrepresents and exaggerates the recommendations of the panel and it is that version, from the summary rather than the panel report, that is repeatedly cited in NCLB and its implementation. Curiously, this same PR company has also represented McGraw-Hill in publicizing its commercial reading programs. These programs are being strongly recommended by the bureaucrats screening state proposals for NCLB money.

Managing Other Players in the Movement

The movement that resulted in NCLB brings together many different groups with different agendas. The managers of the campaign have the job of coordinating their efforts, utilizing particular strengths, and keeping them on mission. All of the groups share some commitment to elements of the conservative agenda but they have their own agendas and their own "causes."

For example, opposition to public education and advocacy of back-to-basics and phonics have historically been part of the agenda of the religious right. For decades they've used demands for phonics programs in reading as a device for electing their candidates for local schools boards. Though they had only meager success in the past, their advocacy of phonics over the years gave the campaign a base to build on and a constituency to exploit.

So in Texas Phyllis Schafly's Eagle Forum provided the troops for demonstrations to pressure elected state commissions to adopt the campaign's testing, phonics, and anti-public schools agendas. Pat Robertson and Schafly market their own reading programs, particularly for use in home schooling.

Another group, which sometimes overlaps the religious right, are back-to-basics advocates. Robert Sweet's Right to Read Foundation and an older group, the Reading Reform Foundation, laid the base for the phonics campaign. Sweet authored a white paper (1989) on illiteracy for the Senate Republican Caucus. More recently, he was majority aide to the House Labor and Education Committee and played a role in promoting the Reading Excellence Act that preceded NCLB. The campaign made good use of him, often with the support of the Eagle Forum, in lobbying for phonics laws in a number of states.

Throughout the twentieth century, no matter what else was happening in reading education there has been a persistent group who authored simplistic, behavioristic phonics programs. Small publishers, such as the Open Court Company, were willing to publish them and found a small market for them.

One particularly aggressive group of special educators was associated with Sigfried Englemann at the University of Oregon. Forty years ago, when behavioristic psychology was popular, Englemann developed the Distar program in reading and math. It controlled teachers by requiring them to adhere to a tightly sequenced script. Englemann and his colleagues were not modest about their claims of success and promoted the program as scientific.

The campaign capitalized on the fact that these claims had been rejected by the mainstream in literacy education, exploited the historic split within literacy education, and began to showcase the immodest authors. That gave the campaign a simple message: phonics has always been the simple, sure way to teach reading but advocates of whole language ruined that by misleading teachers into not teaching phonics.

McGraw-Hill acquired both Open Court and Distar and began to market them heavily in support of the campaign. They succeeded in getting the implementers of NCLB to anoint these programs as among the few that fit the "evidence-based" criteria. Key people in the Oregon group (Douglas Carnine, Ed Kameenui, and Bonnie Grossen) served the campaign well because of their absolute certainty that they are right and everyone else is wrong. The campaign widely distributed a publication by Bonnie Gross in which she claimed to summarize 30 years of research. That was originally developed as a promotional piece for Distar. Richard Allington, among others, has shown that the research summarized in the Grossen piece is comprised largely of obscure, unrefereed studies that do not support the conclusions she draws from them.

I need to reiterate here a theme of this book. NCLB (and the campaign that produced it) is not about reading. Its focus on reading is a device for attacking public education. For the purposes of the campaign then, it actually serves them well if the programs they promote are not likely to be successful. These phonics programs, no matter what their champions claim, have not been successful.

Besides the Oregon group, another group of researchers have been used by the campaign. Notable is Marilyn Adams, a psychologist, a member of the staff of Bolt, Beranek, Newman (BBN), a profit-making company with major research grants from the federal government. Adams is also an author of the Open Court program. Congress mandated that, as part of its funding, BBN do a study of programs for developing beginning reading. The result was a thick volume, technically written by Adams, which supplied the conclusion that learning to read was basically learning to read words, letter by letter.

The campaign used her report in two important ways. First, it widely publicized her conclusions. Second, it produced a smaller, simplified volume which was then widely distributed. Publishers gave copies away free.

What the Adams' work, or rather what the pony edition, did was to lay the base from the claim that phonics as represented in Distar and Open Court was scientific.

But the campaign also tapped another group and used them to serve the movement. These are researchers in educational psychology and special education, many of whom work in medical settings and are funded by the National Institute of Child Health and Human Development (NICHD). Their research tends to look for deficiency in learners such as dyslexia, a cognitive condition that interferes with reading development.

G. Reid Lyon is a special educator who became a bureaucrat in NICHD and supervised federal grants to these deficit researchers. He has became a major spokesman for the campaign and is an advisor to President Bush on NCLB.

To bring these disparate groups together and lay a further mantle of science on direct instruction of phonics, the campaign used its muscle and finesse to sponsor two well-publicized panels. One, funded through NICHD, was under the auspices of the National Research Council. Lyon and his colleagues carefully selected a group of panel members under the chair of Catherine Snow, a Harvard educational researcher. The panel was dominated by those in the deficit group and excluded a wide range of literacy researchers. Their report, "The Prevention of Reading Difficulty" supported phonics as the main tool in dealing with the learning deficiencies they assert are likely to cause difficulties in developing readers.

Close on the heels of this panel, Congress directly mandated that a National Reading Panel be formed to take the Snow report and look at research to decide on the most effective ways to teach children to read. Lyon and NICHD selected the panel members and gave the panel its charge: Tell Congress which programs to write into the law that would become NCLB. The panel came up with a series of criteria but stopped short of naming programs. But everywhere in the law itself where it requires funding to be of programs that are " research based," it is the findings of this panel that are referenced. Or rather it is the summary of the panel report which subtly changes those findings to be more simplistic and more definite.

So NCLB mandates phonics as the national reading method-ology. And those who review state proposals reject anything that doesn't fit the narrow interpretations of the law. They strongly push each state to write their proposals to conform to the law and to require local districts to use only those commercial programs the Washington bureaucrats approve.

This aspect of the law is much more serious than the unfund-ed testing mandate but it is less well understood. There is begin-ning to be recognition that the goals of NCLB are unachievable. But what is not well understood is that the National Reading methodology is not scientific at all and has been carefully designed by the campaign to fail.

Institutionalizing Its Gains
Political campaigns are never over. DeMuth says, "It takes at least 10 years for a radical new idea to emerge from obscurity." The campaign has made great strides under the Bush administration. But it knows he might not be reelected. So it is institutionalizing its gains by writing them into federal and state laws and imple-mentation guidelines along with the creation of agencies to decide what research is, which reading and math programs may be used in each state and district and who may and may not participate in teacher education and staff development.

A key premise of the campaign is avoiding confrontation by co-opting the groups with the most power to defeat the cam-paign. The think tanks understand that change must be bipartisan. They did this in the campaign to defeat a national health plan. They were able to convince the very people who had the most to gain from such a plan that it was not in their best interest . This was done through a massive disinformation campaign and by co-opting senior groups and unions.

Like all other political campaigns, this one also has inherent weaknesses. One is that the disparate groups doing its work can become loose cannons. They can pursue their own agendas to the point where they begin to discredit the campaign. Another is that the campaign can achieve too much success too fast. NCLB is the result of years of careful work by the campaign, but its success could prove its undoing, as the federal bureaucracy begins to interpret the law, label middle-class schools as failing, and force neighborhood schools to close.

In the election campaigns it serves the purpose of the campaign if voters become disgusted with its techniques and decide not to vote at all. In the case of this campaign they would like people to give up on public education and be willing to settle for privatization. Its not likely that most people are going to accept losing their neighborhood schools.

References

Adams, M. J. (1990a). *Beginning to Read: Thinking and Learning about Print.* Cambridge MA: MIT Press.

Adams, M. J. (1990b). *Beginning to Read: Thinking and Learning about Print: A Summary.* Champaign, IL: Center for the Study of Reading.

Archibault, G. (2/17/04) Education Reformers Halt Evaluation, *Washington Times*

Collins, J. (10/27/97) How Johnny should Read, *Time* Vol 150:17 pp 78-81

Flesch, R. (1981). *Why Johnny Still Can't Read: A New Look at the Scandal of our Schools.* New York: Harper & Row.

Foorman, B. R., David J. Francis. (in press). Early Interventions for

Children with Reading Problems: Study Design and Preliminary Findings, *Learning Disabilities.*

Kuttner, R. (7/15/02) Philanthropy and Movements. *The American Prospect*

Lemann, N. (1997, November) The Reading Wars, *Atlantic Monthly*

Lyon, G. Reid. (1997, July 10) Statement of G. Reid Lyon, Ph.D. [testimony]. Committee on Education and the Workforce, U.S. House of Representatives. Washington D.C.: unpublished.

Palmaffy, T. (1997 Nov-Dec) See Dick Flunk, *Policy Review* Vol 86 pp 32-40

Spring, J. (1997) *Political Agendas for Education* Mahwah NJ: Lawrence Earlbaum Associates

Toch, T. (10/27/97) The Reading Wars Continue, *US News & World Report*

Wingert, P. and Kantrowitz, B. (10/27/97) Why Andy Couldn't Read, *Newsweek*, pp. 56-60

GOD'S LATEST PLAN FOR EDUCATION

Patrick Shannon

Editor's note: *Many years ago, when I taught the Constitution in 8th grade, I asked my class why separation of church and state was written into the Bill of Rights. I had in mind the usual platitudes about the noble principles of the high-minded framers of the Constitution. A bright 13-year-old girl summed the matter up concisely: "People brought so many religions with them they had to do that. Otherwise they would have been fighting all the time." In this chapter Pat Shannon puts NCLB and the Bush agenda in the context of a historical religious view. —KSG*

No one assumes the White House is a church and no one thinks they can slack off on their work in the name of religion. But we do understand that the political vision we serve is fueled by faith, and the nation benefits when there are brown-bag Bible studies and before-work prayer meetings in the White House. (Bush White House Aide)

What characterizes the difference between previous school reform plans and No Child Left Behind is its negative tone. NCLB states that schools are not doing their job to educate a productive workforce because teachers know little about teaching literacy and are not working hard enough to ensure students learn the right stuff. Moreover, teachers have not been taught or are unwilling to learn the methods that science says make children learn. Students are not disciplined enough to learn fast enough what is expected of them. And administrators are not hiring properly educated teachers, and then holding teachers and students accountable for their actions (or lack of action).

According to NCLB, school administrators and teachers hide their lack of success with some students by averaging test scores across groups. High-scoring groups—typically white middle- and upper-class students—compensate for low-scoring groups—special education students, English-language learners, and minorities—making schools appear to be successful when many students are not learning what is expected when it is expected.

In order to fix these problems, NCLB proposes a series of punishments for schools' failure to help all children make adequate yearly progress toward state standards as measured by state tests. Repeated failure brings greater sanctions. (Success means only being left alone.) Rallies and other promotional activities aside, advocates of NCLB take a dim view of the current state of public schooling and the individuals who work there. They see little chance of redeeming public schools in their current forms.

Why all the negativism? NCLB's pessimism about human nature (administrators do not want to administer, teachers don't want to teach, and students don't want to learn) stems from a rather Manichaeistic interpretation of Christianity which divides the world simply into two parts—good vs. evil. Public schools with their enforcement of separation of church and state fall, at least currently, on the side of evil, promoting the temptation of secular humanism and popular culture among the young before they can be saved. For this reason alone, public schooling as we know it is to be destroyed in order to open up space in which children can develop and exercise their personal relationship with God, learn right from wrong, and develop skills as productive workers.

George W. Bush's Faith

George W. Bush is a born-again Christian. His rebirth happened gradually during 1985 when he decided that Jesus Christ was his personal savior. The decision changed the direction of his life—away from hedonistic pleasures to a belief in service to others in God's name. Shortly after his rebirth, Bush ran for governor of Texas and won. After his election to a second term, Bush attended services in Highland Park Methodist Church in Dallas. During his sermon, the preacher used Moses as his example to explain, "People are starved for leadership—starved for leaders who have ethical and moral courage."

While listening, Bush thought that the sermon was directed at him. He felt a "call," a sense that God was directing him to run for president. His mother, Barbara Bush, had the same thought during that sermon and turned to say, "He was talking to you." Later, George W. Bush told Rev. James Robinson, moderator of the Christian television program *Life Today:*

> I've heard the call. I believe God wants me to run for president. I can't explain it, but I sense my country is going to need me. Something is going to happen, and at that time, my country is going to need me. I know it won't be easy, on me or my family, but God wants me to do it.

Upon being appointed president, Bush displayed immediately the religious conviction of his Administration. On his first day, he called for a national day of prayer and cut federal spending on sex education and banned information on abortion as one of the options offered to women in federally funded clinics around the world. Weekly Bible and prayer meetings began in government buildings. And he surrounded himself with people of faith: National Security Advisor Condoleezza Rice is a Presbyterian minister's daughter; Attorney General John Ashcroft, son of a minister, is a member of the Assemblies of God; Chief of Staff Andrew Card is married to a Methodist minister; Secretary of Commerce Don Evans attended Bible study classes with Bush in Midland, Texas, and Presidential Advisor Karen Hughes is a Presbyterian elder.

Bush and his associates believe individuals' lack of religious conviction causes America's social problems, and therefore, they call for faith-based institutions to solve them. Shortly after his inauguration, Bush established an Office of Faith-Based Initiatives to propose ways in which religious organizations could qualify for federal funding to address social problems by instilling faith in people experiencing trouble. If given a second term, Stephan Mansfield, Bush's religious biographer, predicts that Bush is likely to push toward a faith-based transformation of American social policy.

Bush's plans are driven by a specific interpretation of the First Amendment. Bush argues that the First Amendment only prohibits the federal government from establishing a national religion. It does not concern religious matters in general, he maintains, and does not prohibit the states from enacting religious practices in schools. This understanding of the original intentions of the framers of the Constitution is based upon the language of the Mayflower Compact, which stated that the pilgrims sailed "for the Glory of God and the Advancement of the Christian Faith." Moreover, members of the First Congress celebrated days of prayer and fasting and presented speeches on the floor of Congress referring to the Christianity of the American people.

Accordingly, the pilgrims' descendants and those of other original colonists feared the consequences of national religions, but sought to encourage freedom of religious worship. The First Amendment declared that Congress could not, "make laws respecting an establishment of religion" or "prohibiting the free exercise" of religion by individuals. Therefore, Bush assumes that no laws restrict states from becoming distinctly religious in their policies or the federal government from promoting religious practices, even though the Supreme Court has interpreted the First Amendment to require complete separation of church and state. As Bush understands it, new social policy built upon faith-based initiatives is a return to the origins of the nation.

The First American Schools Run by Faith
Many among the first immigrants to what would become the United States were intent on building the Kingdom of Zion. In this kingdom, the word of God would provide the rule of law as

a defense against Satan and other temptations of the spirit. In order to accomplish this goal, leaders sought a common understanding of the principles of faith among all believers. Those principles were to be found in the Bible, and the ability to read became a civic as well as spiritual duty of all who inhabited the New World. Children were conceived in sin and must be saved from eternal damnation. As clergyman Cotton Mather explained in Cares About the Nurseuries, "We have in our hands the Holy Scriptures which are a storehouse of saving truths and contain all that must be known by all that would be saved."

As early as 1642, the Massachusetts legislature passed a law requiring towns to make certain that all "youth under family Government be taught to read perfectly the English tongue, have knowledge in capital laws, and be taught some orthodox catechisms, and that they be brought up to some honest employment, profitable to themselves and to the Commonwealth." Families who failed to teach their children to read were subject to a series of penalties—fines, shaming, and pillaring. The Old Deluder, Satan Act of 1647 established formal publicly-funded schools in Massachusetts designed to promote a uniformity of Christian thought through school texts and practices. By the beginning of the 1700s, the New England Primer began with the entry:—"A, In Adam's fall, We sinned all."

Colonial instruction took two basic forms—independent practice after teacher demonstration in which individuals would eventually have to toe the mark in order to render their lessons perfectly, and choral drilling led by teacher or older student until students' performance met the master's expectations. Both practices instilled the authorities of the teacher and the content. This didactic teaching and explicit moral training were considered to be the only way to overcome children's original sin, to constrain their natural tendencies toward temptation, and to make them good. As best can be determined, the ultimate goal of this instruction was the appropriate application of Bible verses to everyday life. The life of faith, not of intellect or reason, would deliver the citizens to the Kingdom of Zion one by one.

A Separation of Church and Schooling

Authorities disagree about the causes of the split between public schools and Christian principles and practices. Bush subscribes to the position that diversity in post-Civil War America perverted the original interpretation of the First Amendment and, eventually, created the separation of church and state at all levels of government. First, changing patterns of immigration produced greater variety among religious faiths within the population, disrupting the uncontested support for Protestant Liturgy in everyday life. Second, Bush suggests that U.S. Supreme Court rulings of the late nineteenth century greatly expanded federal authority over the states. Attempts to provide equal protection to newly freed slaves required that states align themselves with all federal laws and policies. According to Bush, it was then that American diversity and federal attempts to treat citizens equally prevented Christian influence on public life. To quote Mansfield,

> Soon practices once commonly understood as bequeaths of a Christian heritage were somehow deemed violations of the new understanding of a secular state. Courts found that the Ten Commandments posted in government buildings, the prayer that started each day in the public schools, the "release time" that permitted students to study their faith during school hours, and even nativity scenes on government grounds were all in violation of First Amendment safeguards.

In its own way, NCLB is expected to right these wrongs in schools by demonstrating the accuracy of its negative assessment of public schools, imposing penance on them in order to change their character and, therefore, making them good again.

Most educational historians, however, propose a more complex dynamic for the waning of religious authority in American schools. First, they present a different timetable for the separation, challenging Bush's assertion that Christianity enjoyed an undisturbed two-hundred-and-thirty-year tradition of authority in colonial and early America. In the Massachusetts Bay Colony after 1691, enfranchisement was based on property ownership and not religious affiliation, suggesting that wealth and not faith was valued most highly in the growing Northern colonies. Although these historians acknowledge that the American population indeed grew more diverse spiritually and culturally after the Civil War, they attribute the shift away from Christian control of schools to the pursuit of liberty and growing demands of capitalism well before that time.

Of course, Christianity was (and is) compatible with republicanism and capitalism in many ways. God's laws alone, however, would not account for the intellectual arguments necessary for self-government, the production of capital, or the accumulation of property. These pursuits required a more sophisticated school curriculum than the one intended primarily to build the Kingdom of Zion.

Some among the clergy recognized the changing demands in political and economic life and supported more secular ideas within school curricula and civic life. During the Great Awakenings of the 18th century, however, most rural and Southern clergy challenged this drift away from a Christian nation and reaffirmed the religious foundations of schooling. Such intolerance led Benjamin Franklin and others to propose practical school curricula set to aid the average citizen. Franklin encouraged teachers to use Cato's Letters, a text found in half of the private libraries across the colonies, which argued that the development of freedom of thought and commerce were incompatible with schools dominated by religious goals.

The ideas behind republicanism and capitalism projected a more positive view of human nature than the assumption of original sin. For example, John Locke argued for a malleable human nature which experience would direct toward good or bad. Jean Jacques Rousseau posited children as the glorious reflection of nature with unbound potential to develop into a virtuous citizen, if protected from the corruptions of society (including religion) until they were able to deal with them. Educators across Europe and some in the new United States translated these assumptions about human nature into more nurturing methods of teaching, challenging the authoritarian and punitive Christian methods of making students learn their lessons. These assumptions and teaching methods spread slowly across the United States during the nineteenth century and culminated in the progressive education movement by the turn of the century.

New political and economic interests beginning in the late 17th century were gradually reflected in adults' expectations of youth. The young were not expected to create and maintain the Kingdom of Zion in the New World. Their primary virtues were no longer piety and observance of the statutes of the Covenant. Their identities were not to be solely in service of salvation. Rather, American youth were expected to learn to be useful to their country, to know information and techniques for their utility, to act with modesty and civility, to be dutiful to society's needs, and to serve people, not God. Their schooling and textbooks reflected these new expectations. For example, the 1800 edition of the New England Primer began not with a reminder of Adam's sins, but with "A was an angler who fished with a hook."

In any case, it was an 1869 lawsuit brought by the Catholic community of Cincinnati, not atheists or non-Christians, which objected to Protestant prayer in the public schools that brought the definitive court decision on keeping prayer out of public schools.

Caring About What Comes Next
The distrust of public schools and school personnel encoded in NCLB stems from Bush's plans for faith-based social policy. He

believes that NCLB, like all other plans of his administration, is a demonstration of God's plan for schools and the country. Armed with God's will and the original intentions of the founding fathers, Bush is adamant that his policies are correct and are the only true solutions to America's problems. Daily reading from Oswald Chanber's *My Utmost for His Highest* leads Bush to conclude that as a faithful man God directs his decisions and only God can correct his choices. In his book, *A Charge to Keep*, Bush explained:

> My faith frees me. Frees me to put the problems of the moment in proper perspective. Frees me to make decisions that others might not like. Frees me to try to do the right thing, even though it may not poll well. Frees me to enjoy life and not worry about what comes next.

In order to clear the way for NCLB, Bush neglects the controversies over Christian authority in colonial and early national public life. Displaying intolerance, Bush characterizes the separation of church and state in schools as evil caused by expressions of racial and ethnic diversity and attempts to achieve equal justice. His policy, NCLB, punishes this evil and points out the road to salvation. His belief that he is the messenger of God frees him "to enjoy life and not worry about what comes next."

While President Bush is probably referring to the afterlife in that statement, too many Americans are not able to enjoy their lives and must worry daily about what comes next for them on earth. Some of these Americans are hungry (during the Bush Administration 11 percent of Americans are insecure in their food supply). They and others worry about income (although the U.S. economy must produce 100,000 jobs each month to accommodate new workers, three million jobs have been lost during Bush's term in office and 30 percent of employed Americans earn too little to provide for their families with one paycheck). And they are scared (Bush's Patriot Act curtails American's Constitutional rights and a $500 trillion federal budget deficit robs their children of prospects of a promising future).

Yet, Bush intends to meet these challenges with an increased emphasis on individuals' Christian faith and private faith-based initiatives. Faith by definition is irrational, and Bush need not deal with the consequences of his policies because he understands them as God's plan. Are these results what educators and the public have to look forward to in schools as well?

READING WITH REID

Roger Rapoport

Located just below the beltway and only half an hour from the White House, the National Institutes of Health sprawls across Bethesda, Maryland, like a state college campus. Cookie-cutter office buildings in park-like settings are home to bureaucrats like Reid Lyon, who the *Wall Street Journal* calls the most important reading authority in George W. Bush's education brain trust. President Bush may get a lot of kidding about his use of the English language but there's no doubt that in his mind reading and Reid are synonymous.

Lyon's job is to supervise grants under the National Institute of Child Health and Human Development, one of NIH's many institutes. He also translates NICHD research for the White House and Congress and advises Bush on education appointments, research, and policies.

Reid Lyon is the point man in the reading wars. At stake is nothing less than control of American reading education. The signed photographs on his office wall show where the realpolitik of education is headed. George W. Bush, Laura Bush, Secretary of Education Rod Paige, the beat goes on and on.

Before reaching his position of power in Washington, Lyon taught children with learning disabilities, served as a third-grade classroom teacher, and as a school psychologist in New Mexico. Today, he operates as a kind of circus aerialist working without a net. Lyon has staked his entire career on an extreme approach that has elated politicians impressed with his relentless certainty. In the spirit of a corporate takeover artist, Reid Lyon is, depending on who you believe, a godsend or a pariah.

George W. Bush summoned Lyon to the White House on the second day of his administration. The president, who made a name for himself in Texas attacking what Lyon likes to characterize as "the soft bigotry of low expectations" had a question. Lyon says Bush told him, "I want to know what works, how we can do this better. We are going to improve this system."

The president is moved by critics of public education who comprise a neoconservative movement that brings together an odd coalition. Included are politicians, business CEOs, union leaders, parochial school recruiters, private school advocates, libertarians, testing bureaucracies, advertising-driven companies baiting prospects with their phonics hooks, neoconservative think tanks, and, perhaps most important, parents eager to do something about the problems of underfunded multicultural school systems straining to educate children.

The so-called "crisis" in education is an opportunity for politicians eager to show how their bureaucratic initiatives can and will trump seasoned educators. In the same way that war is too important to be left to the generals, it is the belief of many politicians that education is too important to be left to the professionals.

No one believes this more strongly than Reid Lyon, who declared at a public meeting that he would "like to blow up the colleges of education." No, this didn't trigger a house call from the FBI or the Homeland Security Administration. In fact, his comment never made it to the nation's news media but was largely circulated through academe via the internet. There is a story circulating that Lyon was again summoned to the White House and scolded for his indiscretion.

Lyon says he regrets his remark but remains passionate about his campaign. His plan on behalf of "the man downtown" on Pennsylvania Avenue, became a bipartisan solution to a literacy crisis some have called manufactured. The president is absolutely committed to a back -to-basics approach that would have every child, regardless of income or school inequality, reading by the end of third grade.

While Lyon is a bureaucrat, with a doctorate in special education from the University of New Mexico, he is also enough of a politician to understand the opportunity before him. And in many ways his personal vision has a lot in common with Bush. He believes that a lot of what is right and wrong in America is wrapped up in the pedagogy of the nation's system of higher education.

Lyon says that close to 40 percent of children in the fourth grade are not reading at grade level. (Actually by definition 50 percent of all fourth graders are at or below grade level and 50 percent are at or above grade level.) He agrees that part of the problem can be tagged to the home environment of students who perform poorly. He believes that if these kids lived in homes with a rich print environment, "the problem would be reduced to the 10 percent level. Most of the reading failures are coming from backgrounds that weren't print-rich environments and they weren't read to."

In other words, if you could simply move these children into wealthier homes where more print materials were available, along with parents who emphasized the importance of reading every day, the children performing poorly on standardized education tests would be able to develop good reading habits and skills. He believes it is the job of the schools to make up for the lack of attention and opportunity given these children in print-deprived homes.

In 1973, after completing a dual major in psychology and special education, Lyon took a job in a third grade classroom in a lower-middle-class Albuquerque neighborhood where 35 percent of the students were Hispanic.

"About a third of the third graders couldn't read well. They had good awareness, they had print skills, but they were very slow pulling print off the page. Many of them could not read to grade level or read for enjoyment. Most of the kids hadn't a lot of language education in the home or anyone who read to them. Their verbal skills were weak."

Lyon talked to teachers and studied the literature and came to believe that the biggest problem in American education is that a significant number of kids can't read well enough to use print as a vehicle to learn.

He blames the teachers' colleges. "When I was in education courses, there was no depth to the reading curriculum." He says he was shocked by the difference between the psychology curriculum and the education school courses. "Coming from an experimental background there was very little in educational methods courses based on evidence. It was mostly philosophy and assumption on how kids do learn things. The research was qualitative, not quantitative."

In Lyon's view, much of what passed for modern curriculum was actually guesswork. The fact that a man with this view became George Bush's reading advisor is a powerful statement about the gap between the public colleges of education and the politicians who appropriate their budgets.

Lyon says that the controversial reading component of "No Child Left Behind" is the answer to the questions he raised years ago as a rookie teacher in Albuquerque.

Question Number One: How do kids learn to read?

"For a long time no one knew what to do. There was not a lot of converging evidence on this subject. We now know that a number of subskills have to be mastered and integrated."

Question Number Two: How is this curriculum created and implemented?

"Comprehension is the key. Why do all kids not do the same? If a kid is not understanding, even if they can read, they won't continue to read. What gets in the way and what interferes with the program?"

A focus on comprehension requires an efficient delivery system, says Lyon. The key is to "identify the kids who might be at risk. If we are not going to get to kids early enough how can we help them?"

To turn Lyon's belief into legislative mandates of course

requires a strong partnership with elected officials. Lyon says "fortunately, we have enough experience to inform the legislature." And using the power of federal law, Lyon and his colleagues have swept away the right of teachers to personalize assessment. No more automatic promotions. No more high school diplomas based on grading scales that may have been eroded by liberal-minded teachers all too willing to give their students the benefit of the doubt. Like mandatory sentencing, teachers must follow the new federal rule book or risk sanction, even dismissal. These sanctions extend to school districts who can lose federal financing if they break the rules outlined in the many-hundred-page NCLB play book.

Standardized testing has been elevated to do-or-die status. Children must meet or exceed the test du jour or face the consequences: tutoring by approved tutors, summer school, repeating a grade, and sitting on the sidelines cap and gownless as their classmates march to Pomp and Circumstances at the end of 12th grade.

If all of this sounds Draconian, it's important to realize that Lyon and Bush are not going to let up on the people they consider the witch doctors of higher education. "Kids need to know the sounds and teachers have to teach kids how to relate sounds to language. But a phonics-based approach is not a panacea."

"Kids in studies with good phonemic awareness still don't comprehend. They apply these sounds but still don't understand."

Part of the problem, says Lyon, dates back to his own education at the University of New Mexico. "Pervading the early to mid 1970s was the notion that learning to read was a natural process, like listening and thinking. The party line, he says, went something like this:

"Why would you want to teach letters and sounds when what all you need to do is read aloud and have them interested in authentic texts?"

Lyon believes that reading remains fundamentally "a skill like gymnastics. The lack of appreciation for using convergence of scientific evidence has," Lyon believes, "led to a crisis in the classroom."

"It's endemic that the folks that go into colleges of education are typically not driven by using evidence. There is a good deal of post-modern thought which contends that everything is in the eye of the beholder." This leads to a "my evidence is as good as your evidence," approach, "even though there is a marked difference in the quality of the evidence and in the quality of the interpretation."

"We are getting better. We now know that we do have a problem. We know we have a gap between what our teachers know and classroom implementation. The issue is what works in the classroom. There are now materials available that work."

"We can go into a classroom where up to 70 percent of the kids can't read at the basic level and we can bring to bear conditions that would bring this number down to 6 percent."

This astonishing claim, says Lyon, is based on a program that focuses on four components: the sound part (phonics), fluency, vocabulary, and comprehension. "These are criteria that go into reading. Teachers need to assess how the kids develop these skills. They need to know how to go to the textbook literature and the vendors and identify those instructional programs that have been chosen for their effectiveness"

While NCLB mandates that all children must show year-to-year improvement, Lyon concedes that even the best program is not a panacea. "Every study shows that about two to six percent of the children don't respond to any program."

But he firmly believes that everyone else can benefit once the teaching community takes "a more scientific approach to training and implementation."

"The situation we have now is similar to medical schools at the turn of the century. The Flexner report showed that doctors had widely varying training and backgrounds because class content varied from school to school.

"The same thing is true today in the big colleges of education. And we don't have a good system in place for identifying the quality of teaching. If we have a good idea of what teachers need to know that seems to indicate teaching a common language.

"The system we have now doesn't bode well for consistency. Certification does not seem to be synonymous with quality. A degree in elementary education doesn't equal qualification."

Lyon believes a comprehensive national testing program can force schools to mend their past mistakes. So-called failing schools that don't show year-to-year improvement will be required to transport kids to better schools. Lyon says schools "won't have resources taken away for three years. If schools don't improve after three years, decisions will be made at the Department of Education."

Could some of these schools be closed under NCLB guidelines? Lyon backs off. "We are talking 13 years down the line. Even the worst schools can be brought around. Money has to be spent in the right way."

No Child Left Behind offers a total of $1.5 billion for reading programs that align staff development with what Lyon calls "scientific evidence." No state got the money (for reading programs from NCLB) on the first try, "because some of the proposals were "sent by teachers and administrators who don't know shit from shinola."

"Some districts have a home-grown program. The key is using teaching methods that are aligned with scientific methods. We've got data and data trumps everything. In the end evidence accrued over the years will show how effective this has been."

Lyon and his law rule out programs he believes won't work. "People might say they are going to use a whole language approach. That wouldn't be approved because it is based on a faulty conception," such as learning to read "by jumping up and down on a trampoline."

He says whole language is a good example of a type of

instructional delivery that is not based on a comprehensive program. "Some states have told local districts they are limited to a specific program. If they use federal dollars it has to be used for programs that work and are comprehensive. You wouldn't keep a medical school in business if it chose apricot pit therapy. The same is true in reading. We know what goes into it."

"Educational agencies can get educational development from state universities or anyone else as long as content is based on converging evidence. One-third of Texas teachers are being certified outside traditional university colleges. They could contract with Voyager (a private company that provides staff development programs)."

Lyon says his remark about blowing up the colleges of education was a "shot across the bow. This is a way to get the education establishment's attention and say we can do better. If I had to do it over again, I wouldn't use those particular words. I would have said that we need to do a better job of preparing our teachers with content and pedagogy where the results are reflected in student performance."

VANISHED WITHOUT A TRACE, TEXAS STYLE
Ken Goodman

During his election campaign George W. Bush took credit for "The Texas Miracle" in education. He claimed he had raised test scores, eliminated dropouts and improved education. The differences between minority and white achievement had narrowed. In making the changes that resulted in this miracle he got heavy support from the Governor's Business Council headed by Ken Lay of Enron fame. Bush promised to bring the miracle to the whole nation if elected president. A major justification for the unreasonable and unreachable goals of NCLB is in the claimed achievements made in Texas.

The Houston Independent School District also received acclaim. The Broad Foundation gave it a $1 million prize as the nation's best school system. Its website lists both Rod Paige and Kaye Stripling, current HISD superintendent as "Our Heroes":

> Under Stripling, HISD was awarded the inaugural Broad Prize for Urban Education in October 2002 because of its success in dramatically increasing student achievement and in beginning to reduce achievement gaps across ethnic groups and between high- and low-income students. We will continue to watch as Stripling leads HISD on the path of reform that has become a legacy. (Broad Foundation, http://www.broadfoundation.org)[1]

The legacy began with Rod Paige. As president, Bush chose Paige, then Superintendent of Houston Schools, as his Secretary of Education. Paige's rise itself was something of a miracle. He went

---

[1]Note: The Broad Foundation recently joined with the U.S. Department of Education in funding Standard and Poor, a subsidiary of McGraw-Hill, to rate all schools nationally according to NCLB criteria.

from Coach at Texas Southern University to president of the college. He became a member of the board of HISD. While a member of the board, his colleagues chose him as school superintendent. (http://www.ed.gov/news/staff/bios/paige.html)

As Houston Superintendent, Rod Paige got the Harold W. McGraw, Jr. Prize in Education on September 26, 2000 for his achievements which included purchasing the Open Court Reading Program for use in HISD from McGraw-Hill. Open Court and Direct Instruction Reading, both published by McGraw-Hill are two of only a handful of commercial reading programs Paige's bureaucrats at the US Department of education accept in NCLB state proposals.

Chairman emeritus Harold W. McGraw, Jr. told the crowd of educators, "This year's honorees have demonstrated a steadfast commitment to education reform and are truly improving educational opportunities for our nation's children." (http://www.mcgraw-hill.com/community/mcgraw_prize/2000)

Walt Haney, a researcher at Boston College, did a two-year study of the "Texas miracle". Among his revelations is that large numbers of students, particularly minority students, are failing ninth grade and being pushed out of school, though Texas districts including Houston claimed to have few dropouts.

Here are some of his other findings (in italics). Partly as a result of his report, the *New York Times* conducted their own investigation (NYT. 12/3/03). I've added their findings to his.

The recent history of education reform and statewide testing in Texas led to the introduction of the Texas Assessment of Academic Skills (TAAS) in 1990-91.

Haney Report: *The passing scores on TAAS tests were arbitrary and discriminatory. Analyses comparing TAAS reading, writing and math scores with one another and with relevant high school grades raise doubts about the reliability and validity of TAAS scores.*

The *New York Times* reports its comparison of data from the Stanford Achievement Test and the Texas exam (TAAS) :

> Houston students improved from 1999 to 2002 in most grades, but at only a fraction of the rate portrayed by the state exam . . . the gains in the average scores on the Stanford test were about a third of the average gain in the TAAS scores.
>
> Even students with the poorest skills posted high scores on the Texas test. In reading, a passing score of 70 on the test was the equivalent to scores below the 30th percentile in national ranking on the Stanford test in every grade. In tenth grade, passing the state exam was equivalent to the fifth percentile in the national ranking.
>
> Haney Report: *There were problems of missing students and other mirages in Texas enrollment statistics that profoundly affect both reported dropout statistics and test scores.*

Subsequent to the Haney report, Dr. Robert Kimball, then assistant principal at Sharpstown High School in Houston, blew the whistle on the misreporting of dropouts at Houston high schools. *New York Times* writer Diana Jean Schemo reported that "Some 462 other students left the school that year, and Sharpstown claimed that not one had dropped out." She quotes Kimball: "We go from 1,000 Freshmen to less than 300 Seniors with no dropouts. Amazing." Yet at Sharpstown, the entire staff received cash bonuses for the school's performance.

According to the *Times:*

> Sharpstown was not alone. A recent state audit in Houston, which examined records from 16 middle and high schools, found that more than half of the 5,500 students who left in the 2000-01 school year should have been declared dropouts but were not. That year, Houston schools reported that only 1.5 percent of its students had dropped out. . . .

In a third of Houston's 30 high schools, scores on the standardized exams have risen as enrollment has shrunk. At Austin High, for example, 2,757 students were enrolled in the 1997-1998 school year, when only 65 percent passed the 10th grade math test, an important gauge of school success in Texas. Three years later, 99 percent of students passed the math exam, but enrollment shrank to 2,215 students. The school also reported that dropout figures had plummeted 92 percent, to 0.3 percent from 4.1 percent. (NYT, Schemo, July 2003)

Haney Report: *Only 50 percent of minority students in Texas have been progressing from grade 9 to high school graduation since the initiation of the TAAS testing program. Since about 1982, the rates at which Black and Hispanic students are required to repeat grade 9 have climbed steadily, such that by the late 1990s, nearly 30 percent of Black and Hispanic students were "failing" grade 9. Cumulative rates of grade retention in Texas are almost twice as high for Black and Hispanic students as for White students.*

Here's what the *Times* found:

The achievement gap between whites and minorities, which Houston authorities have argued has nearly disappeared on the Texas exam, remains huge on the Stanford test. The ranking of the average white student was 36 points higher than that of the average black student in 1999 and fell slightly, to 34 points, in 2002.

Haney Report: *Some portion of the gains in grade 10 TAAS pass rates are illusory. The numbers of students taking the grade 10 tests who were classified as "in special education" and hence not counted in schools' accountability ratings nearly doubled between 1994 and 1998. A substantial portion of the apparent increases in TAAS pass rates in the 1990s are due to such exclusions.*

The *Times* also reported such exclusions:

> Kathryn Sanchez, head of assessment for Houston's
> schools, said students were doing well on both the Texas
> exam and the Stanford test, given the city's large number
> of poor and minority students. Ms. Sanchez said that
> Houston students had also done well on the National
> Assessment of Educational Progress, a federally mandated
> test widely referred to as "the nation's report card."
>
> On that test, fourth graders in Houston and New York
> outdid children in four other cities in writing, to score at
> the national average. . . . Of all six cities, however, Houston
> excluded most children with limited English from taking
> the national assessment, and some researchers suggest that
> removing such students may have helped raise Houston's
> score.
>
> Haney Report: *In the opinion of educators in Texas, schools
> are devoting a huge amount of time and energy preparing students
> specifically for TAAS, and emphasis on TAAS is hurting more
> than helping teaching and learning in Texas schools, particularly
> with at-risk students, and TAAS contributes to retention in grade
> and dropping out.*

The *Times* concurs:

> And in some places, it seemed to work, said Rene
> Barrios, lead organizer for the Metropolitan Organization,
> a chapter of a group that monitors public services. But in
> many other places, Ms. Barrios said, the system became
> the single most important measure of school success and
> the test itself, for many teachers, became the curriculum.
> "The whole system has been taken over by the test," she
> said.

Haney Report: *The review of GED statistics indicated that there was a sharp upturn in numbers of young people taking the GED tests in Texas in the mid-1990s to avoid TAAS.*

A convergence of evidence indicates that during the 1990s, slightly less than 70 percent of students in Texas actually graduated from high school.

The *Times* investigation shows that this record has not improved since the Haney Report:

Houston school officials acknowledge that the progress in the elementary grades peters out in high school. About 13,600 eighth graders in 1998 dwindled to fewer than 8,000 high school graduates. Though 88 percent of Houston's student body are black and Latino, only a few hundred minority students leave high school "college ready," according to state figures.

Haney Report: *Between 1994 and 1997, TAAS results showed a 20% increase in the percentage of students passing all three exit level TAAS tests (reading, writing and math), but TASP (a college readiness test) results showed a sharp decrease (from 65.2% to 43.3%) in the percentage of students passing all three parts (reading, math, and writing).*

As measured by performance on the SAT, the academic learning of secondary school students in Texas has not improved since the early 1990s, compared with SAT takers nationally. SAT-Math scores have deteriorated relative to students nationally.

The gains on NAEP (National Assessment of Educational Progress) for Texas fail to confirm the dramatic gains apparent on TAAS.

The gains on TAAS and the unbelievable decreases in dropouts during the 1990s are more illusory than real.

For the full Haney Report, go to http://www.epaa.asu.edu/epaa/v8n41.

Dropouts and Pushouts

There can be no doubt from both the Haney study and the *New York Times* follow-up study that there has been widespread manipulation of the key statistics in Houston and other parts of Texas. Even worse, there has been a major coverup of a huge number of Texas young people being pushed out of the schools and denied graduation at the same time a "miracle" was being proclaimed.

The state authorities made the Texas tests (TAAS) easy enough for most white, middle-class kids to pass but hard enough to fail many Black and Latino students. Ninth grade became a key gate. Large numbers of Houston students, including about a third of minority students, failed the TAAS and were prevented from going on to tenth grade and eventual graduation. These students reach the legal age for leaving schools so they drop out or are simply dropped for unexcused absences. At the same time, the authorities bragged that the proportion of tenth graders graduating had improved and that higher proportions of minority students were graduating.

The *Times* study suggests "that perhaps Houston is a model of how the focus on school accountability can sometimes go wrong, driving administrators to alter data or push students likely to mar a school's profile—through poor attendance or low test scores—out the back door."

But the Texas Education Agency, the state education authority, is quite forgiving. The audit recommended lowering the ranking of 14 of the 16 schools from the best to the worst. For now it is rejecting the recommendation of the auditor to rank the district's performance as unacceptable. Instead a state monitor will be reviewing HISD's efforts to improve the way it reports dropouts.

Houston joins only 3 of Texas's 1,040 school districts classed as "Academically Acceptable: Special Accreditation Investigation," whatever that means. The state reduced academic rankings at 15 of the 16 middle and high schools where dropout records were altered , and told Houston to reassign the administrative staff at

Sharpstown High School. The *New York Times* quoted Superinten-dent Kaye Stripling as saying Houston's "accountability rating remains academically acceptable, and we should be proud of our progress."

So, in contradiction to the claim that the intent is to leave no child behind, driving large numbers of students, mostly minority students, out of school and not counting them as dropouts is "aca-demically acceptable" to the State of Texas and the Bush/Paige Department of Education.

No one has been punished and no action has been taken to reconsider the policies that have caused large numbers of pupils to be retained in ninth grade and pushed out of school. These are the fruits of policies developed under Bush and Paige in Texas. The Broad Foundation has not asked for their $1 million prize back. What led Haney, the *New York Times* and others to question the Texas Miracle is the absurdity of the claims being made. No dropouts? Amazing improvements in scores? There is more than careless data-keeping and overzealous advocacy here. Clearly pressure on administrators was a factor. But the Texas Education Agency, Rod Paige, and George W. Bush cannot have been unaware that they were touting absurd results of their policies and that dirty secrets were being covered up.

How many children are being left behind? Texas is not alone in not counting pushouts as dropouts. An estimate in New York, the nation's largest school system is that 20 to 30 percent of stu-dents are being forced out in a manner similar to Texas. And the Bush Administration is also pushing to raise GED requirements, a path to a high school diploma followed by many high school pushouts. Is there a miracle in Texas education? The miracle is that they got away with what they did and continue to boast about what they achieved.

Now NCLB permits states to create their own tests and set the passing criteria. The next step in NCLB requires states to use the same test but they still will set the passing criteria. Some like

Texas have made the tests easy enough to avoid offending white, middle-class parents. Many, however, have not understood how the game is being played. They created tests so hard that the majority of students are failing them including many usually high-achieving middle-class kids.

Richard Rothstein, writing in the *Times*, points out Arkansas whose low-income eighth graders rank very low on the NAEP had no schools rated as failing, but New York whose low-income eighth graders ranked 7th had 19 percent of the state's low-income schools listed as failing, and Massachusetts' low-income eighth graders score about in the middle of the nation in reading but 24 percent of the state's low-income schools are deemed failing.

Secretary Paige has responded to this disparity by scolding states for making the tests too easy.

References

Rothstein, Richard. "How U.S. Punishes States With Higher Standards" *New York Times*, September 18, 2002

Schemo, Diana Jean, and Ford Fessenden. "A Miracle Revisited— Gains in Houston Schools: How Real Are They?" *New York Times*, December 3, 2003

DESTROYING PUBLIC SCHOOLS
IN THE NAME OF SAVING THEM

Ken Goodman

When Trent Lott "slipped" on the nostalgic occasion of honoring 100-year-old Strom Thurmond and professed his belief that if the nation had followed Thurmond's overt racism, as Mississippi a half-century earlier had done, America would be a better place today, he was revealing that the goal has not changed, only the tactics. Then, the confrontations were overt and ugly, with television news showing rights advocates beaten as they demonstrated peacefully and mobs harassing children on their way to school. Now, the forces aiming to destroy social justice and limit democracy have learned to use their money and power and the processes of democratic institutions to accomplish their goals.

Today, they no longer confront, they co-opt and subvert the very groups whose interests they attack. Lott was not punished for admitting his belief in a racist society. It was his nostalgia for the good old days of confrontation which cost him his job. Contemporary racists don't stand in the schoolhouse door, they close down the "failing" neighborhood schools using test scores as their bludgeons. And they do this in the name of "saving" poor children "trapped" in inferior schools.

If the suggestion that No Child Left Behind is essentially a racist and, to some extent, elitist effort to downsize and destroy the public school system sounds like a harsh assessment, perform your own due diligence. Simply get in your car and drive to the minority neighborhood of your choice. Talk to teachers at under-funded schools and ask them how they feel about the possibility of a mandated federal shutdown. Like churches and synagogues and mosques, schools are bedrock community institutions. Without neighborhood schools, minority communities will be stripped of an irreplaceable asset. Will these schools be super-seded by for-profit educational corporations?

Nowhere has the switch in tactics from confrontation to manip-ulation of democratic institutions been more successful than in the schools. The Bush Administration has rolled back the Constitutional rights of Americans by exploiting the fear of foreign and domestic terrorism. In education, a crisis in literacy has been manufactured (see Berliner and Biddle's book, *Manufactured Crisis*) and a subtle, relentless campaign has successfully imposed a national reading curriculum on America's highly decentralized educational system. Through a series of sham scientific panels and reports, the campaign has established that there is a simple solution to the literacy "crisis," supported by a scientific consensus. This phony crisis is so great that it warrants federal interventions in the schools right down to the classroom level. Never mind that the laws and their enforcement clearly violate the U.S. Constitution. Those framing the laws understand that in a democracy if power is taken and then institutionalized it becomes hard to challenge. This is particularly true when the judiciary system that is supposed to be a check against assertions of power is also abused.

Remarkably the campaign has succeeded in centralizing con-trol of the educational system at a bargain cost. Less than 8 per-cent of the national education budget comes from the federal gov-ernment, and the changes mandated by NCLB will cost states and local schools far more than they receive. The cost is so high, in fact, that some conservative officials have already rebelled.

One newspaper reported:

The Ohio Department of Education, for example, released a study last month estimating that the state will spend about $1.5 billion a year—more than twice as much as it now gets from the federal government under Mr. Bush's K-12 initiative—to meet the administrative costs and achieve-ment goals of the No Child Left Behind Act.

And while Virginia's Republican-led House of Delegates didn't have such a study to cite, it nearly unanimously passed a resolution January 23 declaring that "the law will cost literally millions of dollars that Virginia does not have" just to cover administration.

"It is significantly underfunded," argued Delegate James H. Dillard II, the Republican chairman of the chamber's education committee. "The problem now is that states are now just beginning to get an understanding of how much it's going to cost," said Mr. Dillard, who is also vice chairman of the National Conference of State Legislatures' education committee. (David J. Hoff, *State Journal*, February 4, 2004)

Today, schools labeled as failing are required to bus children, at their expense, to another school, which is required to accept them even if there is no room. A key player in the campaign, Chester (Checker) Finn Jr., a former federal bureaucrat and official of the Thomas B. Fordham Foundation, has gloated over the ease of co-opting the local and state decision-makers. They don't have to take the money, he says. But actually they do, because the same forces have been active at the state level.

Secretary of Education Rod Paige, who declined to be interviewed for this book, understands that teachers are a harder sell than politicians. On February 18, 2004, he slipped and referred to the National Education Association as a "terrorist group". In his "apology" he made clear that he regards any dissent as unacceptable. Paige said:

The principal critics of this law—aside from those with issues concerning federalism—fall into three camps: protectors of the education establishment, such as national union lobbyists; some state legislators who have become victims of an organized misinformation campaign; and, perhaps most sadly, some members of Congress who voted for the law and support its ideals but now see opposition as being to their political advantage. These forces have nothing to offer in place of the No Child Left Behind Act but demands for more money to pay for the same programs that haven't worked in the past. They seem to have forgotten what is really at stake here: the best interests of the children. Do they want to condemn a child to a poor education? Are they going to decide whose children will be left behind? (*Washington Post*, 2/27/2004)

The ultraconservative "states rights" advocates who have usually fought federalization have, until recently, been silent. But in conservative Nebraska, Doug Christensen, Nebraska Education Commissioner, says, "The Constitution of this country says education is a state matter, that it's our job, and I cannot in good conscience stand up in front of anyone in this state and say we need to do something because the federal government says we do." The Utah and Virginia and Arizona legislature have considered resolutions to reject NCLB, for the same reason.

Reid Lyon, lauded by the *Wall Street Journal* as President Bush's reading czar and introduced by Education Secretary Rod Paige as one of the president's key educational advisors, made a slip similar to Lott's on November 18, 2002. Just months after 9/11, he proclaimed at a public function attended by many educators and representatives of professional organizations that if he made the laws he would "blow up the colleges of education." Lyon, head of the research branch of the National Institute of Child and Human Development (NICHD), has clout in Washington. He helped the Bush administration select new officials in the Department of Education. But despite his success in shifting the reading curriculum to meet the goals of the White House, he continues to blame the colleges of education for the current "crisis" in the public schools.

Reid Lyon's logic is to blow them up. It is they (the colleges of education) who mislead and miseducate teachers. Incompetent themselves, they fill their students with useless overly complex theory and refuse to teach them the phonics they need to know to teach scientifically. They are unworthy of academic freedom and can therefore be required to clear their course syllabi with state monitors on threat of decertifying their programs.

Perhaps Lyon is impatient with the process because it is becoming increasingly clear that the fail-proof "scientific" reading programs are not working. For example, in Baltimore, one of the first sites where these "scientific" programs were put in place, their failure has sent shock waves through the NCLB team. The dismal results are no surprise since these are warmed-over narrow phonics programs with long histories of failure masked by unwarranted claims of success. But more important, the tactic of censoring teachers and forcing conformity on them neutralizes the more professional teachers, driving many out of the classrooms, while providing a cover for their less competent colleagues. Any program, no matter how well thought out, must be implemented by a first-class, experienced teaching staff. Unless, or until, teachers are allowed to do the job they have learned to do, free from the strictures of NCLB, students are going to have a difficult time learning.

The failure of NCLB-mandated programs becomes an excuse for closing more schools and heaping more abuse on the colleges of education. Since the programs are "scientifically" proven to be fail-proof, the teachers get the blame. They must be "reeducated." They are sent to summer training at great expense, indoctrinated over the internet, and when all else fails, replaced with teaching wannabes who have neither the education nor the experience to do a good job. The only clear winners in this process are a handful of federally certified vendors that publish materials preaching and teaching the NCLB party line.

It has been easy to eliminate or hamstring professionals in the state departments of education and shift power to state boards in places like Arizona, where the agenda can be more easily controlled. In the Texas Education Agency, a key person in reading education was punished for the expression on her face as she left a meeting. Sadly, professional decision making becomes political decision making at increasingly lower levels.

Those who resist the NCLB mantra are increasingly likely to be scapegoated. Listen to Checker Finn, who has given himself the title The Education Gadfly. In a publication of that name he recently said:

> Do not, however, doubt the determination of resisters to stick by the regime under which they have thrived. The most dogged of them may turn out to be the ed schools, which (along with the teacher unions) one might term public education's version of Iraq's Republican Guards.

In another issue he shifts blame for failure of the "scientifically proven methods" to teacher educators and the entire profession:

> How can Congress enact a law mandating that every child in every state will (within 12 years) attain 'proficiency' on state standards if many of those children's classroom instructors have no such expectations? One ought not fault teachers for their beliefs. They are what they've been shaped to be by those who trained them yesterday and supervise them today. For the most part, their attitudes, expectations and priorities, as well as the methods they employ in class, mirror the views of their ed-school professors and their professional mentors.
>
> The problem is that the professors and the profession have not entirely bought into standards-based reform. It goes against their grain. Never mind that it's the law of the land, the centerpiece of education policy in nearly every

state and the strong preference of most parents. We could face an education train wreck if what happens when the classroom door closes does not advance the goals that policymakers and parents so hopefully enshrined in their states' standards.

In the days of Senator Joseph McCarthy, blacklists were overt and focused on public figures. Today, covert blacklists have been established of people, ideas, and practices that may not be mentioned in state or federal applications for support. In education, these blacklists are enforced in staff development designed to reeducate teachers in the federally mandated programs. Teacher educators are forced to demonstrate their acceptance and support of the federal mandates. Lyon and others have suggested the possibility of accusing administrators and teachers of malpractice for non-conformity. And it is certainly true that those attempting to conform with the mandates may find themselves legal scapegoats charged with fraud or misapplication of funds for innocent attempts to ameliorate the effects of the mandates.

It is a curious demonstration of how successful the seizure of power in education in the United States has been that, while Senator Lott's social justice slip was punished and widely criticized, Reid Lyon's advocacy of acts of terrorism was neither reported in the press nor challenged even by the representatives of the colleges of education in his audience that day. This attack on public education is merely the first wave in a sustained campaign to discredit community schools and put them out of business. If the NCLB advocates have their way, the remaining public schools will lack the capacity to accommodate the displaced students. Private schools couldn't afford to take on the additional student load either. Education would be turned over to private corporations, bean counters, and conformists.

Like Trent Lott, the advocates of NCLB are determined to go back in time. Given a chance, they will take our nation back to a time when universal free public education was only a distant dream.

Reference:

David J. Hoff, Debate Grows on True Costs Of School Law, *State Journal*, February 4, 2004

ROD PAIGE, SUPERSTAR:
DOES EDUCATIONAL POLICY NEED A PEP RALLY?
Richard J. Meyer

Editor's note: In April 2002, U.S. Secretary of Education Rod Paige took to the road "to educate parents about the most sweeping change in education policy in three decades—and to ask for their help" . . . a 25-city No Child Left Behind Tour Across America . . . "aims to reach out to parents and working families to ask for their active participation in this process of improving America's schools." . . . The tour . . . unveiled a No Child Left Behind toolkit for parents, featuring an American flag, patriotic pens, two booklets, and an interactive CD "to answer questions and find resources for local information.

Richard J. Meyer, University of New Mexico professor, attended the kick-off rally of the No Child Left Behind Tour Across America in Albuquerque. Following are excerpts from his notes:

The outdoor theater of the National Hispanic Cultural Center has two sets of steep concrete bleachers, thirty rows high. Each row seats about sixty people. The north bleachers with the sun shining on them are packed with students walked or bused from their inner city schools. I'm curious that the speakers at the south-facing podium/stage have their backs to the huge crowd of school kids. East-side bleachers, six rows high, are shaded by a large awning. That is where the dignitaries are seated . . . Above the bleachers commercially prepared signs in patriotic colors read:

RESULTS FOR STUDENT ACHIEVEMENT
USING SOLID RESEARCH FOR INSTRUCTION
INFORMATION AND OPTIONS FOR PARENTS
FLEXIBILITY AND LOCAL CONTROL

Various childrens' groups perform:

> Zuni Pueblo Head Start kids are dancing accompanied
> by two elders singing in Zuni. . . . A young woman comes
> to the center of the stage and says: "Thanks to our presi-
> dent, children like these will not be left behind." She intro-
> duces a dance group from a local high school's Black
> Student Union. Local singer Stephanie Montil thanks Rod
> Paige for inviting her and sings in Spanish about children
> and love. A drill team from Jimmy Carter Middle School
> cheers: "We are here to show our pride, let no child be left
> behind."
>
> They repeat the last part four times and throw American
> flag T-shirts into the audience.

A speaker talks more about leaving no child behind, sharing
information about the NCLB website. . . . New Mexican Olympic
Medalist Tristan Gale speaks next.

> . . . As she's talking, a group is passing out postcard-
> sized American flags. . . . The flags begin to wave. . . . She
> welcomes Rod Paige, who stood at the front of the class
> and sat in the superintendent's chair.
>
> Rod Paige is descending to the podium from the top of
> the bleachers. People are standing, clapping and watching
> him shake hands and wave.

Local political figures take the mike. Senator Bingaman wants "to
see that this legislation works the way it was intended." Next

Representative Wilson repeats statistics about the failure of our schools. Of Rod Paige, she proudly says, he "does not hang around in the halls of theory."

Paige says the "nice rally"reminds him of his football coaching days. He repeats the goals of NCLB, interacts with some students, and calls upon parents to pressure schools to implement NCLB.

> There are flags waving behind Rod Paige, framed against a cloudless blue New Mexico sky. The air is still morning cool for this time of year and the crowd is with him. He talks again . . . that the government will only fund programs based on "scientific research" . . . about flexibility, local control and how special interest groups cripple reform.
>
> Suddenly he . . . is talking about terrorism—"we're gonna win that fight because the military uses solid research" . . . kids are waving posters, "United for results." . . . A singer starts "God Bless America." Everyone rises and sings along. . . . Two huge cannons rise shooting confetti into the crowd. Over the loudspeaker comes "You make me want to shout." The song is loud, the confetti shoots for at least five minutes, flags are waving.

The message is clear: if you are a good American, you'll support the plans of the federal government for killing terrorists and leaving no child behind.

Parent Support for "No Child Left Behind" Is Thin

Ken Goodman

Most American parents who know about "No Child Left Behind" (NCLB) school reforms like the concept, but they also would oppose implementation of any of its punitive terms in their own child's school. So concludes the first national opinion survey since NCLB implementation to specifically zero in on what the parents of school-age children think about the two-year-old initiative. Conducted among 699 parents by Opinion Research Corporation (ORC), the survey is sponsored by Results for America . . . a project of the nonprofit Civil Society Institute. The report says:

> . . . [A] third of all parents (34 percent) who have heard of NCLB see the school reforms as "punishing schools for failure instead of rewarding them for success," a quarter (25 percent) view it as "limiting learning by students,"while fewer than half (46 percent) associate NCLB with "improving learning."

The RFA survey also found almost no parental support (10 percent) for increased spending on the controversial school reform plan. This is true even though there is widespread awareness (78 percent) of NCLB among parents, with two-thirds (68 percent v. 22 percent) of the NCLB-aware parents expressing support for the concept of the school reforms. The report states:

> Many parents have major concerns when the focus shifts from the *abstract* concept of NCLB to the *real-world* specifics of the reforms, including high-stakes testing (only 51 percent support, with just 17 percent expressing "strong" support and 33 percent "somewhat" supportive) and taking

funds from schools deemed to be "failing," particularly those of their children (only 19 percent supporting such a move). Significantly, most parents would prefer to see any additional federal education funds spent on smaller class sizes (52 percent), not enforcement or further implementation of NCLB (10 percent).

"This survey makes it clear that concerns about 'No Child Left Behind' go up the closer it gets to the homes of parents and the schools attended by their children," said Civil Society Institute President Pam Solo. "What you end up with is lukewarm backing for NCLB that resembles what Mark Twain said about the Platte River: it's a mile wide and an inch deep. Parents don't much like the idea of high-stakes testing on which everything rides on the outcome of dubious quizzes or the notion that their own child's school could be branded a 'failure' and penalized." According to the report:

It is worth noting that this does not appear to be a political or ethnic phenomenon; the seemingly schizophrenic view of NCLB's conceptual and 'real world' terms cuts across most demographic and political groupings. . . . Nearly three-quarters (73 percent) say they would not support withholding funds from their child's school for failing under NCLB, with only 19 percent willing to support such a move. . . . Supporters of NCLB are just as opposed to withholding of federal funds from their own schools (72 percent), and 61 percent of Republican parents join most independents (84 percent) and Democrats (79 percent) in opposition to withholding of such funds.

THE 2 VOICES OF (FORMER) ASSISTANT SECRETARY OF EDUCATION SUSAN NEUMAN

Ken Goodman

Voice I: October 2002

A Stockton California newspaper quotes Assistant Secretary of Education Susan Neuman who was principally responsible for implementing President Bush's No Child Left Behind Act:

> "The previous administration was waiving this and waiving that. This administration is serious. We don't intend to waive any of the requirements."

Voice II: Fast forward; it's now March 2004

Michigan faces having to restructure over 100 failing schools by September 2004. Detroit has 53 of those. Nobody's exactly sure what that restructuring means but apparently the whole staff must be moved out and a whole new one moved in.

The *Detroit News* now quotes Professor Susan Neuman:

> "Lansing leaders need to demand that the federal government give schools another year," said Susan Neuman, the former Assistant Secretary for Elementary and Secondary Education for U.S. Department of Education.
>
> "This is a very, very critical point in our history," said Neuman, now a professor of early childhood education at the University of Michigan. "If we don't do this well, we risk hurting kids."
>
> Neuman was responsible for implementing the law until she left the post in January 2003. She says parts of it are unworkable and the federal government needs to be more flexible with its requirements.

SECTION THREE

The School and the Classroom

TEACHING KNOWLEDGE AND EXPERIENCE: DO THEY COUNT?

Yetta Goodman

Vera Milz is a teacher in a Detroit suburb with four decades of experience. She is admired by and receives accolades from her former students, her student teachers, administrators, and colleagues. It is a great pleasure to watch Vera interact with her students in her quiet and supportive manner, respond to parents with confidence and understanding, to listen to her talk about her teaching and children's literature and how kids come to know reading and writing. Those who have spent time researching and student teaching in her classroom sing her praises. She knows about language, language learning, and language teaching. She respects children's innovations and expects them to learn. Her doctoral dissertation research was an analysis of the specific ways in which her first graders developed as writers during a one-year period. She followed up and continued her classroom research over the years using her ever-growing knowledge and experience to construct an innovative learning environment that involves her children in becoming literate as they learn about their world by exploring all kinds of questions related to science, social studies, math, music, and much more.

She involves parents in their children's literacy learning. She brings the finest children's literature authors to her district and her classroom and involves her young authors in writing to their favorite published authors and to write and produce their own stories and books. She is asked to review kids' and professional books for prestigious professional journals. She has been elected and appointed to committees and commissions of professional organizations.

Recently, Vera told me this story: A first-year principal was hired at her elementary school. The principal believed strongly in the importance of self-esteem for students and decided that this would be the theme for the school year that would involve all the teachers and the students. She brought in experts in the area of self-esteem for a three-day workshop during the week before school started. At the end of the in-service, the principal thanked the presenters and said to the teachers, "Please invite me to your classroom in the next two weeks to see your self-esteem lessons."

Two weeks later the principal said to Vera: "You haven't invited me to your classroom to see your self-esteem lessons yet." Vera responded in her calm and direct way, "Every time you walk into my classroom, you'll see my self-esteem lessons. You're welcome anytime."

Why Isn't There Acclaim for Outstanding Teachers?

Ever since I heard this story, I've wondered why a school administrator wouldn't get to know the strengths of the teachers in her building to make use of the knowledge and experience that teachers have to offer the school community. *Why isn't there more acclaim for the capabilities of outstanding teachers in the classroom? Why are the rich resources of years of developing knowledge and professional experience so often overlooked and consciously ignored by many professional educators, parents, politicians, and the public in general?*

I return to these questions whenever I walk into the classroom of an outstanding professional who capably supports an individual learner in awe about something new she is learning. Or I see a teacher who picks up on a comment of one student with excitement and uses it to interest and excite other students into a new study filled with wonder about animals, planets, or a new author. I wonder how as an educational community we learn to value and acknowledge the many teachers who demonstrate daily their ability to create and compose classrooms in which rich and important learning is an ongoing experience for the students.

In the present climate of No Child Left Behind, with restrictive laws at the national and state levels, I see respect for teachers and public education waning as we hear more about underperforming schools than we do about outstanding teachers. At the present time there are those who would do away with certification and make decisions about teacher quality by simplistically testing bits of knowledge. As a result, I see teachers become disheartened about teaching.

I want to share a few teacher stories that exemplify how the profession and the public continue to ignore the knowledge and experiences of great teachers and suggest some reasons for why this occurs.

Ignoring Knowledge and Experience
In the lunchrooms of elementary and secondary schools, at presentations by teachers at professional conferences, on the internet, in newspaper articles, and in graduate education classes at universities, I often hear or read stories about how the knowledge and experience of teachers are being ignored. In my university office, teachers, working diligently on master's or doctoral degrees, often sigh deeply now and consider seriously whether it is not time for them to leave teaching and sell candy at See's or wait tables at Red Lobster. Many of these teachers already have a head start. They work outside of school hours in these establishments or others like them. So much money is wasted on self-defeating bureaucratic initiatives like No Child Left Behind that there isn't enough money to pay teachers what they need to support their families.

I relate some of these stories without names of teachers because, in the present climate, many teachers are wary of being publicly reprimanded for telling their poignant stories.

✎ A Tucson reporter writes about a male, Hispanic fourth-grade teacher who came back to teach in the same working-class district where he attended elementary and secondary school. He was inspired by a dedicated fourth-grade instructor who still teaches in the district. Like a lot of teachers today, he loves working with students but wonders if it is worth it. His school has been labeled "under-performing." The parents, the teachers, and children feel as if they are failures. The teacher is understandably worried about increasing demands, low pay, and diminishing respect. But most of all he feels that he can't be an inspiration to his students when he has to worry about their test scores rather than engaging them in learning about the important issues that face their community.

✎ A group of teachers was talking about the Curriculum Specialist in their school, who believes every teacher there in the school should be presenting reading and writing lessons in the exact same way in order to make sure that the kids can pass the test. This is a little like telling a heart surgeon that he has to operate on every single patient exactly the same way, regardless of the patient's condition. Surgeons improvise because their job demands it. Pilots make allowances for unusual situations because their passengers' lives depend on their experience and judgment. But when teachers try to improvise to meet the needs of an individual—look out. The bureaucrats are focused on short-term test results. Teachers take a far healthier long-range view. Unlike politicians, they are not running for reelection. They know that the chemistry of a well-orchestrated classroom will help children make their dreams come true.

✎ Teachers are told, with a straight face, that the children coming from homes where most parents do not speak English should not be given special consideration because this would be discriminatory. After her team used the district-mandated six-trait rubric to score the writing of all first graders in the school, one teacher noticed a trend. Most English-language learners scored below mastery. The children bused in from the low income area did poorly, as well. But all those children who had attended that school as kindergartners scored "mastery" at the end of first grade. Excited about the documentation of success within the school, she shared her findings with the Curriculum Specialist. The Curriculum Specialist responded, "It doesn't matter if they're low income or English speaking. You can't use that excuse for ineffective teaching anymore."

✎ The teachers in another school have many years of experience and knowledge on the teaching of reading and writing. They buy books, out of their own pocketbook, to enrich the lives of their students. They focus their attention on students who are determined to realize their own potential. And they work with parents to make sure that the home environments support the students' creativity. One of the teachers was assigned the children considered the hardest to teach in the school because she was a master at helping these children develop as readers and writers. This teacher believes one of the reasons her students became more confident readers was that they learned crucial writing skills. She helped them realize the importance of writing about their families and communities. She helped them establish the relationship between reading and writing, between authors and readers.

Now, however, since the school has not done well on the simplistic writing portion of the statewide test (how do you standardize writing?), the Curriculum Specialist has arrived to wave her magic wand. She provides specific probes the children have to write on every week for a specified period of time, and these must be evaluated using a six-trait rubric with the results posted in the hallways and on the internet so they are visible to all—the students, parents and administrators. In a world where well- published writers can spend months on an essay and years on a book, this approach is an insult to the intelligence of both the students and their teachers. These techniques are more appropriate to drag racing than they are to education.

The teacher no longer has time to involve her students in writing compositions based on their own topics of interest over a number of days, to share their work with classmates, and revise based on their responses and then proudly print and illustrate their books.

✎ A university education professor received a letter from a young teacher, one of her former students. This teacher talked about serving on a school team to choose a basal reader (textbook) for the district. She was excited about the program because it seemed to include many of the ideas she learned in her education courses. But things have changed for the teacher.

"I now feel as if all of the good teaching practices I learned in the last few years have been tossed aside. We are back to using worksheet after worksheet after worksheet. There is so much group instruction and 'teacher talk' that by the end of the day, I'm tired of hearing my own voice. Where is the meaningful and inspiring instruction? We are bound to use this program by state requirements as well as the federal Reading First Grant. At an underperforming school like mine, the pressure is very intense. The result will be that teachers will be teaching to the tests, worrying so much about low scores, the true mission of teaching and inspiring students will be lost."

✎ In an urban school district, each high-school teacher must administer a hastily constructed reading test. It's based on a short passage from their textbook selected by, believe it or not, the school secretary, because there was no time to involve teachers in the selection process. Each student reads orally from the short passage for 60 seconds to establish a "fluency score" based on the number of words read free of errors within one minute's time. The score translates into a reading grade-level. One of the teachers told me: "What I know about what my students know is irrelevant because the results of this *quick and dirty* measurement is what is considered accurate."

The issue of ignoring the knowledge and experience of teachers is as problematic for those who are in the early years of developing their professional expertise, as it is for Vera Milz.

Tamzin Sawyer, a third-grade teacher in a Tucson magnet school, describes her development as a conscientious and caring teacher in the new book *Whole Language Teaching, Whole Hearted Practice: Looking Back, Looking Forward* to be published in a volume edited by Monica Taylor in Peter Lang's Scholar Series.

Sawyer discusses her knowledge development from the time of her preservice to her present involvement in getting her master's degree. She describes how she expands on her experience supported by her developing knowledge. By her third year of teaching, she learned to integrate science inquiry curriculum with her reading and writing instruction: "Our science time went from half an hour to an hour and a half, blending science, reading, and writing. Students made predictions, drew diagrams, and wrote conclusions."

She talks about the importance of learning to trust her students to select their own reading materials and to work collaboratively. "I began checking in with my students individually about once a week. . . . we would review what they had read, what they liked about the books they chose, and what book they thought they would like to read next. I wanted them to become independent readers."

She encouraged her students to independently raise their own questions and research topics of their own choosing. The children were excited about their work and wanted to share it with their families and community members. The children, with Ms. Sawyer's support, organized a presentation for their families and community members: "Many of our guests . . . listened expectantly... as each child or group delivered short oral reports. . . . After the oral reports the students took their places by their displays (which included posters, computer-generated banners, and written reports) to answer questions about their topics. . . . Our audience was extremely impressed. . . . I, too, was amazed by how much my students and I learned in the process"

But then came the district-wide mandates in response to prospects of the school being labeled "underperforming." The school reorganized into reading groups based on test scores. Ms. Sawyer remembers: "I was unable to follow through on what they [her students] had learned during reading block time, and I had little idea what to tell their parents about what they were doing. . . . This new plan placed students ranging from ages eight to twelve in the same reading group. "The older students tended to be embarrassed (causing some to act out) while the younger students were shy and hesitant to contribute. . . . We now were required to label each skill taught with a six-digit code using our state standards notebooks. . . . I don't have a problem with being accountable for teaching what third graders need to know . . . but I regret that our motivations were beginning to stem from raising test scores and not from what teachers, the people who interact the most with students, thought their individual students needed."

Teachers and administrators had to tell parents that they were labeled as an underperforming school. Lunchtime was cut ten minutes; social studies, science, music, art, and PE were cut by half an hour a week and taught only in the afternoons; math took up 75 minutes and language arts took 90 minutes each morning. All students in the same grade were given identical assignments and assessments. "Week after week students who struggled to read simple texts were given the third-grade assessment and week after week they failed them."

Ms. Sawyer concludes: "It's degrading to principals, teachers, parents, and students to have their school so negatively labeled. It's degrading for teachers (some near retirement) to be told that what you have been doing for your entire teaching career was wrong. What is most degrading, however, is to take away the passion teachers have for teaching students things they love because there just isn't enough time in the schedule."

Tamzin Sawyer had learned to trust her kids to become learners in the enriched environment she organized with her students. She now was working in an environment where neither the learners nor the teachers were trusted. Her experience and knowledge are ignored by self-proclaimed experts who have their heads buried in testing result spreadsheets. As other sections in this book conclusively document, these tests are often hopelessly flawed and scored incorrectly. Millions of dollars in damages have been awarded to students and their parents victimized by these worthless tests.

Today we are living in a time of the *pedagogy of the absurd,* as Kenneth Goodman has labeled this period in educational history. This is a time when schools across the nation are blessed with many outstanding teachers in classrooms who achieve wonderful results with their students. This is a period of time when more teachers than ever before are extending their knowledge base through advanced degrees, doing research in their own classrooms, writing articles and books and speaking at conferences to continue their own development and the development of their colleagues.

Yet, at the same time, many public-school administrators and university professors are being directed to work against the best interests of public education to deskill teachers. There are even those who believe that all that is needed for students to learn are commercial programs and text books that reflect a dubious set of standards and are measured by machine scored tests.

Because of the sloppy imposition of NCLB regulations, we have moved to a narrow and uninspired curriculum that limits the opportunity for students to become richly literate.

Why Ignore Knowledge and Experience?

Today, more than ever before in my professional lifetime, teacher knowledge and experience are not only being ignored but undermined. Why are there individuals, groups, and institutions who ignore knowledge and experience that are the basis for scholarship in all fields of study? In most places in the world, people with knowledge are revered and supported by rewards and honors. At this period of time, especially in response to No Child Left Behind, not just classroom teachers but those of us who have been involved in professional development of teachers are being ignored and marginalized. Sometimes when we speak out about our considerable research on the teaching and learning of literacy, we are accused of being a special-interest group, or unpatriotic, or terrorists.

It's no secret that publishers of commercial programs and tests worry that the success of outstanding teachers might diminish their power and profits. They are concerned that administrators and school districts might rely less on the sales of commercialized programs if the word got around that teachers do not need to rely on single textbook or text adoptions to be successful in the classroom. In times past, there were publishing companies who labeled their materials "teacher proof." Obviously these companies make a lot more money if districts are forced to adopt standardized textbooks. The idea that teachers and students can build a substantial library in their own classroom or go to a library and pick out their own books is considered somewhat subversive. This helps explain why school library budgets have become significant casualties in today's slash-and-burn world of educational finance.

Students need and deserve the right to pick out the books they want to read. They should not all have to be on the same page of a standard textbook that has been substantially edited to conform to the biases of current politics. It is the job of educators to teach kids how to think for themselves. There is no better way to encourage students how to think and write than to encourage them to make their own reading decisions. It is the ultimate irony that both our federal government and the nation's largest publishers have found common ground with a strategy that forces school districts to squander vast amounts of money on textbooks that are created primarily to enhance the bottom line of a handful of corporations.

When George Bush hires speech writers to craft his state of the union address, you can bet that they are not turning to History or Government textbooks for their ideas and inspiration. Trade books, the same ones that teachers have been encouraging students to read at their own pace, are the heart of an intelligent curriculum.

No matter how hard they try to punish good teachers, the Wunderkinds in George Bush's Department of Education need to understand that children are going to read books that matter to them, books that are up-to-the-minute, not the freeze-dried concoctions of textbook makers who are perpetually behind the times.

There are conservative political groups that are interested in the privatization of schooling. Public schooling needs to be supported by tax dollars, and there are those who have worked for decades to eliminate this expense. For example, the governor of Montana says she has a hard time understanding why her state should spend $6,000 a year to educate students when they can be home schooled for $300.

Most Americans get their information on schools from the news media. Instead of visiting schools and finding out the truth for themselves, they read second- or third-hand information often presented by groups determined to close public schools as quickly as possible. Thanks to the sophistry of the NCLB minions, the American press corps is being fed dishonest stories of allegedly failing schools. As other sections of this book demonstrate, some of these "failures" have nothing to do with math or reading. They may simply reflect the fact that only 94 percent of the federally mandated 95 percent of a student subgroup showed up to take a test. In other words, if a flu epidemic keeps too many students out of class on a testing date, the school flunks and the administrators are sent to the woodshed for a good thrashing.

Concepts related to terms such as grade level, average scores, proficiency levels, phonics, reading abilities, comprehension, and whole language are complex, and reporters rarely have the space to explain them adequately to their audiences. The book you are holding is one effort to correct this problem.

At this crucial time, we as educators have a choice. We can succumb to the manipulation of politicians and bureaucrats and watch everything we believe in be replaced by a hierarchy of statisticians. Or we can tell parents and politicians and reporters and administrators what is really going on in our classrooms. In Sweden, where parents can watch their children in the classroom from three camera angles via the Internet, teachers have nothing to hide. As Vera Milz put it so eloquently, any time outside visitors wish to step into her classroom they are welcome to see what self-esteem is all about.

No Illusion Left Behind: "High Standards" Meets the Real World

Jerry Parks

It's scary when you feel like you're the only sane person.

I'm a recently retired Iowa elementary principal, and I can't figure out why educators all over the United States aren't screaming and yelling about the federal No Child Left Behind law.

It's hard to tell whether this law is more a product of arrogance or ignorance, but either way it's shaping up to be a spectacular train wreck of a collision between bureaucracy and reality.

The main thrust of the bill is that it requires all U.S. school-children to be "proficient" in reading, math, and science by the year 2014. Hard to argue with, until you learn that proficiency has been arbitrarily defined as the current 40th percentile of the nation.

In other words, in 2014 every child will score better than 40 percent of the nation today, or roughly 19,000,000 children. We will be essentially trying to get every child in the nation to be "above average," and should probably change our name to something like the United States of Lake Wobegon.

But it gets worse. The law specifically mandates that children with serious learning problems (our current specialized population) must also meet this standard. In my medium-sized school district of about 4,800 students, last year's testing found 100 percent of special education fourth graders to be below "proficiency." Surprise? Apparently it is to the Department of Education.

These children currently receive targeted instruction, a specialized curriculum, and are often in classrooms as small as eight students. They need these intensive services, but even with this extra help probably will remain well behind the average student. A second group of targeted students are English-language learners, i.e., immigrant children who are just learning English. Is there some educational strategy I've missed out on that can turn a non-English-speaking third grader into an average fourth grade reader in one year? Who writes this stuff?

All schools are supposed to make steady progress toward the outrageous 100 percent success level, and schools that don't keep pace face tough penalties.

State departments of education have recently released the lists of those who didn't make it this year. In my neighbor state of Illinois, 627 schools were labeled as failing, and estimates are for that number to double.

In Iowa, a preliminary estimate found that up to half of our schools could make the failing list, though the final tally for this year was much less. How could half the public schools be failing in a state that has the second-highest ACT college testing scores in the nation?

It's obvious to me that when 2014 rolls around and everyone has to hit the 100 percent standard, almost every school in the country will be labeled a "failing school." Is it possible this bill is an elaborate set-up designed by those hoping to usher in an era of vouchers, charter schools, and other alternatives to public education?

I don't know the answer to that question, but I do know that the draconian provisions of No Child Left Behind will generate increasing amounts of fear, anger, and unjust blame as one year's unrealistic goals give way to the next.

THERE IS NO ONE-PLAN-FITS-ALL IN EDUCATION

John C. Aerni

> Editor's note: *Several years ago I taught a week-long seminar for teachers in a remote part of Alaska. Teachers had to fly in for the workshop. In talking with them I became convinced that what is troublesome about education in the lower 48 becomes absurdity when applied to rural Alaska. So it is with NCLB as this insightful Alaskan teacher says.* —KSG

> John C. Aerni *is a teacher in the Kwethluk Community School, Kwethluk, Alaska, located on the Alaskan Yukon-Kuskokwim River Delta in the Yup'ik Eskimo village of Kwethluk. The Elementary (K-6) and Junior/Senior High School (7-12) are all located in the same building. The combined student body is about 250 students. The village has a population of about 800 residents.*

Despite its ambitious claims, the No Child Left Behind law (NCLB) does not work effectively in some settings and may be completely inappropriate in others. Here in rural Alaska, the NCLB law is hurting students and is creating a situation where many students may be left behind.

Consider the Lower Kuskokwim School District (my employer). Because of new mandatory state graduation exams, three years ago the district completely revamped its curriculum in the hope of having more students pass the exam. This change was discussed for two years prior to that, well before the passage of NCLB. Views in the district differ as to how effective this change is, but it proves to me that parents, teachers, and administrators here care about the success of their students. Moreover, they cared long before the NCLB law came into being.

However, under the provisions of NCLB, most of the schools in the district are failing and have very little hope of ever attaining passing status. Our students are all Yup'ik Eskimo. Yup'ik is the first language for many and English is their second. You will hear mostly a village dialect of English from students throughout the school as it is their language of choice much of the time, but they are bilingual.

The schools here, for the most part, do not make what Mr. Bush, the law, and education departments in Washington and Juneau define as "adequate yearly progress" (AYP).

Our school has a Yup'ik immersion program where the students are taught in Yup'ik from kindergarten through third grade. The community wants to ensure that the Yup'ik language is carried on by the younger generation and the teachers want to connect what the students have learned at home to what they are expected to learn at school.

After third grade in Yup'ik, the students repeat third grade, this time taking the classes in English. It is in the middle of the "second third grade" that the students are tested for the first time to determine if we, as a school, comply with NCLB. The test is given in English to students who have had classroom instruction in English for only a few months. Not surprisingly, we fail to meet the standards for AYP on this test.

NCLB labels a school as failing for not making AYP on 31 different indicators, ranging from test scores at certain grades, to daily attendance figures and dropout rates, to name but a few. Therefore, no matter what else is happening at the school, because of these third grade tests scores, our school will be deemed failing.

My concern here is not about the low test scores for those students who are taking English classes for the first time in their lives, but rather for a law that labels a school failing without looking at why this is happening. Our school would be failing the community if we did not have a successful program to maintain the Yup'ik language and culture among our students.

Among rural Alaskan schools, the dropout rate is another factor that usually throws schools into the failing category. To fail our rural schools for this is culturally insensitive, since many of the students who drop out are leaving to learn the traditional lifestyle of subsistence hunting and fishing from their elders.

To be taken off the failing list, my school would have to pass every single one of those 31 indicators for two straight years. Because of the unique situations that we face in rural Alaska that's not possible, despite our very best efforts. The law is absurdly out of touch with the realities of teaching and life here. According to the law, parents have the right to have kids bused to a more successful nearby school. But there is no other school nor roads for buses to travel on.

We are currently in our fourth year of failing; like many schools around the nation, we have never received a passing mark. It is all too easy to point a finger and punish the faculty for not reaching an unattainable goal. In terms of NCLB, this year the entire teaching staff can be fired and the state government can take over the school. It took decades for native people to get control of their own schools. Would they now accept a government takeover?

Alternately, the law allows the government to hire a private company to run the school. What company would want to take on the task of educating Yup'ik students in the Alaskan bush? What resources would they put toward this? How would they meet the interests of both their shareholders and the students? And how would that company meet the criteria that the President and Congress have put in place with this misguided law.

If the government uses its power to fire those of us who have invested ourselves in the education of these often-forgotten students, where would they find "highly qualified' teachers willing to come to these remote villages to replace us? About two-thirds of the staff is native, two of the non-native teachers have married into the community, and the rest tend to be younger, idealistic people like myself. The native staff is not replaceable; there are few teachers anywhere who speak Yup'ik.

In the interest of educating students, which is my first and foremost priority as a teacher, I argue that while the academic performance of the school on paper appears to be poor, the actual story of the school is a success. We *are* educating students who come to us.

Until 1980, there was no high school in the village and students who wanted secondary education either had to live with a relative in a larger town or had to attend boarding school far from home. Now students can receive an education and live at home. We have had graduates go on to college and currently have graduates working in jobs around the Yukon-Kuskokwim Delta, an area where jobs are scarce.

Our staff is dedicated and highly qualified to teach in this unique setting. But NCLB mandates that every teacher must be "highly qualified" in all areas that they teach by the end of the 2005-2006 academic year. In our small rural school, each teacher teaches five different subjects per day and six or seven over the course of a school year. Our school would have to hire "highly qualified" part-time teachers for each subject since there aren't enough classes in each area for full-time teachers. Where could we find people willing to come for part-time salaries?

Here's my message to those who have given us NCLB: Mr. President, members of Congress. Don't impose your federal standards on education. There is no one-plan-fits-all solution for schools in this diverse nation. Your education secretary, Rod Paige, visited our school district last spring and while he was here, acknowledged that we are facing a unique situation in rural Alaska. The No Child Left Behind Law is not only leaving children behind, but it is also hurting those who are trying to get an education and those who are dedicated to helping them do so.

Reprinted with permission of The Delta Discovery *(2/17/04) and the author*

"WHAT THE DIBELS IS THAT?!"
(A DIRECT QUOTE FROM A FIRST GRADER)

Farin Houk-Cerna

Editor's note: *Many states are being required by the NCLB Washington bureaucrats to use a simplistic test called the DIBELS, published in Oregon. Here's one professional teacher's experience "Dibeling" her kids.*

Fresh from winter vacation, this is a busy time in our kindergarten-first grade combination class. It's time to review our rules, the ones that we all wrote together as a class. Do your best, help others do their best, and treat everyone kindly and peacefully; simple really. We teach the new kids how things work in our class: how to do the calendar, where to find writing materials, what it means when the stoplight is on red (NO TALKING!), and as one says very solemnly "about peace, Ms. Cerna, they have to be peacemakers and help other people." We review the expectations, just in case anyone accidentally forgot them over the long break: how to walk in the hallway, how to do our end-of-the-day jobs, how to be a good listener.

And of course, we pitch ourselves back into the routine of what one possibly delusional teacher calls "joyful rigor": our learning. We remind ourselves how to read all those books that we forgot while we were playing in the snow, we stammer about getting our days of the week back in order, and we resume work on whatever brilliant story we were writing before the break.

And I, as the teacher, have a new job this January. This year, five short months into the school year, I get to go through and sort my kids into categories: at risk, some risk, and low risk. For reading failure that is. It's quite easy actually: all I do is give them a simple test and poof—I get a nice neat graphic that shows me exactly which of my kids are at risk for being struggling readers, and exactly what they need to avoid such a miserable fate.

An absolutely reliable indicator of basic literacy skills and potential, they say. (And even if it's not totally reliable, we'll still call the kids at risk in the meantime.)

All I do is sit down with my kids and test them: how many letter names can they say in one minute? Forget any letter that takes them longer than three seconds (did you still have visions of sugar plums dancing in your head?) It's wrong and they're off down the road to "at risk."

How many phonemes (sounds) can they segment in one minute? OK, when I say "man" you say /m/ /a/ /n/. Easy! Just make sure that if I say "trick", you don't say /tr/ /ick/—that's too many sounds all mushed up together. That might work for real reading, but it won't keep you out of the at-risk category!

And then there's the best indicator of future reading success, the nonsense word test. How many nonsense words can my kindergartners read in one minute? My five-year-olds (all but two of whom speak another language at home) those kindergartners? Aren't they all nonsense words to them? We go through the list: vaj, ov, sim, lut, and my personal favorite, fek. The kids look puzzled. One says, "If you switch these two letters and you put a j at the beginning you'll have 'jump,' teacher!" Sorry, honey, that's wrong and you've used up your time trying to make some sense of these words. Off to the at-risk group you go!

And what does it mean to be "at risk"? Well it means that the kids need intensive, systematic intervention. It means they get lots and lots of focused, methodical teaching so that next time they can really read all of those nonsense words. There won't be much time left for any real reading or any real kindergarten learning, but they'll be able to dissect those words properly.

The thing is, I didn't need any fancy test that the school district invested thousands of dollars in to know which of my kids are at risk. I know that many of my children face serious risks in their lives, only one of which involves reading. After living with these children for five months now, I know which ones don't know their letters; I know which ones don't know a single sight word; I know the ones who have a functional English vocabulary of maybe 100 words. I know which ones need extra help; I know which ones are struggling. And any teacher worth his or her salt knows too.

A good many of my students are in absolute need of intensive, systematic help. But they don't need to be practicing day in and day out until they can name 54 letters in 60 seconds. And they certainly don't need more work in decoding nonsense words.

Want a plan to ensure reading success for all children? Here it is. First, start with some good prenatal care, nutrition, and education. Second, when the children arrive, make sure that their parents don't have to work 3 jobs in order to keep their spot in a rundown, cramped public housing unit. That way they can spend more time talking, playing, and reading with their children.

Then, as the children grow, make sure that they always have plenty of healthy food around to eat. Having a mediocre meal once a day at school because there's no food at home, or because mom's at work and there's no one to cook is no way to ensure reading excellence.

And if you really want to make sure that we don't leave anybody behind, include some great birth to age three programs that emphasize language and concept development, good purposeful play, and quality parent education. As the children enter school, let's be focused and systematic about their health care.

And [finally] , if you want all kids to be great readers, make sure they have great schools, with tons of good books, lots of money and time for field trips, plenty of materials, and the best-trained, highest-quality teachers to be found.

Give that intensive systematic plan a good try and I promise, all of our children will be readers.

But in the meantime, I trudge through, sorting my children, this one "some risk," that one "high risk," inflicting upon them the next round of band-aid solutions to misinterpreted deficits. It's enough to drive a good teacher to say, well, fek.

Reprinted from the Tacoma News Tribune

TENTH AND PENN SCHOOL

Roger Rapoport

George W. Bush, I'd like you to meet Frank Vecchio. It's not diffi-cult. Don't come by helicopter. There's a lot of marginal housing around which the wind blasts could damage. Hop aboard the Bieber Bus line and it'll take you to Vecchio's hometown of Reading (Listen George, it's not "read" like "reed," it's "read" like "red"), Pennsylvania.

Chances are he'll even pick you up at the bus station and run you over to his K-5 school, creatively named Tenth and Penn. As principal, Vecchio is responsible for 510 students. But you'd bet-ter come soon. Thanks to your No Child Left Behind law, Tenth and Penn, a recycled bank that is now home to 27 classrooms, could become a casualty. Considering the fact that Tenth and Penn won an award in 2001 for its performance on the statewide achievement exam, the local folks find it a little hard to under-stand why your guys put it on the federal "school improvement" list. They believe in Tenth and Penn. It's an inner-city school with 87 percent of the students eligible for free and reduced price lunch. But Principal Vecchio says, "As far as I'm concerned, our kids and staff can compete with anyone given the same criteria across the board."

And that, Mr. President, is why the Reading School District (remember, like "red," not "reed" or "Reid") has become the first in the nation to file a lawsuit against No Child Left Behind. For all Tenth and Penn's success on state tests and within the communi-ty, your law is seriously threatening it because NCLB demands year-to-year improvement in unreasonable and irrational ways.

By NCLB criteria the school failed to show an improvement in its fifth-grade reading test scores in 2003 because the majority of the kids who took the test were not allowed, as required by NCLB, to take the test in their native language.

"I drove home in the middle of my vacation last summer to get the results," says Vecchio. "And when I saw them I cried. We had flatlined in reading." The reading "problem" in Reading (remember "red," not "reed") reflects significant changes in the city's ethnic makeup. "When I was a little boy," says Vecchio, "the city was primarily ethnic Italian and Polish. People didn't even bother to lock their doors. Today, the immigrant families are working overtime to establish themselves in a culture that has significant crime, and they are fighting hard to close down crack houses. They move a lot to find safer places to live or homes that they can afford. And a lot of them send their kids to Tenth and Penn.

"Opened in the fall of 1997, this school teaches English to many new immigrant students who come from homes where English isn't spoken. The school is like a turnstile. Kids are constantly transferring in and out. In some years the number of transfers actually exceeds the student population. We are being measured on very strict criteria. Unlike other districts, where the students are all native speakers and stay put for the . . . academic years prior to the No Child Left Behind test, our kids are expected to go through a miraculous transformation. We must take kids who are new to the English language and turn them into superb test takers in just six months."

The irony is that Tenth and Penn and the city's other inner city schools do a superb job at teaching English says Mackie Wickert, an 18-year classroom veteran who is the school's reading coach. "Under the old system," she explains, "English-language education was structured week by week. The idea was you went from unit to unit all year long. We had to integrate vocabulary with social studies, health, and science instruction. Children don't all learn at the same pace, and we now know that it's impossible to keep everyone on the same page and teach to the test. Every kid is different. Every classroom is different."

Because the NCLB assessment focuses on fifth graders, the

school is under a lot of pressure to make sure these students become proficient in English, but many kids have had little or no formal schooling prior to enrollment at Tenth and Penn. "Then in a matter of six months they are supposed to be ready to pass a major exam in English because the state does not provide the crucial test in Spanish, as required by the No Child Left Behind law," says Wickert. "When you realize that it takes five to seven years to learn another language, you understand why the government's testing yardstick for NCLB can't work here. Even if they are working at grade level in their own language, there is no assurance they can pass the test."

After Tenth and Penn was placed on the government's "school improvement" list, in the first step of a process that can lead to school closure, parents were notified that they could request the district to bus their kids to another school. "None of them were interested," says Vecchio. "We have a lot of support. They see what we are accomplishing in our classroom. When they visit, as we encourage them to do, they are impressed by the job we are doing.

"The government is saying we don't see any bang for our buck. What they fail to realize is that our teachers have to do many things before they can teach. "We have to be the guidance counselor," says Wickert. "Our pre-learning function is to make sure that kids feel safe. In many cases we have to be surrogate parents.

"The difference between our schools and the suburbs is the hard culture of poverty," says Vecchio. "Here, everything is based on survival. Do you have a place to sleep tonight? Do you have food?

"Public education still works, as it has for more than 200 years, in this country. Teachers as educators have not changed their commitment. We believe that if a kid fails, it's our failure. We're always looking for better ways to help kids succeed."

While teachers are working extra hours to help students score better on the state exam, the extra work is no guarantee that Tenth and Penn will avoid being closed. "No Child Left Behind requires every school to increase its test scores year to year," explains Vecchio. " That isn't always possible."

Down the line there are even more unrealistic expectations in NCLB. "The federal goal of making all kids proficient by 2014 is a statistical impossibility," says Vecchio. "The idea that struggling special-ed kids are going to grow at a fixed percentage is unrealistic. We could do a tremendous job, but if there is not improvement in this one subgroup from year to year there are sanctions imposed on this building."

Tenth and Penn's future is dependent on the performance of a small group of children, says Vecchio. "Statistically, if I have four or five kids who move from basic to proficient our school is no longer in school improvement. That is very important when you look at the big picture. We are now pulling reports and looking at particular kids and looking at the skills they are struggling with. Our school is being forced to take this approach for our survival. It's certainly not the ideal way to teach, but here it's a necessity.

"When you look at NCLB over a period everyone should be at 100 percent proficiency . . . They are raising the bar so much that everyone will be in school improvement. We don't have a problem with standardized tests or being accountable. Standardized tests are an objective measurement that we take seriously. But there is no way that every child is going to perform at the 100-percent level.

"We are in the people business," adds Wickert. "We are not robots. From a cognitive perspective everyone is not created equal."

What will happen if Tenth and Penn is forced to close? "That's a hard question to answer," says Vecchio. "It's hard to imagine, given all of our successes and the loyalty we enjoy with the community, that this will help the kids. To tell you the truth, a lot of teachers don't really want to work in the inner city. We're fortunate to have such a dedicated staff. I don't really think they can be replaced."

Leading a tour of the building, "Look at all the creativity in our classrooms," he says. Turning a corner to the immaculate boy's restroom, he turns boastful. "Look how clean it is. Does this look like what you'd expect to find at an inner-city school?"

Walking down the halls, showing off the music rooms, the library, the classroom picture books teachers have purchased at garage sales, and the science exhibits, his pride is understandable. "I wish more people would come here and see how much we are accomplishing. Then people would understand just how good our public schools really are."

On the way out, Veccio and Wickert lead the way to the school cafeteria. "Many kids qualify for breakfast and lunch," says Veccio. "When we learned some children didn't receive dinner at night, our staff set up another program with the food bank. These kids received three meals a day at school. Where are they going to get that kind of help if Tenth and Penn closes?"

Those Who Can't Teach, Can:
Assessing the Impact of No Child Left Behind
on Teacher Education

James V. Hoffman and Misty Sailors

Critics of the No Child Left Behind Act have tended to focus their attacks on such issues as the heavy-handed requirements for accountability and "high-stakes" testing, the intrusion of the federal government into states' rights and responsibilities in educational decision-making, and the absence of federal funding to help states in meeting the NCLB requirements of this legislation. In this chapter we focus attention on teacher education, a topic that has received far less attention in the public arena discourse but is no less critical. Our analysis of the impact of NCLB on teacher education will rely on evidence from both macro (the national debates and ideology) and micro levels (a case study of what is happening to teacher education in the state of Texas).

The "Teacher Gap"

Education Week's 2003 national "Quality Counts" survey focused on the "teacher gap." In this report, Olson (2003, p. 9-10) described "the fact that students in high-poverty, high-minority, and low-achieving schools have the least access to skilled instructors." The data documenting the severity of this gap came from original data collected through the Quality Counts survey, existing data gathered through the National Center for Education Statistics, and current research in teacher preparation. The report states that "nearly one-third of the students in high-poverty schools, and one in four students in high-minority schools take at least one class with a teacher who hasn't even minored in the subject. That compares with fewer than one-fifth of students in low-poverty or low-minority schools" (p. 10).

In the same Quality Counts report, Park (2003) describes

efforts by school districts to meet demand for qualified teachers. Teachers assigned "out-of-field" is only one strategy that has been used by districts to meet the demand. The creation of "alternate certification routes" is another. Park says "Although some alternative routes graduate effective new teachers who stay in teaching, other programs permit individuals to enter the classroom with minimal prior training or experience working with children" (p. 18). The majority of teachers certified through an alternative route end up in "high-need areas" (Blair, 2003).

While there is a growing consensus on what makes a good alternative teacher education program, the variability across regions, states, and districts is great. Again, it is the low-income, minority communities that are impacted most by the most questionable alternative certification programs (Blair, 2003).

Teacher Quality and No Child Left Behind

For decades, to become a professional teacher in the United States someone must get a teaching certificate by completing a program for preparing teachers at a college or university approved by the state. National professional associations regularly review the quality of these programs. For the first time, through NCLB, the federal government is determining "teacher quality." NCLB requires states to ensure that all teachers in high schools and middle schools of the core academic subjects (English, reading or language arts, mathematics, the sciences, foreign languages, civics and government, economics, history, geography, and the arts) are highly qualified in every subject they teach by the end of the 2005–2006 school year. Given the severity of the "teacher gap" just described, these requirements place an enormous burden on states to make substantial changes in the teaching force. They are particularly difficult for smaller rural schools and middle schools to meet.

A positive spin on this requirement might have led states and districts to examine complex issues of teacher retention, teacher recruitment, and professional development. It might have led states to invest more resources into existing teacher preparation programs that would attract, prepare, and retain teachers to work in areas of high need. But these positives have not appeared. Blame it on the fact that NCLB was not fully funded and was without specific provisions for investing in teacher quality. Blame it on the declining economy that left individual states facing enormous deficits. Or, blame it on the mounting conservative political agenda to privatize education that also has set its target, as Cochran-Smith (2001) argues, on the systematic destruction of teacher education in America.

> There is . . . a well-publicized and well-funded movement to deregulate teacher education by dismantling teacher education institutions and breaking up the monopoly that the profession (schools of education, professional accrediting agencies, and many state licensing departments) has, according to its critics, too long enjoyed. The deregulation movement is well-funded by conservative political groups like the Heritage Foundation, the Pioneer Institute, and the Fordham Foundation (p. 5).

Dismantling Teacher Education

Four years ago Chester E. Finn Jr., the president of the Washington-based Thomas B. Fordham Foundation, laid out this campaign in a report titled, *The Teachers We Need and How to Get More of Them: A Manifesto* (Fordham Foundation, 1999). The report argues "for teachers, and for the schools in which they teach, the surest route to quality is to widen the entryway, deregulate the process, and hold people accountable for their results—results judged primarily in terms of classroom effectiveness as gauged by the value a teacher adds to pupils' educational experience."

The Abell Foundation (2001) in Baltimore, Maryland, has taken a similar stance, calling for opening the doors to teaching to anyone with a bachelor's degree of any kind. According to this campaign, the hiring institutions or local service agencies should be the ones to provide for a minimal preparation period (typically two or three months) leading to full-time teaching responsibilities. On-site mentoring and training will supposedly help smooth the transition.

It is one thing, of course, for a conservative "think tank" or "foundation" to propose deskilling and deprofessionalizing teachers. It's quite another when this becomes the stance of the federal government. In July 2002, Rod Paige issued the Secretary's Annual Report on Teacher Quality (U.S. Department of Education, 2002). In this report, titled *Meeting the Highly Qualified Teachers Challenge*, he essentially argued for the dismantling of teacher education systems and the redefinition of teacher qualifications to include little professional preparation for teaching. He asserts that current teacher certification systems are "broken," and that they impose "burdensome requirements" for education coursework that make up the "bulk of current teacher certification regimes" (p 8). The report argued that certification should be redefined to emphasize higher standards for verbal ability and content knowledge and to de-emphasize requirements for education coursework, making student teaching and attendance at schools of education optional and eliminating "other bureaucratic hurdles." Paige echoed the Abell Foundation that there was is "little evidence that education school course work leads to improved student achievement" (2002, p 19). Paige's new model of teacher preparation would essentially bypass colleges and university programs.

The "dismantling" argument reached the level of absurdity when Reid Lyon said that we should begin the reform effort in teacher education by "blowing up colleges of education" (Lyon, 2002). Lyon got carried away but what he voiced is the national policy agenda the Bush Administration has formed within the NCLB legislation. This national policy agenda interacts in important ways with initiatives underway at the state levels.

Teacher Education in Texas: a Case in Point

We focus on Texas to illustrate the processes of institutional change spurred by NCLB, in part because of our first-hand experiences in teacher preparation in this state. But more importantly, many of the elements included in NCLB are national manifestations of changes that were initiated under the leadership of then-Governor George Bush, and even earlier in Texas.

The relationship between colleges of education and state policymakers in Texas became contentious in the mid-1980s when the Texas Legislature imposed an "18-hour cap" on education course work to prepare a teacher (Watts, 1989). NCATE (The National Council for Accreditation of Teacher Education) took the lead in a series of national protests, arguing that this action by Texas policymakers was an intrusion into professional autonomy and responsibility. The University of Texas at Austin, facing the potential loss of accreditation, withdrew from NCATE. This action was praised by Texas legislators and was followed quickly by the withdrawal from NCATE by several other colleges of education within the state. The number of NCATE-accredited institutions in Texas fell from over thirty in the 1980s to just ten in recent years (NCATE, 2004).

Through the decade of the 1990s, the Texas Education Agency, drawing on the Regional Service Center network and various school districts, took an active role in supporting the development of alternative certification programs. The public argument in support of this movement was to create a larger supply of teachers to meet shortages in the state. However, there was the implicit argument that traditional teacher education programs were inadequate, or worse, unnecessary. Currently, there are over 60 approved alternative certification programs in Texas, matching closely the number of college and university-based teacher preparation programs.

During the 1990s, the state developed a set of certification tests for teaching in subject areas and related fields. It was no longer sufficient for a graduate to complete an accredited program, he or she must also pass the state tests.

More recently, state regulations provide that a teacher who has received initial certification could gain additional certifications by simply passing the subject area exam in a field. There would be no requirement for individuals to complete an accredited program prior to taking the test. These actions set in place the conditions for broadly opening the doors to teaching, though not necessarily as a profession. All that was needed was a catalyst for change like the NCLB act.

The more attractive school districts could, of course, choose to hire new teachers who had completed programs in the colleges or universities. So again those who had little or no professional education were more likely to wind up teaching poor and minority kids.

In January of 2003, Carol Strayhorn, the state comptroller issued the Texas performance review report, *Limited Government, Unlimited Opportunity.* It outlined savings and additional revenue suggestions that would help address the pending budget crisis. One recommendation related directly to teacher preparation and certification. "State law should be amended to allow anyone who passes the state's teacher certification examination (ExCET) in a subject area and holds a bachelor's degree in the same area to be fully certified without completion of a teacher training program." The comptroller went on to state: "Educational research does not support a need for training programs for prospective teachers. The emphasis instead should be on supporting new teachers during their first few years of employment, when turnover rates are highest."

Only days later, a bill was introduced (Texas H.B. No. 318) that was focused on alternative certification of persons holding a bachelor's degree. According to this bill, the state board may issue a teaching certificate to a person who: 1) holds a bachelor's degree received with an academic major or interdisciplinary academic major, including reading, other than education, and 2) performs satisfactorily on the appropriate examination prescribed under Section 21.048. The bill, although garnering support from Texas Governor Rick Perry, was rejected by the legislature.

Next, proponents of the failed legislative bill successfully placed an almost verbatim version of HB 318 as an action item on the November agenda of the State Board for Educator Certification (SBEC). Created in 1995, SBEC issues teaching certificates and sets standards for teacher preparation courses and certification exams in Texas. Appointed by the governor of the state, SBEC has the power to alter certification requirements within the state. The proposal to SBEC called for the creation of a Temporary Teaching Certificate that would follow an "alternative certification" plan. The documentation supporting the proposal to SBEC says:

> The federal requirements under "No Child Left Behind" for "highly qualified" teachers . . . requires the teacher to have full state certification and have demonstrated subject area mastery. For new elementary teachers, this is accomplished through passing the elementary certification examinations. For middle and secondary teachers, this mastery can be demonstrated by either passing the appropriate content certification exam or by having an academic major or equivalent in the content area. Section §200.56 allows individuals who have not obtained full state certification to meet the requirements of "highly qualified" by being in a state-approved and regulated alternative route to certification. An alternative route, according to the federal requirements, must provide a field-based practicum or internship with "high quality professional development that is sustained, intensive, and classroom focused prior to and throughout the assignment." Further, the law requires that supervision of this practicum or internship be conducted

"with the structured guidance and regular ongoing support of an experienced educator who has been trained as a mentor."

On Friday, November 7, 2003, SBEC passed the rule authorizing the issuance of a two-year Temporary Teaching Certificate for degreed individuals who pass the required examinations. During the two-year probationary period, the district would provide "intensive support" including mentoring and professional development concerning the state laws, standards, and behavior management.

At the end of two years, the school district would then recommend the individual for permanent state certification. Under this rule, these individuals may achieve certification without completing a teacher preparation program or receiving a recommendation from a preparation entity, and parents would not have to be notified that their child's teacher had not received a traditional recommendation.

After four hours of public testimony that, for the most part, attacked the rule, SBEC members voted 5 to 4 favoring the proposal. Board members reported that there had been heavy pressure from the "Governor's office" to pass this rule (Harmon, 2003). Approval by SBEC, however, is not binding. The State Board of Education, the governing body for the Texas Education Agency, reviews all decisions made by SBEC and has the power to overturn its actions.

The Texas Education Agency (TEA) is responsible for the day-to-day operations of the educational system. The Commissioner of Education (the director of TEA) is appointed by the Governor. On January 12, 2004, just weeks after the passage of the SBEC rule on temporary certification, Governor Perry appointed Shirley Neeley as Texas Commissioner of Education. In an interview with the *Austin American Statesman* (Jan. 30th, 2004), Neeley stated her full support for the Temporary Teaching Certification plan.

Austin American-Statesman: Do you support the State Board for Educator Certification proposal that would permit college graduates to bypass teacher training programs such as the alternative program or traditional college teacher preparatory programs?

Shirley Neeley: I support SBEC's position 100 percent, and that has just opened a wonderful window of opportunity for principals and superintendents to fill some vacancies in an area where we have a critical teacher shortage. I don't think there is any reason to be afraid of that, because good principals are going to look for the best teachers.

Austin American Statesman: So much of what you're saying depends on the good will of "good principals," and that's not the total reality out there. If that is in fact your goal—to find and hire the best teachers—then why not get all of those college graduates and put them through the alternative certification program, which is there to do what SBEC wants to do in the first place, instead of opening the door to an unproven system?

Shirley Neeley: Because we still have a critical shortage of teachers. It's a supply and demand issue; that's the bottom line. Many districts cannot fill teacher vacancies. That's very frightening when a parent comes in the first day of school and they want to meet their child's teacher and there may be a substitute there. And what has happened in the past is you could not put a teacher in there because they weren't certified.

SBEC's recommendation on the temporary certificate was brought before the State Board's Planning Committee for discussion and public testimony on February 25, 2004. Of the 30 (plus) individuals and groups presenting testimony to the Planning Committee, most opposed the creation of the certificate. At one point in the proceedings, the Chair of the Planning Committee asked Richard Kouri, representative of the Texas State Teachers Association (an NEA affiliate), if he was a "terrorist." There was some uncomfortable laughter in the room as Kouri ignored the comment and testified that the proposed rule was a "wrong cure for a misdiagnosed problem." He further went on to say that Texas is "denigrating the teaching profession" by making it easier for someone to call himself or herself "a certified teacher" and that this is "diminishing the teaching profession." Karen Soehnge, representative of the Texas Association of School Administrators and Texas Association of School Boards, spoke in favor of the rule as a way of helping to bring school districts into compliance with NCLB.

On Friday, February 27, 2003, the full State Board considered the proposal. The final vote was eight members voting to reject and seven members voting to approve. Because the action came to the State Board as recommended from SBEC, it would take a two-thirds vote of the Board to reject the creation of the temporary certificate. The proposal, despite the majority of state board members rejecting it, was therefore passed. Interestingly, not one of the state board members who voted in favor of the certificate spoke publicly of their reasons for support. All of the discussion offered at the State Board meeting came from members who opposed the rule.

So—Those Who Can't Teach, Can

It seems reasonable to assert the following regarding NCLB and teacher quality.

- The requirements of NCLB for a quality teacher in every classroom will be used, not to leverage resources for needed reforms in the teaching profession, but as the primary basis for bringing less-qualified teachers into classrooms.

- These actions will create the illusion, in the short-term, of reducing the "teacher gap," but the reality is that the bulk of those entering teaching through these fast-track programs will "learn to teach" in the schools serving poor and minority students.
- More states will follow the path of Texas in the dismantling of university-based teacher education programs through alternate certification of teachers. Georgia, for example, most recently passed a law very similar to the one passed in Texas.
- Finally, and most assuredly, the efforts to dismantle teacher education programs will not stop at the secondary level. Similar plans for temporary certificates for middle school, elementary school, and early childhood education are soon to follow.

These are probabilities, not possibilities. Reform efforts must focus on the complexity of teacher quality, teacher recruitment, teacher preparation, and teacher retention and not on simple solutions that take us back rather than forward.

Next Steps

None of the arguments offered in this paper should be interpreted as an endorsement of the status quo in teacher preparation and professional development. We must explore alternatives that involve creative collaboration between universities and school districts that provide alternative routes. But these efforts must produce well-prepared teachers rather than serving policy mandates routed in ideology or the politics of balanced budgets.

What if NCLB were NPLB (No Patient Left Behind) and the reform took on the preparation of medical doctors and nurses? There is no question that we have a "medical gap" in this country that needs to be addressed (i.e., the disparity in health care services available to the poor and the wealthy). How would the public respond if we just took actions to certify anyone as a qualified health care provider who had earned a bachelors degree and could pass a paper-pencil anatomy test? There would be outrage, just as there should be outrage at the impact of NCLB on teacher preparation and teacher certification. The professionalization of teaching is one of the great accomplishments of American democracy. All over the world, nations are recognizing the need for raising the level of professionalization of teachers to achieve what they perceive Americans have.

The language surrounding "a highly qualified teacher in every classroom" was put forward as a goal that would rally consensus for a bold undertaking. The bipartisan support in Congress for NCLB reflected national concerns over equity and educational opportunity. But the truth is out on NCLB. It has become a tool for coercion and subversion of education. The efforts to dismantle traditional forms of teacher education and deskill teachers through the requirements of NCLB cannot be ignored. NCLB must be thrown out or radically rewritten to address in positive ways the need for quality teachers.

What is needed is a positive alternative to NCLB's law that would create the conditions and the resources for professionals to address the complex challenges that face our educational system, not mandate solutions. The alternative needs to focus on the real issues in teacher education (resourcing of teacher education programs; retention of highly qualified teachers; the teacher "gap" between schools serving the children of low-income vs. middle- and high-income communities; and research in effective teacher preparation). The alternative needs to move away from the discourse of sanctions and punishments and into a positive discourse of support. It needs to broker honesty and trust between the educational community and the public such that all parents can rest assured they are placing their children in the care of highly qualified teachers.

References

Abell Foundation (2001). *Teacher Certification Reconsidered: Stumbling for Quality.* The Abell Foundation. Baltimore, MD. Retrieved March 26, 2003, from http://www.abell.org/publications/detail.asp?ID=62.

Blair, J. (2003, January 9). Skirting tradition. *Education Week.* XXII, No 17, pp. 35–38.

Cochran-Smith, M. (2001). Constructing outcomes in teacher education: Policy, practice and pitfalls. *Education Policy Analysis Archives, 9* (11). Retrieved March 18, 2003 from http://epaa.asu.edu/epaa/v9n11.html.

Fordham Foundation. (1999). The teachers we need and how to get more of them: A manifesto. Retrieved February 28, 2004 from http://www.edexcellence.net/foundation/publication/publication.cfm?id+16.

Grusendorf, K. (2003). H.B. No. 318. *A bill to be entitled an act relating to certification to teach school of individuals who hold bachelor's degrees.* Retrieved March 18, 2003 from http://www.capitol.state.tx.us/tlo/78r/billtext/HB00318.htm.

Harmon, D. (2003, November 14). Perry pressed for new teacher rule appointee says. *Austin American statesman.* Austin, Texas.

Kouri, R. (2004, February 25). Testimony given before the Planning Committee of the State Board of Education, Austin, Texas.

Lyon, R. L. (2002, November 18). *Rigorous evidence: The key to progress in education?* Paper presented at the forum of the Coalition for Evidence Based Policy. Washington, DC.

National Council for Accreditation of Teacher Education (2004). NCATE accredited institutions in the state of Texas. Retrieved February 29, 2004 from http://www.ncate.org/list-institutions/central.htm#texas.

Phillips, A. & Lowery, D. (2004, January 30). System needs changes to deal with teacher shortage. *Austin American Statesman.* Austin, TX.

Olson, L. (2003, January 9). The great divide. *Education Week,* XXII, No 17, pp. 17–18.

Park, J. (2003, January 9). Deciding factors. *Education Week,* XXII, No 17, pp. 17–18.

State Board of Educator Certification. (2003, November 7). Action Agenda 16. Discuss Possible Creation of a Temporary Teacher Certificate. Retrieved February 29, 2004 from http://ww.sbec. state.tx.us/SBECOnline/brdinfo/agendas/2003_11/dagenda.asp.

Strayhorn, C. K. (2003). *Limited government, Unlimited opportunity. Recommendations of the Texas Comptroller.* Austin, TX: Texas Comptroller of Public Accounts. Retrieved January 18, 2003 from http://www.window.state.tx.us/etexas2003.

United States Office of Education (2002). *Meeting the Highly Qualified Teachers Challenge: The secretary's Annual Report on Teacher Quality.* Office of Postsecondary Education, Office of Policy Planning and Innovation. Washington, DC. Retrieved March 26, 2003, from http://www.title2.org/secReport.htm.

United States Office of Education (2003). *Inside No Child Left Behind.* Retrieved March 25, 2003 from http://www.ed.gov/legislation/ESEA02/pg2.html#sec1119.

Watts, D. (1989). Ncate and Texas Eyeball to Eyeball: Who Will Blink? *Phi Delta Kappan, 71,* 311–18.

SECTION FOUR

Children Left Behind

REAL STORIES OF CHILDREN LEFT BEHIND

JoBeth Allen

> Editor's note: *When Marion Wright Edelman, head of the Children's Defense Fund Action Council, came up with the slogan "Leave No Child Behind" for her charitable foundation, she never dreamed that George Bush's Department of Education would plagiarize her idea and turn it into an Orwellian slogan for a national campaign against public schools. Like the Patriot Act that destroys civil liberties and the Healthy Forests Act that is trashing America's treasured woodlands, No Child Left Behind is a subterfuge. In this piece, University of Georgia Professor JoBeth Allen, who spends a lot of time in schools, looks at some of the extraordinary ways No Child Left Behind discriminates against children regardless of race, color, creed, or special need.*

No Child Left Behind has four arenas in which the Bush Administration is trying to change educational policy. To quote the official website, ED.gov, their ideals are:

1. Stronger Accountability for Results
2. More Freedom for States and Communities
3. Encouraging Proven Education Methods
4. More Choice for Parents

While the goals, as stated here, sound reasonable and even democratic, the way they are being enacted is damaging children, teachers, families, and schools all over the country, at all grade levels, in all kinds of schools. Here are some of their stories.

Ideal One: Stronger Accountability for Results

Realities: In his 13th annual report on the state of public education, Gerald Bracey called The No Child Left Behind Act "a weapon of mass destruction targeted at the public schools," pointing to the proliferation of high-stakes tests in schools. NCLB requires competency in all subject areas in the next 3 years. Georgia has already implemented high school exit exams.

A teacher of English as a Second Language (ESOL) who asked not to be identified (because "I'm already on the 'hit list' at the county office for fighting to keep upper elementary students in ESOL until they have enough reading comprehension skill to be successful in the regular classroom") wrote,

> I had to give the Cognitive Achievement Test and the Iowa Test of Basic Skills to a Japanese student who has been in the U.S. 2 months and had no previous English instruction. The first day, 30 minutes into the test, she broke into tears. Our school last year was the only school in our cluster that was not on the Failing List. We were also the only elementary school that served ESOL students a segment of Social Studies instruction to teach them how to read nonfiction, how to take notes, and stressed building vocabulary by paraphrasing the vocabulary they understood. We had 93 percent of our ESOL students meet adequate yearly progress. Yet we're being pushed to stop giving these students this second segment. We've had to limit services to 18 students when we have 50 who are eligible for support.

Brad, a teacher in a very high-performing middle school, reports that teachers in his school are told to "make sure those students you believe will fail the Gateway exam fail your class so that there is no discrepancy between grades and standardized test scores." The Gateway exam is a Georgia county version of federal high stakes testing, designed with an "acceptable failure rate" in the name of accountability. Brad told me, "I would love to become vocal about this system. But as you know, our district doesn't tolerate teachers who voice their opinion." So the children in Brad's classroom and countless others can work as hard as possible, make great progress, and their teachers may be forced to fail them anyway.

Children Left Behind

Gwen, an English teacher in a rural school reported, "This year 97 percent of our students passed the Georgia High School Graduation Test. At a recent meeting we were told that the state feels that so many students are passing this test that it is probably too easy and they plan to "ratchet" up the test. Are the children not supposed to pass the test? Are we deliberately trying to fail students, and in the process teachers and schools?"

Kristi, a Writing Project colleague of Gwen's in an urban high school, put a face on the travesty of this policy: "One of my students, Cammi, an incredibly considerate, thoughtful, upbeat student who was pushing herself so that she could attend college, has not been able to pass the science test after several attempts—missing a couple of times by a mere point or two (she has passed all the others). Although not a great writer, Cammi completed every writing activity we worked on, was willing to revise portions of her work that were lacking, stayed after school for extra help, and was the top reader in my class of 25 students. She took College Preparatory classes, attended a weekend program for high school seniors at Agnes Scott College, had survived her mother's alcoholism and her parents' divorce, and was determined to 'make it.' Cammi received a certificate of attendance when she walked across the stage at graduation, instead of a diploma. I saw her at school a couple of days ago. She was going to try one more time. In the meantime, she's working at Ryan's Steakhouse."

Cammi is a Child Left Behind.

Ideal Two: More Freedom for States and Communities

Realities: More freedom for states? Reading First grants in many states got rejected until they wrote in the adoption of a "core reading program"—otherwise known as a phonics-based reader.

A wonderful K-8 school with only 150 students in a small, rural community has worked hard to address the needs of all students, including those with special needs. They have an award-winning special education teacher. Through inclusion, children with special needs are an integral part of all aspects of school life. There are 15 children in the fourth grade—the grade that takes the test. One of those children has severe autism. Children in the class accept her, and understand that she interacts differently; one child told her mother, "She doesn't say words yet, but some day she might, and it will be so exciting!"

The fourth graders did well on the test. The "cut" score in that state is 23; they scored 91, the highest score in the state. But they are a failing school. They failed in the category of special education because the child with autism, who did come to school the day of the test, cannot hold a pencil. Because she could not write her name on the test, she was counted as absent. They asked if they could score her as a "zero" but that's against the rules. No Child Left Behind! Now as a failing school, they must take corrective action—the whole school. Do you know what the action is for the children with special needs? They must spend hours learning how to write their names.

Ideal Three: Encouraging Proven Education Methods
Realities: In the name of compassion and high expectations for all children, politicians have created a bureaucratic game of dominoes that falls ultimately on those with the least power in our society. The provision that an acceptable percentage of children in each category take and pass the test—a just and equitable requirement on the surface—has resulted in some bizarre consequences, like the "failing school" with the highest scores in the state.

DIBELS is the reading test mandated in Georgia for schools receiving Reading Excellence Act and now Reading First money. An Associated Press article reported that principals in Gadsden, Alabama, decided to end naptime in kindergarten. The time will be used to prepare for the DIBELS.

These are the sleepy Children Left Behind.

Last spring an estimated 33,000 Florida third-graders were denied promotion to the fourth grade because they failed the reading portion of the state-wide achievement test. Retention may reap monetary as well as "test-score gains" advantages from NCLB. The fact is, being held back makes the child 50 percent less likely to finish high school (and 90 percent less likely after two failures). What proven education method involves retaining 8-year-olds?

These are Children Left Behind

Ideal Four: More Choice for Parents
Realities: One school that became a failing school because not enough children took the test is considering suing the parents for not getting their children to school. The parents made a legal choice. The school was punished unjustly. Good people, when pushed too far and punished unjustly, will do bad things and retaliate where they can.

I am working with two elementary schools in a true partnership involving the school district, the university, and representatives of the community (social service agencies, leisure services, businesses, and interested citizens). We are involved in comprehensive school re-visioning and reform.

We have created new partnerships with parents through Family Resource Centers. We are redesigning a literacy and math curriculum and assessments. All children are attending school 195 rather than 180 days; there are additional weeks of enriched curriculum involving educational field trips and projects with university faculty and students focusing on art, science, and recreational opportunities that are also educational.

Both these schools were in "corrective action" when the partnership began. Regardless of all the efforts that are focused on the schools, the principals had to send a letter home to each parent that says, "Your child is in a failing school. You can leave and attend a superior school, a passing school since we are in need of improvement." Who do you think left? Was it the children who struggled the most, the children who did not do well on the tests, the children NCLB is supposed to serve? No.

All of the students in the partnership schools who took the state criterion reference test, including large numbers of students with special needs at one school, and 40 percent English-Language Learners at the other, showed gains ranging from an improvement of 14 percent to 34 percent of children who met or exceeded standards.

Now for the bad news: one school didn't make Adequate Yearly Progress for the second year in a row. They didn't make the 60-percent "cut" score in reading. They are now facing restructuring. The other school is out of corrective action, which decreases funding.

The work of the partnership will not be able to continue. Parents who chose these two schools and who have participated in their design will *not* have more choice, but less.

These are Families Left Behind

Looking in the Faces of Children Left Behind: What Can We Do?
I admire all those who are working hard for the children who have been inadequately served by public education. Parents, teachers, teacher educators—all of us have to become advocates for The Children Left Behind. And we have to oppose political decisions that hide the faces of the children left behind while pretending to help them.

MORE CHILDREN LEFT BEHIND
Ken Goodman

Editor's note: *As in other parts of this book, some teachers have asked that their names be withheld—for obvious reasons.*

There's a new kind of urban folklore developing among teachers and administrators. Except that these are true stories of the children No Child Left Behind leaves behind. They take on a chilling significance as the mayor of New York and the governor of Florida mandate retaining third graders who fail the test. Here are a few we have authenticated

Getting Left Behind Again
The folk term among kids when they fail is they "got left behind. This child already has been "left behind" once in third grade and is caught in a system he's sure will leave him behind again. One teacher told us this story:

His name is "Zack" and he is in the third grade for the second year because he "failed" the FCAT test last year (Florida's test—third graders must pass with a certain score or be retained).

Anyway, the school had a wonderful speaker for an assembly today who hooted, hollered, had the kids dancing, and preached the gospel of eating well, resting, and "relaxing" before the big test. At the end of the session, while all of the excited boys, girls, and teachers celebrated and danced the "I Can-Can", there sat "Zack", on the media center floor, crying. He tried to keep his tears hidden, but I couldn't help noticing him because he was the only child sitting on the floor, and I was afraid he was scared of all the "hoopla."

I went to him, gave him a hug and said, "What's the matter, Zack?" He completely broke down and said, "I'm worried . . . I'm going to have to go to the third grade again next year if I don't do good on the FCAT test. I don't think I can do it, and I'm supposed to think I can, but I can't."

He cried and cried, and there I stood hugging him as all the kids and adults around us celebrated and "hooped it up."

I walked him to his class, encouraged him to give his dad the note I had sent home earlier in the week announcing his ribbon award for his artwork at our county fair. I told him to tell his dad I would very much like it if they would go and see the artwork and then have fun on the rides. He said he was sorry for forgetting to give his dad the note . . . he has to do FCAT Explorer (test preparation) for 40 minutes every night when he gets home from school and he forgot to give his dad the note.

I went to my assistant principal's office and broke down myself. Zack's dad has been "driving" him all year at home. He is in extended-day tutoring, and at the end of the day the other day, while all the other children celebrated their "Fun Friday," he was in the media center on FCAT Explorer. He has just "had it."

I am so upset. I teach art. Zack clearly excels in art (especially painting), but testing preparations and past failure did not allow him opportunity to be proud of his accomplishment of being the *only* child in our school to place in the competitive juried exhibit. I told him to go to the fair, go outside and play every day, if he can, and try to forget about the test as much as possible, and do art as much as possible because he's so good at it. I told him he is as prepared as a human being can be, that he needs to be proud of how hard he has worked and relax until the test comes. He said he was afraid he would forget everything.

Folks, this is a sweet, sensitive, shy child, not a rebellious sort at all. I am *so* sad. I wish Jeb Bush could have seen what I saw and heard what I heard today. I hope his dad takes him to the fair.

Tell It to This Kiddo

Many administrators advocate for and support the children in their schools to diminish the impact of NCLB. Mary Korth-Lloyd, a principal in Columbia, Missouri, tells this story:

I had a child transfer to my school from another state where children have to pass a test to be promoted to the next grade. This child was in his third year of fourth grade. We promptly promoted him to fifth grade, gave him the support he needs, and he is doing fine. Imagine, *No Child Left Behind???* Tell it to this kiddo!

Bubble Children

This story comes from a teacher in California. With the stress on getting the mean scores up many schools are using desperate strategies to raise the mean. One way is to focus on those kids on the bubble (just below passing).

Early in the school year my principal announced that teachers were to target three kids in each class. We were to choose those who were just below "proficient," move them to the front of the room, tutor them after school, and meet with their parents frequently.

When I asked "What about the others?" my principal said, "Forget them." I quit my job.

Since then, I've heard the *triaged* children referred to as "bubble children"—those on the bubble just below the surface of "proficient." That is in my old district.

Last week I heard from another teacher that another district calls kids "pushables" (those you can maybe push into "proficient") and "slippables" (those who might slip below the surface).

DON'T GET BEHIND:
UPDATE OF THE GADSDEN SCHEDULE CHANGE

Steven L. Strauss

Recently, kindergartners in Gadsden, Alabama, discovered that school administrators had eliminated naptime in order to not lose precious seconds preparing for standardized tests.

To be sure, a vanguard among these clever tots will not take the news sitting up, and are debating various forms of civil disobedience. One proposal currently circulating among the 5-year-olds is to request frequent passes to the lavatories, and grab a few extra winks while nestled on the commode.

Already, Washington is developing counterinsurgency plans. Not to be outsmarted by some uppity pre-literates, the House Committee on Education and the Workforce is putting the finishing touches on legislation that will require children's bathrooms to be equipped with toilet paper whose individual squares contain letters of the alphabet.

Bush, in fact, has been holding round-the-clock meetings with his pals at McGraw-Hill, trying to convince them to collaborate with Charmin.

Planning a major media blitz in conjunction with his re-election campaign, the Bush team is promoting "wipe for literacy," in which teachers will be required to have children "decode on the commode."

The NICHD has been given the go-ahead to solicit research proposals for a major study on wiping techniques that best promote phonemic awareness. They plan to include a neuroimaging grant to identify the brain-behind connection.

Democrats are all excited about Bush letting them name the next revision of the Elementary and Secondary Education Act. They are thinking about "No Brain No Gain" and "From the Brain to the Behind: A Top-Down Approach to Reading."

Reference

Schools drop naptime for testing prep, October 2, 2003, Associated Press, Gadsden, Alabama.

SECTION FIVE

Why the Focus on Reading and Testing?

If the Underlying Premise for No Child Left Behind Is False, How Can That Act Solve Our Problems?

David Berliner

The fundamental premise underlying the legislation known as the No Child Left Behind Act (NCLB) is that the public schools of the United States are failing. But that is a half-truth, at best. When government legislation is built on a faulty premise, accepting half-truths and ideology as facts, the legislation can never solve the problem it is designed to address. Discussed below is the evidence about the faulty premise underlying NCLB, a description of the real educational problems that confront America's schools, and a suggestion about a school reform agenda that might work.

Are American Schools a Failure?

The answer to this deceptively simple question will always elude us because each individual's response is deeply rooted in personal beliefs about what should be accomplished by our schools. Some want to look primarily at academic achievement, concentrating on what students know and are able to do in reading, science, and mathematics. Others want to emphasize the civic knowledge our youngsters acquire. Different individuals want students to learn an appreciation for cultures other than their own. Still others judge schools primarily on whether or not they can provide safety for their children. The list of outcomes that are valued by one group or another is lengthy.

Depending on the outcomes chosen to judge our schools, and the weight we assign these various outcomes, different answers about the effectiveness of our schools are forthcoming. With that understanding, I examine a few of the trustworthy indicators available to help frame at least a partial response to the question about whether or not our schools are failing.

The SAT tests for college entrance. For over 60 years the College Board has surveyed high-school graduates and judged their potential for doing college-level work. The scores on their test, the SAT, were recalibrated almost a decade ago, and there exists a common scale for measuring achievement from 1981 to the present. Thus, we can look at high-school verbal and mathematical learning over the past two decades. When we do that, we learn how easy it is to convince someone that nothing much has happened in our schools, despite the best efforts of our politicians and teachers and the investment of a good deal of money. This case is easily made because the average verbal score on the SAT achieved by high-school seniors in 1981 was 504, and the average verbal score achieved in 2002 was exactly the same, 504. There appears to be no gain. On the surface there is nothing to indicate an improving public-school system. But appearances are often deceiving and digging beneath the surface is a recommended strategy.

Looking closer at these data we find that American Indian high-school test-takers, as well as students of Mexican descent, and white students, the great majority of all the test-takers, each gained an average of 8 points over that time period. Puerto Rican test-takers gained 18 points. Black high-school students gained 19 points. Asian high-school students gained 27 points. *Every subgroup for which we have data shows gains,* but the overall average score didn't move up at all.

How is this possible? The issue is a well-known one in statistics, called Simpson's paradox (Bracey, 2003), and is not at all difficult to understand. White students in America, in general, are of a higher social class than minorities, and ordinarily they have access to better educational systems. Those demographic characteristics bestow advantages to white students such that they usually score higher than minorities on the SAT. Over the time period we are looking at, America became home to more immigrants, and many more minority students sought higher education.

Thus, eventually, the higher-scoring and constantly improving white students became a smaller percent of the SAT test-taking population. The percent of all SAT test-takers who were white shrunk from around 85 percent in 1981, to around 65 percent in 2001. Since more minority students and more students with lower social-class backgrounds sought a college education, we can consider this a triumph for American public education. But this triumph brought into the pool of test-takers many more people with poorer educational histories, and so the average scores on the SAT remained constant, while evidence abounds that every subgroup in America improved its performance on the test.

The gains made by urban black and Puerto Rican students were particularly large, and these large gains showed up on the math portion of the SAT test, as well. On that test, over these two decades, black students' scores went up 36 points, while Puerto Ricans gained 23 points. American Indians also gained 20 points and white students gained 24 points. So the critics of our schools are accurate when they say that overall scores in verbal skills are not rising. But they are not telling the whole truth about the scores on that test. And they are simply ignoring the real and dramatic gains made by all students in mathematics, where even the average scores were up approximately 1 point a year for the last 20 years! Data such as these make me question the basic premise of NCLB, namely, that our public schools are failing.

The National Assessment of Educational Progress (NAEP). The NAEP tests are considered by many to be the best assessments we have of our students' performance over time. How have we done on the reading, mathematics, and science assessments? From approximately 1971 to the present, these tests have shown steadiness or growth, and a reduction of the gap between white students and non-Asian minority students (Berliner and Biddle, 1995). Steadiness or growth in NAEP scores, and a reduction in the achievement gap, has occurred despite the fact that over the past

30 years the poorest 40 percent of all U.S. families have lost real income, that all families have had to work more hours simply to hold their place in the economic system, that special-education and language-minority children exist in our nation's largest school systems at much higher rates than they used to, that immigration has risen to rates not experienced since the turn of the 20th century, that medical insurance is missing for a large share of poor families, and so forth. It would not be illogical to regard holding even, or showing only slight growth in achievement in the face of so many social problems, as a sign of success for the public schools.

Nevertheless, because the gains have been quite modest (averaging only a few points on the NAEP scales for 9-, 13-, and 17-year-olds), and the gap between white and non-Asian minority students has remained too wide, critics appear to have grounds for concern. But as Bracey (2003) documents, Simpson's paradox is operating here, as well. Let us look just at NAEP reading scores. From the 1970s until 1999, white 9-, 13-, and 17-year-olds gained 4, 6, and 9 points, respectively. If we look at the gains for Hispanics across the three age groups we see gains of 1-, 12, and 10 points. And if we look at the gains made by black students across the three age groups, we see scores rising by 28, 16, and 16 points, respectively.

In science, the situation is the same. From 1977 to 1999, total scores increased only an average of about 8 points for our 9-, 13-, and 17- year-olds. But across the three age groups, the scores for whites were up an average of about 9 points, the scores of Hispanics went up an average of 14 points, and the scores of black students went up an average of 16 points. In mathematics, from 1978 to 1999, the same trend is evident. For all 9-, 13-, and 17-year-olds, the scores went up an average of around 10 points. But over this time period, white scores for the three age groups increased an average of 11 points, black scores increased 15 points, and Hispanic scores went up 16 points.

The case for failing schools cannot be made easily with NAEP data because that data show only improvement! Advocates for NCLB, such as President Bush and Secretary Paige, ignore the steady growth in NAEP scores and argue instead that the NAEP shows too low a level of performance for American youth, particularly in reading. But that charge can be examined by looking at three recent international comparisons, PIRLS, PISA and TIMSS, with which we can benchmark U.S. performance.

Progress in International Reading Literacy (PIRLS). A few years back, reading tests were given to fourth graders or 9-year-olds in 35 countries. The data from the PIRLS study has recently been analyzed by a federal agency, the National Center for Educational Statistics (2004). It is quite instructive. In this reading test the United States ranked 9th out of 35 countries, which is certainly a respectable showing. But it is more important to note that the U.S. was beaten statistically by only three other nations that competed in this study. The performance of U.S. students in this literacy study provides no evidence of a public-school system that has problems teaching literacy! Furthermore, the PIRLS test and the NAEP tests share some common approaches to assessing reading. They both define "reading" similarly, as a constructive process. They both expect reading to be informed by what students bring to the test. They each expect students to develop interpretations, make connections across text, and evaluate what they have read. Each uses literary passages drawn from children's storybooks and informational texts as the basis for the reading assessment. And both tests use multiple-choice and constructed-response questions in about the same ratio. It does appear, however, that the PIRLS was designed for third and fourth graders, while the NAEP is designed for the fourth and fifth graders. Thus NAEP is the more difficult exam, and may be assessing what fourth-grade students do not know, rather than what they do know.

The U.S. 9-year-olds showed some remarkable achievements

in reading compared to their international competitors. For example, scoring above the international 90th percentile were 19 percent of U.S. students. Only one other country had a larger percent of students scoring in the top 10 percent on this international test of literacy. Similarly, 41 percent of the U.S. students ranked above the international 75th percentile, a record exceeded by only one other nation, Sweden, which in this study also had the highest average literacy score in the world.

Sweden is a small, economically and ethnically homogenous white nation. Yet if the millions of white children of the U.S., both the rich and the poor combined, had competed as a separate nation, they would have had the highest average literacy score in the world. U.S. white students would have beaten Sweden by a considerable amount. Although scoring considerably below white children, black and Hispanic children in the U.S. were still at or above the average score for the international community. So even our public schools' poorest minority children seem to be getting appropriate literacy education compared to the children in other nations.

The results of the PIRLS study resemble quite closely the results of another study of reading, about a decade earlier, where the performance of our 9- and 14-year-olds were assessed. Statistically, we either tied the highest-scoring nation in the world (little, homogeneous Finland), or we were tied for second place behind Finland (Berliner and Biddle, 1995). It is curious how President Bush, Secretary Paige, and others who criticize our nations reading programs can reconcile these remarkable facts about our youngsters' world-class performance with their statements that U.S. public schools fail at teaching reading.

Perhaps the most important issue that the PIRLS study revealed is that schools with under 10 percent of its children in poverty (schools for advantaged children) had scores that were considerably above the average for U.S. white students, and thus dramatically above Sweden's scores, the highest-achieving nation in the world. Money matters! On the other hand, but still illustrative of the point that money matters, is the fact that poor children in the U.S. did not score well in this international comparison. For children in schools where poverty was a predominant characteristic (schools where more than 75 percent of the children were eligible for free and reduced-price lunch), the average score on PIRLS was as low as in some of the lowest-achieving countries in the world. Our poorest students economically are also our poorest students in international assessments of achievement. Money matters. This is a repetitive theme when we examine other achievements of our U.S. students.

Program for International Student Assessment (PISA). The second recent international survey of students was PISA, which assessed 15-year-olds in mathematics, science, and reading (Lemke, Calsyn, Lippman, Jocelyn, Kastberg, Liu, Roey, Williams, Kruger & Bairu, 2001). The items on this test most resembled IQ or problem-solving tasks, rather than items that dealt directly with the secondary-school curriculum. PISA was designed to assess how students would cope with work and other complex environments as they reach the age when they might leave school. So how did our 15-year-olds do? The answer is, not bad, in aggregate, but not good if you care about equality of achievement in America. What was found was that on the tests of reading, mathematics, and science, our nation was at the mean. We were at the overall international average, a cause neither for celebration nor despondency, though critics were quick to point out that average scores were not good enough for the United States. Forgotten, however, is that with data such as these, most countries will inevitably be bunched close to the average score. But apart from wanting to live in Lake Wobegon, where all the children are above average, how did the various ethnic groups in America do? The answer to this question provides a clearer picture about the success and failure of American education.

Looking at mathematics, we find that the U.S. average score on PISA was near the international average, about the same score obtained by Germany, the Czech Republic, Norway, and Hungary. I don't think those countries are such embarrassing company to be in for mathematics learning, but we were still way below the highest-scoring nations. Yet if we pulled out from the U.S. data only the scores for white 15-year-olds, those students would have ranked as about the 7th-highest-scoring nation in the world, beaten handily by only Japan and Korea. America's black and Hispanic 15-year-olds, however, would have been beaten by all but two nations in this study. Our minorities exceeded the scores only of students in Mexico and Brazil, countries that are not thought of as fully developed. Apparently, when we pool together America's white students of all social classes, they compete quite well with the students from other industrialized nations. On the other hand, America's black and Hispanic students compete quite well only with the students from underdeveloped nations. This is, or should be, an embarrassment.

The data in science is roughly the same. The U.S. average score hides both the successes and the failures of our public education system. In science, our students are approximately tied with those of Norway, France, Hungary, and Switzerland, and well above the students from Germany and Denmark. Once again, this suggests to me that we are not in such terrible company. But as usual, the important information comes from disaggregating the U.S. data. If they had competed as a separate nation, our white students would have ranked 4th in the world against students from other developed nations. Our black and Hispanic students would have beaten the students, however, from only two underdeveloped nations, scoring near the bottom on this survey of science achievement.

The data on reading in this international study of 15-year-olds' achievements show about the same thing. The U.S. average places our students in the middle of the pack, approximately tied with Austria, Iceland, Norway, France, Denmark, Switzerland, and others we regard as developed nations. When we disaggregate these data our white students rank second in the world, beaten only by the students from tiny, economically and culturally homogeneous, Finland. Our black and Hispanic students once again placed near the bottom on this international assessment.

Third International Mathematics and Science Study (TIMSS). In the middle of the 1990s, and again about five years later, data from the TIMSS study and its replication (TIMSS-R) were made available (Gonzalez, Calsyn, Jocelyn, Mak, Katzberg, Arafeh, Williams & Tsen, 2000).

The original TIMSS informed us that American fourth- and eighth-graders scored at about the same level as those in 41 other nations, but well below some Asian nations in math and science. In TIMSS-R, the United States once again came out about average among the 38 nations whose eighth graders competed, ranking only 19th in mathematics and 18th in science. Since average scores are always unacceptable in the U.S. the alarm went out with the release of each of these reports.

Although newspapers were reporting the awful news that we were average, The TIMSS study also revealed that some of our schools were doing fine. The U.S. average, as always, masks the scores of students from terrific public schools and hides the scores of students attending shamefully inadequate schools.

Illinois is an example of this. Along Lake Michigan, north of Chicago, are 20 public-school districts serving predominantly wealthy suburban families. They banded together, calling themselves "The First in the World Consortium" and gained permission to compete in TIMSS as a separate nation. The results indicated that these advantaged public-school students were, indeed, on a par with the top students in mathematics and science in the world. Statistically, "The First in the World Consortium" was beaten by only one nation in mathematics, and was not beaten by any other nation in science! These spectacular achievements are ignored by those who claim our public schools are not working. But let us also focus on southern Illinois, where East St. Louis is located. For decades, this poor minority community has been served by awful schools, which should have been, but were not, an embarrassment to a nation as rich as ours. Yet any suitable random sample of U.S. schools for an international assessment includes both kinds of districts, those similar to East St. Louis and those that resemble the North Shore of Chicago. Put them together, and you hide important distinctions between schools in different communities.

The same sorts of distinctions exist among states, as well, when you separate them out from the overall statistics. In TIMSS, at the eighth-grade level among the 41 nations, 32 of these nations statistically outscored Louisiana in Mathematics. Worse, 36 nations outscored the District of Columbia, our nation's capital. On the other hand, only six nations in the world beat Iowa and Nebraska in mathematics. In science, 26 nations outperformed Mississippi, and 37 nations beat the District of Columbia. But only one nation, Singapore, scored above Colorado, Connecticut, Iowa, Maine, Massachusetts, Minnesota, Montana, Nebraska, North Dakota, Oregon, Utah, Vermont, Wisconsin, and Wyoming.

So which academic performance record should we talk about when we talk about schools? Are we talking about the performance of students in the District of Columbia or the performance of the 14 states that placed second in the world? This question makes an important point even clearer: Average scores mislead completely in a country as heterogeneous as ours. We have many excellent public schools, and many that are not. Those who want to undermine our public schools often condemn the whole system rather than face the inequities within it.

When the TIMSS-R data were released, the news media and public-school critics seemed also to have missed something important. The highest-achieving nation in the world exceeded the United States—even when we are looking only at the average score for our nation—by getting exactly 4 more items out of 48 correct. This is not the kind of huge difference between nations that will make the sky fall on America!

In mathematics, we did not do as well. Students from Singapore, the leading nation, got an average of 40 of the 48 items right. Even though American students scored above the international average, they only got 30 items correct. But at least one reason for that was evident from the TIMSS-R report. In the United States, only 41 percent of math teachers hold math degrees. The average among other countries is 71 percent. Perhaps, instead of condemning public education on the basis of these average scores, unhappy citizens should advocate paying teachers enough money so we can attract mathematicians and scientists to public-school classrooms.

I understand that NCLB will identify schools that are failing. But we already know all we need to know about that. For example, in science, for the items common to both the TIMSS and the TIMSS-R, the scores of white students in the United States were exceeded by only three other nations in the world. But black American school children were beaten by every single nation, and Hispanic kids were beaten by all but two nations. A similar pattern was true of mathematics scores. This was exactly the same pattern we saw when analyzing the results of the PIRLS and PISA studies. Together, these independent assessments convincingly argue, from trustworthy data, that our American public schools are *not* failing, overall. Equally clear from PIRLS, PISA, and TIMSS is that public educational systems *are* failing to provide quality education to most American children living in communities characterized by poverty. Poor children, whose schools are embedded in the culture of poverty, are not receiving a decent education.

It is worth asking if NCLB can ever improve the schools that serve our poorest children when the programs offered to fix schools identified as failing do not address the social and economic factors that affect those schools or the inadequate support they are getting. Rigorous standards, increased testing, withdrawing resources form failing schools, and other features of NCLB cannot solve the problems caused by devastating, community-destroying, family-stressing economic poverty.

The Role of Civic Education. One of the goals we have for our students is that they be prepared for the responsibilities of citizenship in our democracy. As we all know, America's voting-age population does not participate in our democracy at the rates expected, or needed, for a democracy to thrive. It is easy to blame the schools for that. Critics often blame watered-down social studies courses and not enough rigorous history teaching for the failures of adults to register and vote. But we have trustworthy data that inform us this is not so.

In a recent international assessment of the civic knowledge of 14-year-olds, or ninth graders, U.S. students actually did well (Torney-Purta, Lehmann, Oswald, & Schulz, 2001). Twenty-eight nations participated. On the measurement of civic content U.S. students ranked 10th in the world, and on the measurement of civic skills U.S. students ranked first. In total civic knowledge, no other nation's students were statistically ahead of U.S. students. Social studies is apparently taught better in the U.S. than in other parts of the world.

Our students also seem to understand a good deal about democratic values and the nature of an ethical society. For example: 92 percent of our students thought that the government had an obligation to insure that there are equal political opportunities for men and women; 91 percent of our students believed government was responsible for providing a free basic education to all citizens; about 90 percent of our youth said that everyone should have the right to speak out freely; 88 percent of our youth said that government must provide basic health care for everyone; and 87 percent of our youth thought government must provide an adequate standard of living for old people.

Arguably, our youth are better prepared to run a humane democratic society than are those from either party who now run our government.

But all is not well. The scores indicating increased civic knowledge were nearly perfectly correlated with the number of books in a child's home. And civic knowledge was nearly perfectly correlated with the highest level of parental education. There were ethnic differences, with white, Asian and multiracial students scoring quite high, and black and Latino students scoring much lower, although still above the international average. These differences in civic knowledge and skills are adequately explained by the educational differences that exist between various ethnic groups. Not only does a poor education for non-Asian minorities limit their economic and social well-being, it also stunts the development of their democratic values. That may be as serious an effect of providing an inadequate education for our poor students as the academic deficits from which they suffer. Nevertheless, the general conclusion from this study, when we use other countries to benchmark our own civic education, is that our ninth-grade children are very well-educated in civics.

International Survey of School Violence. Many Americans worry more about the safety of their children than almost any other school characteristic. The media's constant selling of violence and the actual occurrence of violence in our schools frightens us all. I join the school critics who say that violence of various kinds—verbal, physical, and that which occurs through exclusion and intolerance—should be of greater concern to American school administrators than it is now. But we should put our concerns in perspective. We can compare our schools with those of other nations because, like us, no society promotes school violence, and all societies condemn such violence.

When we make these comparisons, we don't look bad at all (Akiba, LeTendre, Baker, & Goesling, 2002). For example, students in 37 nations were asked if they were victims of school violence at least once during the previous month of the survey. Despite all our worries, the U.S. seems to be at the international average. Students in the schools of Hungary, Romania, the Philippines, Cypress, and South Africa seem to be far above the international average. They seem to be nations in which it is unsafe for children to go to school. On the other hand, Denmark and Singapore, in particular, seem to be places that are safest for children to attend school.

What about unruly and disruptive students, the kind that are so unmanageable that teachers cannot teach well? Korea, Spain, and Cypress were countries where this was reported to be a big problem. On the other hand this was hardly a problem at all for teachers in countries such as Israel, the Netherlands, and Austria. As is so often the case, teachers' reports about the U.S. showed us to be near the international average.

One of the most important questions asked of teachers in this survey was: Are you limited in your teaching by threats to your or your students' personal safety? From this survey, teaching appears to be hell in Romania, Kuwait, Iran, and Columbia. And such threats to one's person seem to be nonexistent in the Netherlands, and quite low in Scotland, Sweden, and the Czech Republic. The good news is that the U.S. was below the international average in the percent of teachers who said their teaching was limited by personal threats of violence.

The conclusion to draw from this survey of students and teachers in 37 nations is that our schools are not the easiest in the world in which to learn or teach, but they are also a long way from being the most difficult to attend. Our students and teachers are victims of violence more often then we should ever tolerate, but when we use other nations as a benchmark, we see it is a problem not unique to the U.S. Given the media attention to incidents of violence in the schools, and the poor public perception of youth and our schools, it is reassuring to know that we are coping with school violence as well as most other nations. This is a small achievement, to be sure, but an achievement nevertheless.

Conclusion

I started by asking if our schools are failing. The answer now seems clear. American schools are not failing, overall, but they are failing some of our students. The students we fail are primarily the urban and rural poor, and in particular, the poor who are minorities. As a nation we have known this for decades. Thus the accountability practices in NCLB will yield nothing new about the problems of education, or their location.

More important to me, however, is that NCLB focuses almost exclusively on the deficits of students, teachers, and administrators, and dismisses the everyday problems that communities of poor people face. Many of these problems can be addressed by our government if we demand that it do so.

I suggest that the accountability system we push for be two-way, rather than just one-way. The obligation of our schools to be accountable to the communities they serve is matched in equal part by the obligations that the governments of those communities be accountable to their schools. Governments must be held accountable for providing the fiscal and social opportunities for families to raise healthy, high-achieving children in safe, high-performing schools.

In the case of poor communities, government accountability is lacking if it fails to provide high-quality preschools so that advantaged and disadvantaged children can start school more evenly matched. Data inform us this could help.

Government support is needed for full-day kindergartens of small class size, rather than half-day or no kindergartens for our poorest children. Data inform us this could help.

Government should see to it that poor children have classes that are small in size for the first three years of schooling. Data inform us this could help.

Governments must provide pay scales and mentoring programs to attract the best of the newly certified teachers to the schools that serve the poor, rather than allowing uncertified teachers or those from alternative teaching-training programs to begin their careers at those schools, learning to teach at the expense of the poor. Data inform us this could help.

Governments need to provide incentives and better working conditions to attract Nationally Board Certified Teachers and well-regarded experienced teachers to our poorest schools. Data informs us this could help.

Policies need to be in place to find teachers that regard color, ethnicity, and language variations among children as strengths to be drawn upon instead of deficits to be overcome. Data inform us this will help.

Government support is needed to bolster community-based youth programs serving those who are in middle schools or their teen years. Data inform us these programs are unusually successful and very cost-effective.

The list of evidence-based interventions to help schools that serve the poor to do better is much longer. But it is clear to me that any of these potential ways to improve schools that serve the poor are not likely to be initiated as a function of the NCLB legislation, because the accountability system is only one-way. NCLB seems designed primarily to identify schools that we already know are achieving well or poorly, and Zip Codes can provide that information at much less cost.

Actually, Zip Codes, or the percent of those in a school receiving free and reduced-cost lunch, or the percent of children who are English-language learners does predict academic achievement remarkably well. Thus, any reasonable plan to improve the schools of the poor must be concerned for the communities in which the schools of the poor are embedded. Otherwise, as Jean Anyon (1997) reminds us, reforming the schools is like trying to clean the air on one side of a screen door.

To make any serious attempt to improve the schools of the poor might require job-training programs for adults in the community, along with medical clinics and language learning programs for the parents of recent immigrants. We may need to ensure that transportation is dependable enough in the neighborhoods of the poor so that people can get to work, and when they do work, that they earn livable wages instead of poverty wages.

Other suggestions that might break the cycle of poverty in neighborhoods abound. But what we are offered in NCLB is one-way accountability, a reliance on the mistaken assumption that the problems in schools that serve the poor are caused solely by those who inhabit the schools. If NCLB focused more on two-way accountability, it would address the fact that the problems of our schools are also in our tax and housing codes, wage structures, the lack of medical coverage provided to families, the location of and subsidies for public transportation, and other social issues.

We need to urge our government representatives to recognize the strengths of many of our public schools and acknowledge the existence of many dedicated teachers and high performing students. Evidence informs us that many such schools exist, and that refutes the major premise underlying NCLB.

This is legislation we can probably do without. But with or without NCLB, our representatives need to be reminded that many unsuccessful schools are that way because of the social conditions in which they exist. We must stop attributing all the blame for failing schools to deficient students, incompetent teachers, lazy administrators and uncaring parents. Responsibility for those failing schools lies also in our communal failure to demand that our state and local governments be as accountable to their communities as we expect our schools to be accountable to our local and state governments. This may be the most important school reform agenda to promote.

References

Akiba, M., LeTendre, G. K., Baker, D. P., and Goesling, B. (2002). Student Victimization: National and School System Effects on School Violence in 37 Nations. *American Educational Research Journal*, 39, 4, pp. 829–853.

Anyon, J. (1997). *Ghetto Schooling: A Political Economy of Urban Educational Reform.* NY: Teachers College Press.

Berliner, D. C. & Biddle, B. J. (1995). *The Manufactured Crisis.* New York: Random House.

Bracey, G. W. (2004). Simpson's Paradox. *American School Board Journal*, 191 (2), 32-34.

Gonzales, P., Calsyn, C., Jocelyn, L., Mak, K., Kastberg, D., Arafeh, S., Williams, T., and Tsen, W. (2000). *Pursuing Excellence: Comparisons of International Eighth-Grade Mathematics and Science Achievement from a U.S. Perspective, 1995 and 1999.* Washington, DC: National Center for Educational Statistics, Department of Education. Retrieved February 26, 2004 at http://nces.ed.gov/pubsearch/pubsinfo.asp?pubid=2001028.

Lemke, M., Calsyn, C., Lippman, L., Jocelyn, L., Kastberg, D., Liu, Y., Roey, S., Williams, T., Kruger, T., and Bairu, G. (2001) *Outcomes of Learning: Results from the 2000 Program for International Student Assessment of 15-Year-Olds in Reading, Mathematics, and Science Literacy.* Washington, DC: National Center for Educational Statistics, Department of Education. Retrieved February 26, 2004 at http://nces.ed.gov/pubsearch/pubsinfo.asp?pubid=2002115.

National Center for Educational Statistics (2004). *Progress on International Reading Literacy.* Washington, DC. Retrieved February 26, 2004 at http://nces.ed.gov/pubs2004/pirlspub/index.asp.

Torney-Purta, J., Lehmann, R., Oswald, H., & Schulz, W. (2001). *Citizenship and Education in Twenty-eight Countries: Civic Knowledge and Engagement at Age Fourteen.* College Station, MD: University of Maryland.

How Well Can U. S. Adults Read?
Government-Centered vs. Learner-Centered Estimates
Tom Sticht

Editor's note: Tom Sticht, a leading world authority on adult literacy, provides some convincing data indicating that a very high percentage of American adults are quite satisfied with their ability to read for life needs and work. He suggests their self-assessment may be more useful than test data.

Author's note: The following brief discussion raises questions about the need for massive reforms of reading teaching in the public schools. If the purpose of K-12 literacy instruction is to produce literate adults, and if almost all adults think they read well enough to meet their daily needs, then is it appropriate for the government to call them "functionally illiterate" based on fallible standardized tests? Perhaps instead of trying to improve all K-12 reading instruction through the No Child Left Behind approach, a focused approach to research on improving reading instruction would be more useful. —TS

The 1992 National Assessment of Adult Literacy (NALS) tested a representative sample of adults 16 years of age and older on three tests of literacy: Prose, Document, and Quantitative. Scores on each test were divided into five levels of literacy, with Level 1 being the lowest level and Levels 4 and 5 the highest levels. Results on the three types of tests were very similar so only the data for the Prose test are used here.

Using the Prose test, some 21 percent (40+ million) of U.S. adults were placed in Level 1 and 27 percent (50+ million) in Level 2. These two lower levels included almost half (47-48 percent) of the adults in the U.S. and this was the basis for a press release of 8 September 1993 from the U.S. Department of Education with the headline LITERACY LEVELS DEFICIENT FOR 90 MILLION U.S. ADULTS.

Interestingly, the press release went on to say, ". . . most of these adults describe themselves as being able to read or write English 'well' or 'very well.'" The press release goes on to quote then Secretary of Education Richard W. Riley making the extraordinary statement: "It paints a picture of a society in which the vast majority of Americans do not know that they do not have the skills they need to earn a living in our increasingly technological society and international marketplace." In short, this statement about adults' insights into the adequacy of their skills simply dismissed the adults' judgments about their skills in favor of the results of the standardized tests made by the government sponsored testing experts.

From 1992 up to the present, numerous reports using the data for adults on the Prose, Document, and Quantitative tests have appeared. The NALS methodology was also used in developing the International Adult Literacy Survey (IALS), which was eventually administered in over 20 nations. For the U.S., a subset of the NALS data for 16- to 65-year-olds were used in the IALS. Like the NALS, the IALS used the three literacy tests as their primary means of literacy assessment, and they also used self-ratings of how well adults thought they read. And again, as with the NALS, the IALS research has led to many reports about the percentages of adults in various nations with "deficient" literacy skills using the test data, but almost no attention has been given to the self-rating data presented in the technical reports.

This paper brings together data that reveal some interesting and important differences among adults in the U.S. in their beliefs about their reading skills. The data are summarized below in a number of questions and answers.

Q1: How many adults 16 years of age and above in the U.S. think they read English "well" or "very well"?
A1: 93 percent thought they read "well" or "very well' while 7 percent (13.4 million) thought their reading was

deficient. This differs greatly from the government's estimate of 90 million adults with deficient reading skills based on its standardized tests.

Q2: How many adults 16 to 65 years of age think their reading skills meet their *daily* needs for reading "moderately well" "good," or "excellently"?
A2: 94 percent "moderately," "good," or "excellently"; 87 percent "good" or "excellently."

Q3: How many adults 16 to 65 years of age think their reading skills meet their main *job* needs "moderately well," "good," or "excellently"?
A3: 94 percent "moderately," "good," or "excellently"; 87 percent "good" or "excellently."

Q4: How many adults 16 to 65 years of age think their reading skills "are not at all limiting," "somewhat limiting," or "greatly limiting" of their job opportunities?
A4: 87 percent "not at all limiting," 9 percent "somewhat limiting," 4 percent "greatly limiting."

Q5: How many adults aged 16 to 59 who were White, Black, or Hispanic thought they read English "well" or "very well?"
A5: Whites, 98 percent; Blacks, 94 percent; Hispanics, 68 percent.

Q6: How many adults aged 60 years or age or higher who were White, Black, or Hispanic thought they read English "well" or "very well"?
A6: Whites, 95 percent; Blacks, 83 percent; Hispanics, 54 percent.

Q7: How many prison inmates thought they read English "well" or "very well"?
A7: 88 percent.

Q8: How many adults age 16 years or higher said they got "a lot" or "some/none" help with completing literacy forms of some sort?
A8: 12 percent "a lot," 88 percent "some/none."

Clearly, the government's test-based estimates of adult reading/ literacy skills differ considerably from the adult population's experience-based estimates of their reading/literacy skills. This raises the question of how each type of information might be best used in establishing the scale of need for resources for adult literacy education.

Of course, it might be argued that neither type of information is the best information for establishing the scale of need for adult literacy education and that instead we ought to focus on the numbers of adults who present themselves for educational services each year and argue for funding needed to provide adequate services for those who present themselves for education.

Finally, if some 9 out of 10 adults think they read "well" or "very well," and that their reading skills meet their daily needs and their needs at work, and that their reading skills do not limit their job opportunities, then what does this imply for policy for reading instruction in the K-12 system, which is where most adults acquire most of their reading skills. Does this suggest that there is a need for massive reforms in the teaching of reading in the K-12 system, whether evidence-based or not?

Why NCLB Puts Its Focus on Reading

Ken Goodman

It must puzzle some reporters when their editors repeatedly assign them to do stories or a series of stories about reading instruction and achievement. Major newspapers like the *Los Angeles Times* and the *Baltimore Sun* have assigned full-time staff to write about reading. It must also puzzle them that news media are literally overwhelmed with slick propaganda from think tanks, foundations, and groups with names like the Reading Reform Foundation, Citizens for Literacy, Parents for Better Schools, etc., all with the same simple message:

- Increasingly large numbers of American children aren't learning to read.
- Many are even graduating from high school virtually illiterate.
- This is largely the result of misguided and miseducated teachers.
- Direct instruction of phonics and phonemic awareness is a method which research proves will teach all children to read by third grade.
- This scientific method requires use of a small number of scientifically-tested commercial programs.
- The crisis is so imminent that it requires new federal and state laws to assure that all children are taught in this scientific way by teachers trained in this scientific way by teacher educators limited to teaching prospective teachers to teach only in this scientific way.

This view has been so repeatedly promoted by a well-coordinated campaign extending over almost two decades that it has come to be regarded as the truth by much of the public and by large segments of the press. The view is now built into President Bush's Reading First Initiative passed into law under the No Child Left

Behind Act. Several books have documented this campaign, most recently Allington (2002).

Why Focusing on Reading Is Good Propaganda

There are several strong reasons why the focus of this campaign is centered on reading:

1. Parents worry their children will not succeed in school if they don't learn to read and write well. Parents of poor children and minorities are vulnerable to the argument that school failure could be the result if their kids are not being given the simplistic phonics programs that work for other children.

2. There is a long history in the United States of controversy over reading instruction, with vocal groups calling for simplistic phonics methods over more complex methods that focus on meaning. Often the claim is made that in the past all children learned to read easily and well. As Berliner and Biddle have shown in their book, *Manufactured Crisis,* there never was such a Golden Age in education and, in fact, there has been a steady improvement in the success of American children in reading development.

In the past, it has mainly been fringe groups concerned about "Godless" schools putting dangerous ideas in the heads of their children who advocated simplistic phonics programs. Now this simplistic phonics solution to reading instruction is the central part of the Bush administration's education agenda.

3. Our public schools are not serving all groups in our complex society equally well. This reality is apparent in any comparisons of test performance, dropout rates, and rates of graduation. But, by focusing their attention on methods of teaching, public attention can be directed away from such factors as poor support of schools, inadequate facilities and equipment, unqualified teachers, lack of diversity and flexibility in curriculum, and real prejudice.

The "Reading Wars"

There are real issues and disagreements in the teaching of reading. American researchers are not unified on how to study reading or on the findings of research on literacy, literacy development and literacy instruction.

Beginning in 1994, a campaign was started to label these disagreements as the "reading wars," with advocates of "whole language" on the one side and "phonics" on the other. Actually, there are a wide range of positions of reading instruction. Whole language emerged as an inclusive, holistic pedagogy that opposed the massive commercial basal reading programs with their emphasis on controlled vocabulary and sequential skill instruction. Whole language teachers used real children's literature and other authentic texts. Writing was encouraged from the beginning, with children allowed to invent spelling for words they needed. Whole language teachers built on the language, culture, and interests of pupils of all populations. A boom in the sales of children's literature accompanied the growth of whole language and greatly increased the quality, quantity, and variety of books for children. Children of color found themselves in these books, and all children found that their problems, values, and interests were available in books. Many fine authors, including authors of color, found ready markets.

Whole language was an ideal target. It was counter-intuitive so it could be portrayed as a faddish "philosophy" rather than rigorous, sequential methodology. And there were reputable researchers willing to fight the "war" on behalf of phonics and sequential skills.

Confusing Differences with Deficits

Researchers have often sought the source of reading difficulty in the learners. A few decades ago, it was popular to blame intelligence differences between ethnic and racial groups. Cultural deprivation was another popular excuse. Bilingualism was used to explain lack of success of some immigrant groups. More modern variations find pathological reasons for differential success. People approaching reading from medical models and from special-education perspectives seek to classify learners as dyslexic, emotionally disturbed, learning disabled, etc. Somehow these conditions seem to be epidemic among minority pupils, English learners, and poor folks in general. All these views confuse "difference" with "deficiency." Researchers who believe that reading difficulty lies in finding things wrong with learners and then remediating them do research to find deficiencies—and they find them.

Those deficit researchers then design instructional studies, using medical models, specifically attacking the identified deficits. Different "treatments" are given to different children. In one highly-publicized study in a suburb of Houston, the treatment was a commercial program that uses a heavy phonics focus. Control groups had what the researchers labeled whole language and embedded phonics. Success was judged on the basis of scores on tests of nonsense words and words out of context.

Before the study was completed, it was being reported at scientific conferences and in the press as proving that phonics works and whole language doesn't. With other studies funded by the National Institute for Child Health and Human Development (NICHD), this study became the basis for the definitions in present and preceding federal and state laws for defining what is and what isn't "research-based" in reading instruction.

In 1999, Congress passed the Reading Excellence Act with bipartisan support, which essentially established direct instruction of phonics as the national reading curriculum. Funding under this act required exclusive use of materials based on "reliable replicable research," a phrase that occurs dozens of times in the bill. When NCLB was written, "reliable replicable research" was renamed "scientific" research.

To further the reading campaign, the NICHD developed a

series of two panels. The first was funded by NICHD but administered through the National Research Council. It was chaired by Catherine Snow of Harvard. Members were carefully selected to be sure that the report that eventually emerged would support the goal of the campaign. It consisted, in the most part, of psychologists and medical researchers and excluded perhaps 90 percent of the range of prominent reading researchers. The title of its final report is a giveaway of its deficit view, *Preventing Reading Difficulties in Young Children.* (Snow, et al.)

The campaign now shifted its rhetoric. The reading wars were over. A consensus of the scientific community agreed that phonics worked and whole language (or anything else) didn't.

Following that, NICHD itself was authorized by Congress to convene the National Reading Panel (NRP) to take the Snow report and decide what research shows works and doesn't work in teaching reading. Again, the panel was composed of a hand-picked, unrepresentative group of scientists. They are publicly reported to have reviewed "all of the research—literally many thousands of studies." Actually, the criteria they used to screen studies for inclusion reduced this number to 38 studies. To be included, a study had to be an instructional experiment with results judged by pre- and post-test data. Predictably, the panel produced a report that favored direct instruction with a heavy emphasis on phonics.

Both panel reports were voluminous and fell short of saying that science equals phonics. But on the day the NRP report was publicly released, the PR firm hired to disseminate its findings already had a slick, beautifully illustrated summary for release to the press. The summary made the panel's findings into what the planners had wanted. It is this summary, and not either report itself, which is the basis for the definitions of research, of reading, and of scientific reading methodology contained in the federal law. Garan has done a detailed comparison of the summary and the actual report, which shows claims in the summary exaggerate or misrepresent the findings. Here's one extreme example:

Claim: The NRP's results indicate "what can be accomplished
  when explicit, systematic phonics programs are implemented
  in today's classrooms" (Summary p. 13).
Contradiction: "There were insufficient data to draw any conclusions about the effects of phonics instruction with normally-
  developing readers above the first grade." (Reports of the
  Subgroups, p2:16)(Garan in Allington, 2002).

Still, the campaign had what it wanted. What remained was for
laws to be written which enforced the national reading curriculum and a federal reading instruction method which all teachers
in all schools would be required to use. No child would be left
behind because all would be taught with the same materials in
the same way. In interpreting the law, Secretary of Education
Paige and his assistants have made clear that only a short list of
commercial programs are acceptable, based in research as now
defined in the law.

Richard Allington, who has carefully studied the research on
direct instruction in phonics, recently summarized what the law
had accomplished:

"Given the almost complete failure of phonics-intensive
direct instruction in programs for children identified as
learning-disabled, we might ask whether we have invested
more funding in any other educational program and ended
up with less to show for it. It would have made sense to me
if the politicians had stepped in and eliminated the NICHD
and the Office of Special Education and Rehabilitation
Services because of their almost complete failure to educate the learning-disabled children entrusted to them. But
putting the special-education direct-instruction gurus in
charge of reforming American reading instruction—even

Orwell wouldn't have imagined such an outcome." (Allington p. 275)

The Realities of Reading

In reality, reading test performance has been stable for the last four National Assessment of Educational Progress reports. Although eighth and twelfth grades were also tested in the other years, only fourth grade was done in 2000. NAEP tests a sample of learners in each participating state. The National Center for Education Statistics reports the NAEP 2003 scores, "No significant change was detected in fourth-grade reading scores since 1992, though eighth graders show an overall gain since 1992."

Changes in particular states and local schools for different populations are more likely to be the result of changed demographics and levels of school support than changes in methodology of reading instruction.

The 1998 NAEP showed a 198[1] mean in fourth grade for those eligible for free or reduced-price lunches compared to a 227 mean[2] for those not eligible. That suggests that relative poverty is at least as important as race and ethnicity in reading test performance. One-third of all fourth graders tested fell in the free lunch group but of course a high proportion of black, Hispanic, and Indian children are poor.

Girls also score higher than boys. Fourth-grade mean for girls was 220 and for boys 214 in the 1998 data. That suggests girls adjust better to reading programs and tests than boys. There was a similar gender difference for eighth and twelfth grades in 1998. The range of performance on any test such as NAEP within any group is considerable. So the mean NAEP scores of white, black, and Hispanic students are different. But many white students score below the black and Hispanic means and many black and

---

[1] Possible NAEP scores range from 0 to 500.
[2] Mean is the statistics term for average.

Hispanic students score above the white means. The mean for Indians is low and Asian/Pacific Islanders is high, but both groups show a wide range.

Some tests, like California, Iowa, and Stanford tests, are norm-referenced. Scores represent average performance by a sample group at each grade level. It is a statistical impossibility to have all third graders reading at grade level. By definition, half will always be below and half above the mean. If all improved the mean would go up. Items are thrown out of the test if everybody gets them right or wrong. And new items are added to spread the test-takers out.

Tests like NAEP, however, are created based on arbitrary performance criteria. A committee is asked to set criteria for what would constitute an adequate score for readers with a particular degree of competence. Such criterion-based scores are thus arbitrary and do not mean that the test items are equally appropriate for all kinds of children in all regions.

The greatest confusion in over-interpreting scores on the National assessment comes from the use of terms to designate criterion scores on the tests as "Basic," "Proficient," and "Advanced." The NAEP test is supposed to be criterion-referenced, meaning that the items deal with what the test writers believe readers should know and be able to do. The committee set the criterion levels to divide pupils into achievement groups. No single score can divide non-readers from readers, weak readers from strong etc. If 30 percent or so of those tested had scores below the score called "Basic," that doesn't mean they are non-readers. If 70 percent of those tested fall below the score called "Proficient," that doesn't mean that they are not proficient readers. In fact, a range of scores on any test around any point must be considered statistically equivalent.

A letter from Secretary of Education Paige to Chief State School Officers reflects this misrepresentation of what these labels for arbitrary scores mean. In it he says: "When more than two out of three fourth graders can't read proficiently on the National Assessment of Educational Progress, we know there is a problem that requires decisive action." (Letter dated October 23, 2002)

President Bush also misrepresents scores as realities: "Yet, earlier this year, we found that almost two-thirds of African-American children in the fourth grade cannot read at basic grade level." (Bush, 8/1/01)

In this statement he is referring to the percent of fourth graders whose scores fell below the NAEP Basic score. But he confuses the meaning of this criterion-based score with the definition of the mean score for fourth graders on a norm-referenced test.

Apparently the consistent conclusions don't matter anyway. In Fall 2002, according to Paige, NAEP scores reflected a "problem." However, a November 13, 2003, press release claims the similar results indicate, "that the education revolution that *No Child Left Behind* promised has begun. We are slowly picking up steam and the reforms are starting to work. . . . The 2003 scores continue to be well above 2000 and 1998 levels."

Reading proficiency is not a score on a test. It is the complex ability to make sense of what you're reading. Research by Goodman and many others has shown that most fourth graders in all populations can make sense of a variety of well-written texts that fit their background and interests. (Goodman, 1979)

What's the Reality Among American Pupils?
Almost all U.S. students learn to read and write. It is hard to find a fourth-grade pupil who is a "total" non-reader or non-writer. However, test performance does vary. All tests are constructed to spread the test-takers out. Those who attend poorly supported schools staffed by underpaid and unqualified or minimally qualified teachers, do not do as well on the tests. Among those children are disproportionate numbers of the poor, of children of color, of recent immigrants, of bilinguals.

READING AND THE FEDERAL LAWS
Ken Goodman

In this section, we'll examine how the mandates of the federal laws and agenda are affecting reading development of children, including those traditionally failed: children of color, poor children, and also kids in general. One avowed purpose of NCLB is to eliminate the gaps between white middle-class and minority children in school achievement. But NCLB thinks that is to be accomplished by treating all children alike.

Phonics and Phonemic Awareness
NCLB implementers insist on use of programs that narrowly focus on phonics and phonemic awareness. These programs do not allow for differences between different dialects of English; in fact, they erroneously assume that speakers of all dialects have the same phonics. But phonics is different for different dialects— how the spellings relate to speech depends on the way each dialect group produces the sounds of English. Consider, for example, how different speakers might pronounce this written sentence:

Aunt Mary is going to take a walk over to my house.

White middle-class children growing up in Atlanta, Boston, New York, and Chicago would each produce a different pronunciation. But in each place they would be taught as if the sounds in each word, for example "over," were the same for all of them. If they speak the high-status dialect of their region, their teachers might teach the standard phonic associations but not hear the deviations in the reading since they speak that way themselves. But what happens if we transplant that child to another region. The Chicago teacher will find the "ovuh" of her Boston or Atlanta pupils unacceptable. The New York child may be corrected in Boston or Chicago.

Now suppose that the child is a poor, rural black child in Atlanta, a Dominican immigrant in New York, an Appalachian migrant to Chicago, a Spanish-dominant child in Tucson. In each case, it is more likely that they will produce pronunciations unacceptable for their teachers and the phonics program will confuse them more than it helps.

The programs being mandated by the new federal law place a heavy emphasis on early instruction in "phonemic awareness," which treats the ability to segment monosyllabic words or nonwords into component speech sounds as a prerequisite to successful reading development. A speaker of Midwestern dialect might be able to hear four sounds in the word "help." But speakers of Southern or some African-American dialects hear three sounds in "he'p". In Midland dialects such as in Oklahoma the word is "hey-ulp." A correct definition of phonics is the set of relationships between someone's sound system and the orthography of the language. We standardize spelling across American dialects but there is no standard sound system.

In many cases teachers feel justified in "correcting" the speech sounds of children of color and low-status white speakers because it "isn't really language." At best, this shows an unscientific and elitist view of language difference but at worst it introduces confusion for the children who don't know why they are being corrected.

For second-language learners, such an early emphasis on producing exact speech sounds diverts them from making sense of their new language while they concentrate on hearing subtle sound differences they have learned to ignore in their first language. A speaker of an Asian language may have trouble hearing and producing the difference in the initial sounds in rate and late. Such a heavy focus on speech sounds in reading instruction leads to second-language learners becoming able to produce an oral response to an English text while having no sense of the meaning.

Phonemic awareness is measured by asking kids to break words down into their sounds. But research summarized by Allington and others shows instruction in abstracting sounds out of their phonological context is of little benefit to most pupils. Some children can do it without instruction, some can't do it but are already reading, some can't profit from the instruction, and a few seem to be helped.

In 1969, Goodman found a flaw in virtually all research that compares differences in achievement of speakers of different dialects:

> Studies relating to literacy and language programs in school are hopelessly confounded by elitist views that make one sound system, one syntax, one vocabulary right and all others wrong. The entire language curriculum is built on a base of linguistic misconceptions. We have virtually no reliable data on IQ, achievement, or learning ability because of the elitist yardstick for language built into the research designs and into the most revered and time-honored tests.
>
> We think when we show that a test correlates with later success in school we have demonstrated the validity of the test when in fact all we have demonstrated is the irrelevance of both the test and the curriculum. (Goodman, 1969)

Treating Reading As an Autonomous Skill

An old belief in reading instruction is that children must learn to read before they can read to learn. A more scientific view is that language, including written language, is learned best in the context of its use. The federal law and similar state laws impose a view of reading as an autonomous skill which is independent of the uses being made of it and which must be learned out of context before it is used. That turns written language into a set of decontextualized abstractions, hard to learn and without any intrinsic motivation for the learner. Young readers are not getting information or a good story from their reading. It is skill for skill sake, not very easy for any learners and a particular problem for children already confused by the unfamiliar sounds they are being expected to use.

NCLB strong-arms schools and teachers to use so-called "decodable texts" in early reading instruction. These texts follow the principle that all words in the text must fit a phonics rule already taught or be learned as an individual word. But that produces very strange-sounding texts with little meaning for the learners. That's why whole language with real books written for children became popular. Because the books used language familiar to the kids, they found them predictable—the young learners could anticipate what was coming from the patterns and rhythms of the language they already spoke.

Beyond "Color Me Brown"

The Civil Rights movement forced developers of reading materials to include the full range of American diversity in their stories and illustrations. Inititially, this led to a quick "color me brown" response. Publishers literally took the existing illustrations and darkened the complexions of some of the children portrayed and occasionally changed their hair texture but left the content intact.

But that still left children reading about people who lived in idealized suburbs with mother at the door in her apron saying goodbye to father going off to work with his briefcase. So that created a pressure to make the content of instructional material more realistic, with the experiences and cultures represented inclusive of all the diversity of America. Now children had characters who not only looked like them but who lived where they lived and had problems and experiences similar to the ones they had. The increased market for children's books cited earlier and the demand for diversity in children's literature brought an explosion in the scope and variety of books written for children. That made it easy for publishers to find well-written stories to include in their programs and for teachers to set aside the basal programs and use the rich diverse literature to teach children to read. There was also a growing awareness that all learners learn best with authentic texts—which are predictable for them because they resonate with their own language, culture, experience, and interests.

The programs being mandated for schools by the federal bureaucracy in interpreting the new law are designed not around diversity and predictability but around decodability. In these programs, "stories" are built using letter-sound correspondences and "sight-words" explicitly taught through "direct instruction." That results in artificial texts, with minimal storylines and a return to "color me brown" tokenism. There may be an illustration with a brown skin or slant-eyed character but nothing in the text relates to a diversity of culture or experience. The focus is on reading as an autonomous skill.

Direct Instruction
There are times when any teacher focuses on a particular skill or concept at the point a child or a group of children seems to need or is ready for such focus. The teacher may want to call attention to a spelling pattern such as "ough," introduce a concept in math such as negative numbers, help with a term like "latitude" or show kindergarten children how to safely cross a busy street near their school. In this sense, the instruction is "direct" (in contrast to less direct focus where the learners are guided in developing knowledge in the context of meaningful and functional experiences). And all teachers make use of such direct instruction.

But there is a view implicit in federal reading mandates that reading consists of a hierarchy of skills which can only be learned through direct instruction. The federally-mandated programs being pushed by the federal bureaucracy in their interpretation of the new federal law have this view in common. Reading is broken down into a series of skills to be hierarchically arranged and explicitly taught and tested. Each skill is considered prerequisite to what follows, so it is directly taught until mastery is demonstrated. Learners in this view are interchangeable and the only aspect of the program which can be varied is the pace __ all children repeat the same task until they show mastery on a test of the specific skill. Teachers are encouraged or required (depending on the program) to group and regroup learners for instruction around their level of mastery of the component skills.

What invariably results is that many children of color, second-language learners, and other poor children accumulate in the lower rungs of this ladder (condemned to repeating over and over what hasn't been working for them and denied access to the more meaningful latter stages of the program, including any opportunity to experience real books).

The logic of the program is that the explicit and direct instruction will assure "success for all." But for many children it assures failure, including retention in grade and eventual dropouts.

Controlling Teachers and Teacher Education

The rigidity of the programs being mandated is compounded if knowledgeable teachers capable of differentiating the instruction to suit the needs and abilities of the learners are prevented from doing so by administrators or program monitors who insist on close adherence to the program. In schools using Slavin's Success for All, an old system called the Joplin plan (for Joplin, Missouri, where it originated) is used to divide pupils by scores on a reading test administered every few weeks. Each teacher gets a group on the same level, not those they have in their own rooms, for reading instruction. The program and the test determine instruction, and monitors paid for under the school's contract watch teachers closely and report deviators to the principal.

In California, several districts have been funded by the Packard Foundation to buy the time of monitors from the Open Court program of McGraw-Hill to assure fidelity to the program. One teacher was told by her principal she would have to remove the extensive library of children's books that she had purchased with her own money from her classroom because they were not part of the instructional program the district had agreed to follow.

That teachers are finding ways of subverting the mandates and following their own professional judgments is evidenced in the complaints of leading advocates of the federal mandates. Louisa Moats complains in a monograph, "Whole Language Still Lives." In it she makes it clear that nothing short of complete adherence to the program is acceptable, including "balanced reading," an attempt to combine holistic programs with skill programs.

Chester Finn, head of the Thomas B. Fordham Foundation and a fellow of the Hoover Institute, is a major architect of the federal mandates. He has complained that now the war has been won, it is up to teachers to "follow the law of the land." (You may have thought that was the Constitution.) He blames teacher educators for leading teachers astray.

And, indeed, in California and several other states, each professor who teaches a reading course is required to submit a syllabus of their courses to the state. The state can withdraw approval of the college's program if the syllabus has omissions or inclusions that are deemed as deviations. A blacklist seems to exist in those states where all syllabi referring to specific researchers or experts are never approved.

The federal law requires that each state submit a proposal which delineates how the law will be implemented. Susan Neuman, then-Undersecretary of Education, made clear that proposals which do deviate will be rejected and funds denied until the state gets them right.

In Hawaii and Puerto Rico, the federal government rejected members of the committee chosen by local leaders to write the proposals. This is only more evidence that a blacklist has been established with the names of those who may not participate or be cited in bibliographies of proposals.

There is a strong attack nationally and in several states on teacher certification and tenure and an increased use of tests to qualify teachers. Minorities have historically been screened out of teaching through such tests.

Ironically, NCLB requires that states hire qualified teachers without defining what qualified means. For teacher aides, however, the new law specifies that they must be high school graduates. Heritage language programs in Arizona, Hawaii, and Alaska have already been forced to close down because aides, generally tribal elders, who speak the languages must be fired. A program in Tucson for Indian language is being suspended for that reason.

Districts still under court order to desegregate are having to set aside part of their desegregation funds to allow for the money "failing schools" are required to use for busing children to other schools. And that puts the schools out of compliance with the federal courts in order to be in compliance with the federal law.

Control of Materials

One aspect of the increasing globalization of power in the world is the mergers and takeovers in school publishing which has reduced the field to five multinational corporations. Vivendi, the French multinational, announced in 1991 when it bought Houghton Mifflin that it was now the second largest media company in the world. (More recently, Vivendi sold Houghton Mifflin.)

These companies control all forms of media and communications. They also control all aspects of school publishing. McGraw-Hill publishes several reading programs formerly independent including Open Court and Mastery Learning (formerly Distar). These are two of the small number of programs that the federal bureaucracy considers "research-based." The same company is a major test publisher and has a large share of the lucrative test-scoring contracts with states and local districts. The new requirement for testing every child in grades 3–8 in every state will greatly increase the size of the test and test-scoring markets. The McGraw family has long ties with the Bush family. Secretary of Education Paige won the Stanley McGraw prize as Superintendent of Houston Schools.

Here's a press release from the company, which shows how they are profiting from new federal and state legislation:

NEW YORK—(BUSINESS WIRE)—OCT. 22, 2002—The McGraw-Hill Companies (NYSE:MHP–News) today reported revenue for the nine months increased 2.4% to $3.62 billion . . .

The McGraw-Hill School Education Group gained share in an elementary–high school market that is off 9.9% after eight months, according to the most recent Association of American Publishers statistics.

We expect to capture more than 31% of the available adoption sales opportunities this year, up from 29% last year. . . . Although our basal reading program did not meet expectations in Oklahoma and Florida, a strong performance by our *research-based reading products and literature programs* produced excellent results in adoption states and the open territories. Our programs captured more than 33% of the K-8 reading adoption market in California and more than 20% of the Florida market.

"We also received a major new order in the third quarter from Detroit, Michigan, for more than $18 million. We believe it is the largest adoption this year in the open territories. Detroit used a blend of local, state and new federal funds from the Reading First program to purchase three of our products: Open Court, Reading Mastery and Corrective Reading. Michigan received a grant of $28.5 million this year from the U.S. Department of Education for its Reading First initiatives and is one of the first states to release funding in 2002. So far this year, 16 states have received Reading First grants from the Department of Education."

"Prospects in the testing market continue to improve, but timing factors resulted in third quarter softness. We recently won new statewide testing contracts in Connecticut, West Virginia and Maryland."

The law is written in such a way that it takes away from districts and teachers the right to use literature programs instead of basal readers. Former Congresswoman Pat Schroeder, now head of the American Publishers Association, wrote Secretary Paige to complain about limiting choice under enforcement of NCLB. Paige responded that any program which is correctly research-based could be approved, though it would be up to the state or district to prove that it was research-based if the feds were to approve it.

Will Communities With Failing Schools Have Access to the Same Choices As Affluent Districts?
Mayor Richard Daley of Chicago finds himself in an intolerable dilemma. Thousands of Chicago children are in schools the state has labeled failing. By law, parents have the right to demand that their children be transferred to "better" schools. But there are almost no places in Chicago's non-failing schools to receive them and suburbs certainly won't make room for them. Where does a failing school in the middle of Alaska or the Navaho nation send its children?

Furthermore, the law contains time bombs set to go off as long as a dozen years from now. Under NCLB the achievement levels for being judged failing is raised in successive years. The law states that the bar for being considered successful schools in reading and other key test areas will be the "Proficient" level in year 2014. The bill writers had the NAEP Proficient level in mind. But Congress in passing the bill gave the states the choice of texts and each state defines its own criterion scores.

The charts included in Figure 1 show the percentages of each defined population over last 4 fourth grade reading NAEP administrations. Though there have been very modest "improvements" in those reaching the "proficient and above" scores in most groups the possibility that even the White and Asian/Pacific Islander groups could ever move the lower-scoring 55 to 60 percent of students up to this level is a statistical impossibility. The level was deliberately set to be hard to achieve. In fact, it is likely that the changes shown here are reflections of a phenomena that has nothing much to do with increasing reading proficiency. Pressure and extra test preparation time has its greatest effect on higher achievers in any group. Those already high can be pushed to score a bit better.

In no year did even 20 percent of Black, Hispanic, and Indian populations reach the proficient level. The effect of raising the bar will be that the higher the proportion or such minority pupils in a school, the more assuredly it will become labeled a failing school. Recognizing this goal is impossible to achieve, some states have begun to redefine the test scores that will be considered proficient.

Questions That Need to Be Asked

Granted that literacy is important in modern society. But why should that require federal and state laws to determine the curriculum and methodology of teaching of reading. Why should we

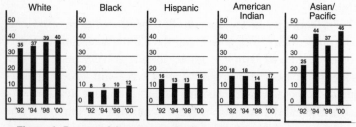

Figure 1 Percent of those tested scoring at or above the score labeled proficient on NAEP – 1992–2000

impose narrow limits on the professional educators? Why should control be taken away from local and state authorities and centered in Washington bureaucrats? Why should reading test scores be used as criteria for closing schools and transferring students to other schools? Why are schools mandated to deny promotion and graduation to students with low scores on tests of reading (and to a lesser extent writing and math). Essentially, we are being told that a political solution became necessary because the educational system has failed and cannot be trusted to do the job without being coerced.

How can all this be mandated by federal law, when the United States Constitution has made education a state and not a federal responsibility? What ever happened to local control?

Some questions can only make sense if we understand that all this fuss about reading was never about reading. It is about privatizing American education and ultimately eliminating the tax burden on business for the expense of supporting public education. In many parts of the world, access to education depends on the means of parents. Those who can afford to do so send their children to private schools and hire tutors if their children are not doing well there. The working poor send their children to overcrowded and poorly-funded public schools. And the children of the non-working poor spend little time in school at all.

The same forces that successfully kept access to health care private are campaigning to privatize education. But there is a widespread belief in the United States that free, universal public education makes it possible for every American child to achieve full participation in the economic and political benefits of our democratic society. So the campaign centers around demonstrating that public education is a failure. And what better way to do that than showing that the schools are so bad they can't even teach children to read?

SETTING THE RECORD STRAIGHT: FEDERAL OFFICIALS ARE HOLDING SCHOOLS TO IMPOSSIBLE STANDARDS BASED ON MISINTERPRETATIONS OF THE RESEARCH

Richard L. Allington

> Editor's Note: *Richard Allington has devoted much of his energy in recent years to debunking some the misinterpretations of research offered in support of NCLB. Here he analyzes the claim that research shows that with appropriate instruction 90 to 95 percent of poor readers can be brought to grade level. He also shows the tremendous cost of the tutoring it would require to accomplish this under the most optimistic research interpretations.* —KSG

Proponents of the federal Reading First mandates of the No Child Left Behind Act have routinely misrepresented and exaggerated what the research shows about effective classroom reading instruction and early reading interventions. The legislative impetus for the new laws and regulations resulted from a recent policy consensus that "90 to 95 percent of poor readers can be reading on grade level if provided with appropriate instruction." Yet there is no evidence that classroom instruction of any sort can come close to meeting the needs of the readers who struggle most. Research does show that expert, individual tutoring produces on-level reading achievement with many struggling readers. But is that how we should define "appropriate instruction"? If so, it will come with a hefty price tag.

But questions persist. What evidence supports the assertion that 90 to 95 percent of poor readers could be reading on grade level if only educators would offer appropriate instruction? And what exactly would it cost to provide such instruction to every student who needs it?

Interpreting the Data

Locating the source of the 90 to 95 percent figure is easy. G. Reid Lyon of the National Institute of Child Health and Human Development (NICHD) provided that figure in his testimony before the U.S. Senate Committee on Labor and Human Resources in April 1998. That figure has stuck like glue. Quoting Lyon (1998):

> We have learned that for 90 to 95 percent of poor readers, prevention and early intervention programs that combine instruction in phoneme awareness, phonics, fluency development, and reading comprehension strategies, provided by well-trained teachers, can increase reading skills to average reading levels. (p. 7)

What research did Lyon use to establish this success rate? He provided no citations in his testimony, but in that same year he coauthored a paper (Fletcher & Lyon, 1998) citing two studies (Torgesen, Wagner, & Rashotte, 1997; Vellutino et al., 1996) that supported his assertion.

Vellutino and colleagues studied approximately 200 at-risk primary-grade students from six suburban school districts. They divided the students into two groups: treatment and control. The treatment students received individual, expert tutoring for one semester, typically for 30 minutes per day, for an average total of 70 to 80 sessions. Some students continued to receive tutoring for a longer period. Almost half (44.7 percent) of the tutored students achieved average reading levels (the 45th percentile) after tutoring.

Torgesen and colleagues provided 20-minute tutoring sessions four days a week for two and one-half years to approximately 100 primary-grade students. Teachers and aides provided daily tutoring on an alternating basis. Tutored students received one of three possible interventions, each of which produced similar outcomes on the word-reading tests.

Although the Vellutino and Torgesen interventions did demonstrate the power of intensive, expert tutoring, the outcomes indicated that these interventions raised roughly 50 percent of the poor readers—not 90–95 percent—to the 45th percentile or above, or to average reading levels.

Did Lyon misinterpret the data in the two studies? I suggest this because the intensive, expert tutoring of struggling readers (in addition to other efforts the schools initiated) reduced the proportion of poor readers in the school populations to approximately 10 percent of all students. In the Torgesen study, the very poor readers after intervention accounted for approximately 2.5 percent of the total population, and the students reading below the 45th percentile accounted for approximately 8 percent. In the Vellutino study, 3 percent of the original suburban students in the larger sampling population had very poor reading skills after tutoring, with 9 percent of the total population still falling below the 45th percentile. Using the 45th percentile criterion, 91 percent of all readers would be at average achievement levels.

But 90 percent of all students reading at or above average achievement levels is quite a different matter from 90 percent of poor readers achieving average levels of proficiency. To clarify, imagine Normal Elementary School. It has 1,000 students whose reading achievement just happens to be perfectly distributed along the traditional bell curve. Thus, 450 students fall below the 45th percentile, and 200 fall below the 20th percentile (a typical cutoff point for identification as a struggling reader). Getting 90 percent of the struggling reader population above the 45th percentile would require a program that solved the problems of 180 of the 200 struggling readers. But getting 90 percent of the total population (1,000) above the 45th percentile would require a program that solved the reading problems of only 100 struggling readers. In the first scenario, after the tutoring intervention, the school has 20 students (200–180) struggling to learn to read; in the second, the school has 100 struggling readers (1,000–900). Simply put, it is harder and more expensive to design interventions that reduce the pool of poor readers to 2 percent of the population (20 students) than to design one that leaves 10 percent of the population (100 students) still struggling.

The two studies indicate that when expert, intensive remedial tutoring supplements good classroom reading instruction, half of the poorest readers in any given suburban elementary school will still lag behind their peers, unable to read grade-level texts independently. Moreover, Vellutino and colleagues removed from the pool of poor readers all students with measured IQs below 90. Approximately 30 percent of all students have measured IQs below 90, according to the bell curve distribution. In other words, this study demonstrated that intensive, expert tutoring could accelerate literacy development in half of the struggling readers with IQs of 90 or higher, resulting in average levels of reading proficiency in this group by the end of second grade.

Both studies demonstrate that many struggling readers can achieve average levels of reading proficiency; that these students are not learning-disabled in the traditional sense but are simply instructionally needy; and that expert, intensive tutoring is a powerful intervention. But neither study shows that 90–95 percent of poor readers can achieve average reading levels with appropriate instruction, even when that appropriate instruction is expert, intensive tutoring.

An Expensive Solution

The Vellutino and Torgesen studies demonstrate that expert tutoring can be highly effective as an early intervention tool (see also Shanahan, 1998, and U.S. Department of Education, 2003). But schools don't normally provide such tutoring to struggling readers. Why not? Let's look at the costs involved.

In both studies, the students received 30–75 hours of expert tutoring; students in the Torgesen study received an additional 30 hours of tutoring from a paraprofessional. The expert tutors were typically certified teachers, including several with M.S. degrees and advanced certification in reading remediation. Such a teacher would cost a school approximately $50,000 annually (National Center for Education Statistics, 2003).

Tutors following the Vellutino model would work with 10 students each day. In our Normal Elementary School example, the program would require approximately 20 full-time tutors for a single semester or 10 full-time tutors for an entire year to teach the 200 students who qualified for tutoring. Tutors following the Torgesen model would work with four more students each day for an additional one and one-half years, which would mean hiring additional paraprofessionals. Either model would cost the school at least $500,000 annually (10 full-time teachers with a salary of $50,000 each).

In the NICHD studies, poor readers who did not qualify or were not selected for tutoring still received small-group remedial or special education instruction, as did some of the tutored students who completed the program. We will assume that existing revenues at Normal Elementary will continue to fund those services. Even so, developing the necessary tutoring expertise, adding a supervisory component, and creating tutoring spaces would most likely add to the cost, which would be substantially higher than $500,000 per year.

But many schools do not have such a normally distributed student population. Consider a recent study of students enrolled in urban, high-poverty schools (McGill-Franzen, Allington, Yokoi, & Brooks, 1999). The average pre-test performance of this group of randomly selected urban kindergarten students was the 13th percentile, well below the cutoff that both Vellutino and Torgesen used for tutoring eligibility.

Consider the tutoring costs for a school such as this, which we will call Abnormal Elementary. Let's say the school serves 1,000 students in a high-poverty neighborhood and two-thirds of the students—667— qualify for tutoring. That would require 34 additional full-time expert tutors, at a minimum cost to the school of $1.7 million annually (34 @ $50,000). And even with this added tutoring, we could still expect approximately half of the tutored students' measured reading achievement to fall below the 45th percentile.

One final consideration: Although Vellutino and colleagues and Torgesen and colleagues provide powerful testimony about the potential of early, intensive, expert instructional intervention, we have no data that suggest how permanent the tutoring effects will be. If we generalize the data from Reading Recovery (Hiebert, 1994), we can assume that many students will remain on this normal achievement track. But early intervention is not a vaccine that protects students from further difficulties: Without continued intensive instructional support, many students will gradually fall behind. Few schools seem to have the resources to provide intensive tutoring for students who get off-track in the later grades. Ensuring that all 6th graders read on grade level would cost even more.

It's time to face the fact that some students will need expert, intensive intervention for sustained periods of time—possibly throughout their entire school careers—if they are to attain and maintain on-level reading proficiencies. But we haven't yet developed interventions that ensure that all students will be reading on grade level.

What the Evidence Really Says

The implied premise of recent federal legislation emphasizing evidence-based instruction—that 90 to 95 percent of poor readers, or 98 percent of all students, would be reading on grade level if only teachers would follow the research—exaggerates what the evidence actually reports. No intervention has raised the achievement of 90 percent of poor readers to the 50th percentile. Moreover, no research suggests that classroom teachers can help 90 to 95 percent of students acquire grade-level reading proficiencies by learning more about phonology, using a scripted curriculum, teaching systematic phonics, or following some "proven" program. Programs that most reliably accelerated the literacy development of struggling readers relied on costly, expert, intensive tutoring, which raised the achievement of only about half of the poor readers to average (45th percentile) levels.

Given the potential costs of initiating a tutorial intervention for all struggling readers and maintaining student on-level performance, no one seems to be advocating—much less funding—research-based tutorial interventions. The current emphasis is on buying new, "scientific" reading materials (Kame'enui & Simmons, 2002), which is surely a less expensive option.

Struggling readers are instructionally needy. Classroom teachers will never have the time to provide the one-to-one support that so many of these students require. Research has shown that tutoring is an effective intervention that can provide this one-to-one support and raise student achievement. It is, however, costly. If legislators and other policymakers are going to mandate adequate yearly progress on the basis of research that measured the effects of individual tutoring, then they should fully fund that research-based tutoring for all struggling readers. Either that or admit to the public that we plan on leaving many children behind.

References

Fletcher, J., & Lyon, G. R. (1998). Reading: A research-based approach. In W. Evers (Ed.), *What's gone wrong in America's classrooms*. Stanford, CA: Hoover Institute Press.

Hiebert, E. H. (1994). Reading Recovery in the United States: What difference does it make to an age cohort? *Educational Researcher, 23*(9), 15–25.

Kame'enui, E. J., & Simmons, D. (2002). Consumer's guide to evaluating a core reading program. Institute for Development of Educational Achievement, University of Oregon. Available:

http://reading.uoregon.edu/appendices/con_guide_3.1.03.pdf.

Lyon, G. R. (1998, April 28). Overview of reading and literacy initiatives: Statement of G. Reid Lyon. Testimony before the
Senate Committee on Labor and Human Resources.
Washington, DC. Available: http://156.40.88.3/publications/
pubs/jeffords.htm.

McGill-Franzen, A., Allington, R. L., Yokoi, L., & Brooks, G.
(1999). Putting books in the room seems necessary but not sufficient. *Journal of Educational Research,* 93(2), 67–74.

National Center for Education Statistics. (2003). Digest of education statistics tables and figures 2001 [Online]. Available:
http://nces.ed.gov/programs/digest/d01/dt079.asp

Shanahan, T. (1998). On the effectiveness and limitations of tutoring. In P. D. Pearson & A. Iran-Nejad (Eds.), *Review of research
in education,* 23 (pp. 217–234). Washington, DC: American
Educational Research Association.

Torgesen, J. K., Wagner, R. K., & Rashotte, C. A. (1997). Prevention
and remediation of severe reading disabilities: Keeping the
end in mind. *Scientific Studies of Reading,* 1(3), 217–234.

U.S. Department of Education. (2003). Identifying and implementing educational practices supported by rigorous evidence: A user-friendly guide [Online]. Available: www.ed.gov/
rschstat/research/pubs/rigorousevid/index.html

Vellutino, F. R., Sipay, E. R., Small, S. G., Pratt, A., Chen, R., &
Denckla, M. B. (1996). Cognitive profiles of difficult-to-reme-
diate and readily remediated poor readers. *Journal of
Educational Psychology,* 88(4), 601–638.

Reprinted from Educational Leadership, *March 2004, with permission
of the author and the ASCD*

Penalizing Diverse Schools?
Similar test scores, but different students, bring federal sanctions

John R. Novak and Bruce Fuller

Key Findings

This brief details how schools serving diverse students in California are less likely to achieve their growth targets and be subjected to stiff federal sanctions. Schools enrolling more demographic subgroups do serve students who tend to score lower on standardized tests. Yet even when students display almost identical average test scores, schools with more subgroups are more likely to miss their growth targets under federal rules set by the No Child Left Behind Act.

Schools serving middle-class children, for example, are 28 percent more likely to be labeled "needs improvement" by the feds when serving five student subgroups than schools serving one group. This disparity exists even though average test scores are just five percentile points apart between schools. Also, schools with large numbers of Latino students from low-income homes display especially low odds of hitting growth targets.

Is it fair or motivating to label a school as failing simply because it serves more diverse students, not because its overall achievement level is lower?

Playing the Odds: Student Diversity and Growth Targets

We examined which schools successfully achieved their AYP targets during California's initial two years under the federal accountability reforms. These results were recently announced, following the spring 2003 round of student testing. We then asked how the odds of hitting AYP targets are driven by average test scores or the number of subgroups, after sorting schools into similar communities, ranging from well-off to poor neighborhoods. . . .

Table 1 shows how we divided schools into four sets, based upon the percentage of their enrollments made up of children who come from economically disadvantaged families. The top group of schools includes those with less than 25 percent coming from disadvantaged families. The bottom group includes schools where over 75 percent of their students come from such homes. We assumed that schools with more student subgroups were more likely to be situated in lower-income communities, so this grouping of schools helps to control for the effects of social-class background.

Table 1 then splits the schools based on the number of student subgroups they enrolled during the 2002-03 school year. We included all schools with enrollments of at least 100 students and reporting complete data to the state department of education. Rows with fewer than 25 schools are not shown.

What's most striking is that the percentage of schools hitting their AYP growth target is strongly related to the number of student subgroups. In addition, schools serving lower-income families and their children, on average, are less likely to have achieved their AYP growth targets. Look, for example, at the top set of schools, those with enrollments of less than 25 percent disadvantaged children. Among schools with two student subgroups, 80 percent met their AYP targets in 2002-03. Even for those schools enrolling between 50 and 75 percent disadvantaged kids, fully 74 percent of the schools with just two student subgroups met growth targets. But look within any of the four sets of schools split by economic disadvantage and observe the falling share who meet AYP targets as the number of subgroups increases.

Within schools serving less than 25 percent of children who are disadvantaged, the share of schools meeting AYP growth targets falls from 83 percent for schools with one subgroup to 55 percent for schools with five subgroups. Among schools with 50–75 percent of enrollees from disadvantaged backgrounds, a similar drop in AYP pass rates is observed. Seventy-four (74) percent of schools

Table 1: Odds of Hitting AYP Targets by Count of Student Subgroups for All California Schools

Families economically disadvantaged	Count of student subgroups	Count of schools	Percentage of schools that met AYP
Less than 25%	1	616	83%
	2	458	80%
	3	364	76%
	4	215	58%
	5	107	55%
	6	30	53%
25% – 50%	1	54	67%
	2	259	76%
	3	389	63%
	4	567	55%
	5	303	49%
	6	77	39%
50% – 75%	2	141	74%
	3	360	59%
	4	746	55%
	5	274	38%
	6	110	21%
More than 75%	2	79	53%
	3	951	40%
	4	698	37%
	5	198	23%
	6	74	16%

in this band with just two subgroups met AYP targets, compared to just 21 percent for schools with six subgroups. Are particular kinds of students driving these sharp differences? We did discover that schools with large concentrations of Latino children from disadvantaged families face the lowest odds of hitting AYP targets.

Let's look again at the poorest quartile of schools, those with

NCLB: FIRST YEAR REPORT

Mary L. Fahrenbruck

The Civil Rights Project from Harvard University has released a series of reports that summarizes the results of the first year, 2002-2003, of NCLB implementation in 10 urban school districts throughout the United States (Kim, Orfield and Sunderland 2004). Harvard professor, Gary Orfield says:

> We in the Civil Rights Project decided that this bill [Bush's No Child Left Behind Act] was the most important thing to affect the education of minority young people over the next five years.

The reports examined four issues: the role of the federal government, accountability, school choice, and supplemental educational services. These issues are summarized in the following sections.

Role of the Federal Government

Orfield (2004) focuses specifically on the relationship between the federal government and the states. In the past, according to Orfield, educational decisions were largely left up to states and local communities and supported by the federal government. States were offered incentives, given time to implement policies, and resources were channeled to low-performing schools as a sign of support. With the passing of NCLB, the federal government expanded its role. It mandated equal educational outcomes for all students by desegregating subgroups including economically disadvantaged students, limited-English proficient students, students with disabilities, and students from major racial and ethnic groups. It imposed time lines for raising all groups to proficient level by the 2013-2014 school year. It expanded test-based accountability to all students in public schools, not just those in schools receiving Title I funds. It specified penalties for noncompliance by states and mandated specific sanctions for under-performing schools. (p17)

The report documents the funding issues incurred during the first year of implementation. The government allocated $13.5 billion to schools that qualified for NCLB grant monies. However, during the 2002-03 fiscal year, all fifty states experienced budget shortfalls. Since educational funding comprises a large portion of states' budgets, education departments were effected by the shortfalls, especially as states incurred additional costs as a result of NCLB implementation.

Under NCLB, Title I funds during the 2002-03 fiscal year increased by 18 percent to local educational agencies. However, during the 2003-04 fiscal year, local educational agencies received only a 9.7 percent increase. The figures for 2004 are lower yet. States have come to realize that their costs exceed the revenues.

Though the U.S. Department of Education claimed all states are in compliance with NCLB, actually by June of 2003 only 11 states had approved plans.

Accountability
Another important aspect of the law is mandated testing. Kim and Sunderman (2004c) report the hardships faced by states as they complied with the accountability requirements under NCLB. Three of those hardships include test adoption, Adequate Yearly Progress (AYP), and disaggregating data. In Arizona, 289 schools labeled "needing improvement" under NCLB met or exceeded state achievement goals standards

The authors concluded that since states valued their own educational goals and assessments, they adopted a second test rather than revise or eliminate preexisting state tests. As states attempted to compare the federal governments achievement and performance labels with their own, confusion resulted. For instance, in Arizona, 289 Title I schools labeled "needing improvement" under NCLB met state achievement standards at "performing" or "highly performing" levels. In Virginia, 723 schools failed to meet federal annual yearly progress goals, while only 402 of these schools failed to meet state accreditation standards.

School Choice

Supporters of NCLB emphasized increased parental choice. Districts are required to offer transfer options to all students who attend failing schools. Kim and Sunderman (2004b) found that less than 3 percent of families requested transfers and that transferring schools were not significantly better than sending schools.

In Arizona some districts studied had no transfers. In Fresno, Buffalo, Atlanta, and DeKalb, less than 1 percent of eligible families requested transfers. Furthermore, districts were not in a position to grant approval for all transfer requests.

Parents perceived that the receiving schools were unlikely to be much better than the neighborhood schools. Despite the differences in school labels between sending schools and receiving schools, Kim and Sunderman found all sending schools had a higher percentage of low-income students than the receiving schools. In addition, both types of schools made similar gains in math and reading scores.

Supplemental Educational Services

School districts that fail to make Adequate Yearly Progress (AYP) for a third consecutive year are required to offer supplemental educational services to increase the academic achievement of students, which must be provided outside the regular school day. (2004d, p 6)

The authors found that such services were not widely used in these districts even though thousands of students were eligible. They concluded that student enrollment was low "simply because the services are offered outside of regular school hours and away from their school building." (2004c, p 21)

Districts were also burdened by administrative issues as they provided for supplemental services. Districts were required to develop, implement, and monitor the programs. Time-line constraints and service-provider demands also complicated implementation of supplemental services. Many schools received word in December 2002 that supplemental educational services were to be offered at the beginning of the 2002/03 school year. Districts scrambled to comply; however, many did not offer services until the spring of 2003. Another concern documented by The Civil Rights Project study was that supplemental educational services were implemented with little or no accountability. Under NCLB, services must improve the achievement level of students within a time frame and provide information to students, parents, and school officials of progress (Kim and Sunderman 2004d). Since districts did not receive additional funds to monitor and evaluate supplemental educational service programs and the time was short for implementation, districts relied on "rudimentary evaluation plans" to evaluate the effectiveness of services rather than "sound and rigorous evaluations" (p 31).

Conclusion

The reports show the problems of districts and states as they implement the mandates of No Child Left Behind. The findings reveal many similarities across the diverse districts:

1. Schools rated as successful by state criteria are often labeled failing by federal criteria.
2. Regardless of label, tests scores show similar improvement across schools. Parents are unlikely to prefer to send their kids to a school other than their neighborhood school, and their skepticism that the school was unlikely to be much better was supported by the study data.
3. Few parents want to have their children sent off campus after school for supplemental educational services.

4. Implementation of NCLB mandates for supplemental services fragmented previous Title I services.
5. There is little control on the quality of supplemental services since it must be provided by outside groups and no funds are available for monitoring.

Orfield concludes, "The reality for too many public educators is confusion and frustration as No Child Left Behind is leaving too many children . . . and teachers . . . behind."

References

Kim, J., Orfield, G., & Sunderman, G.L. (2004). *Inspiring vision, disappointing results: Four studies on implementing the No Child Left Behind Act*. Retrieved February 16, 2004, from The Civil Rights Project at Harvard University Web site: http://www.civil rightsproject.harvard.edu

Sunderman, G.L. & Kim, J.,(2004a). Expansion of federal power in American education: Federal-state relationships under the No Child Left Behind Act, year one. In *Inspiring vision, disappointing results: Four studies on implementing the No Child Left Behind Act* (part a). Retrieved February 16, 2004, from The Civil Rights Project at Harvard University Web site: http://www. civilrightsproject.harvard.edu

Kim, J., & Sunderman, G.L. (2004b). Does NCLB provide good choices for students in low-performing schools? In *Inspiring vision, disappointing results: Four studies on implementing the No Child Left Behind Act* (part b). Retrieved February 16, 2004, from The Civil Rights Project at Harvard University Web site: http://www.civilrightsproject.harvard.edu

Kim, J., & Sunderman, G.L. (2004c). Large mandates and limited resources: State response to the No Child Left Behind Act and implications for accountability. In *Inspiring vision, disappointing results: Four studies on implementing the No Child Left Behind Act* (part c). Retrieved February 16, 2004, from The Civil Rights

Project at Harvard University Web site: http://www.civilrights
project.harvard.edu

Sunderman, G.L. & Kim, J., (2004d). Increasing bureaucracy or
increasing opportunities? School district experience with supplemental education services. In *Inspiring vision, disappointing
results: Four studies on implementing the No Child Left Behind Act*
(part d). Retrieved February 16, 2004, from The Civil Rights
Project at Harvard University Web site: http://www.civilrights
project.harvard.edu

NCLB's Reading First and Multilingual, Multicultural Learners

Jill Kerper Mora

Educators whose research and teaching focus on multilingual and multicultural populations are deeply concerned about the negative effects of federal reading education policy. Reading First is an ideology of reading instruction rather than the product of a professional "consensus" about how young children should be taught to read and write.

In our multilingual society, researchers in sociolinguistics, psycholinguistics, second-language acquisition, biliteracy, and multicultural education have identified multiple factors that affect the literacy achievement of language-minority students. However, researchers in these disciplines are not included on the Reading First review panel because they don't predict an answer before doing their research. The so-called "scientifically based" research (studies that do predict an answer) included in the National Reading Panel Report on which federal policy is based, includes almost no research into multilingual literacy or the challenges faced by students who are learning English as a second language.

A visit to the Reading First website[1] illustrates the nature of the problem. The government's "Facts about Reading First" defines "the challenge" of reading education and then offers "the solution." In addition to the arrogance of a government agency claiming to have found a monolithic solution to the multilayered and complex sociological, linguistic, cultural, and educational challenges in today's diverse society, we see the misuse of "science" to disguise the underlying objectives of federal reading education policy. Ostensibly, federal policy provides a means for turning 35 percent of America's fourth graders who, according to

---

[1] http://www.ed.gov/programs/readigfirst/index.html

the 2000 NAEP data, read only at the "basic" level into "proficient" readers by grade three.

They propose to do this by focusing on teaching the "basics" of reading, which supposedly these students have not already mastered. Educators are directed to disregard the multiple reasons why readers are not reading at the "proficient" level in the first place. This is despite the fact the 2002 United States census shows that 17.9 percent of Americans speak a language other than English in their homes.

Educational policies are schemes that govern access to society's fiscal, human and physical resources within a bureaucratic system. Policy initiatives and programs are not politically neutral, despite claims that they are based on "science." These policies are a means of achieving specific educational, cultural, social, and economic goals. It appears that the federal government's goal is to homogenize our diverse multicultural society. We must be gravely concerned about the current administration's heavy-handed regulatory intrusion into the spheres of decision-making of local school districts, which must be responsive to the particular challenges, resources, and values of their linguistically and culturally diverse populations. In California, as an example, 41 percent of the student population is comprised of children and youth who are or have been formerly classified as limited in English proficiency and are therefore bilingual learners.

The inevitable result of a stifling uniform federal policy will be the inability of local educational jurisdictions to adapt to their socio-cultural and linguistic contexts. This is a lamentable, but not unavoidable, consequence for our public schools, which for generations have been vehicles of equity, democracy, and progress in our growing and changing society.

Reference
http://www.ed.gov/programs/readingfirst/index.html

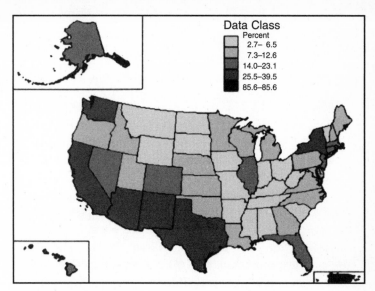

Percent of Persons 5 Years and Over Who Speak a Language Other Than English at Home: 2000
Census 2000 Summary File 3 (SF 3)—Sample Data

ERRORS IN STANDARDIZED TESTS:
A SYSTEMATIC APPROACH

Kathleen Rhoades and George Madaus

Editor's note: *Are misuses and errors in high-stakes tests hurting students? The National Board on Educational Testing and Public Policy, created as an independent monitoring system for assessment in America, located at the Boston College School of Education, systematically researches this question. This report shows that errors in tests of several kinds are widespread and that the increased weight given to these tests in life-changing decisions such as promotion, graduation, and admissions is resulting in personal tragedies for many young people. The report provides chilling examples of the impacts of test errors and indicates that many such incidents go undetected and/or unreported. Because of the technical nature of the report, we did not include references, available with the full study at* www.bc.edu/nbetpp.

Educational testing results can open or close doors of opportunity from kindergarten through school and beyond, into one's job as a firefighter, sales clerk, or lawyer. Decisions based on state testing programs in elementary school can influence the type of secondary education one receives, and decisions at the high-school level can affect one's path after graduation. Many proponents of high-stakes testing take a technological view: they choose to ignore the cumulative effects of test-based decisions, and view test-takers as objects (Barbour, 1993; Foucault, 1979).

Moreover, they ignore the fallibility of testing. Like any measurement tool that produces a number—whether a simple blood pressure reading or a complex laboratory test—tests contain error. The widespread belief in their precision does not admit this inherent fallibility.

In the K–16 educational testing system, *active errors* are often made by the testing contractor—for example, when a test item is scored incorrectly, a score conversion table is misread, or a computer programming error is made.

Latent errors may stem from poorly conceived legislation or policy mandates, or from a faulty decision made at a department of education. For example, latent error in testing resides in the following:

- Legislation requires a single test be used to determine graduation—a requirement that goes against the advice of the test developer or published test standards, or is in conflict with the test design.

- A state department of education demands that test scores be reported faster than can be dependably accomplished by the contractor.

- A mandate requires that school test scores increase by x percent per year. This directive projects growth estimates that are not realistic.

Difficulties with Detecting and Correcting Errors in a Closed System

In contrast to the airline industry, where the reporting of mistakes is considered advantageous, and the consumer products sector, where publications like *Consumer Reports* publicize errors, the testing industry is shrouded in secrecy (Mathews, 2000a). Its inner workings, in particular the arcane psychometrics of Item Response Theory (IRT) and standard setting, are outside the experience of most consumers. The National Commission on Testing and Public Policy (1991, p. 21) pointed out:

Today those who take and use many tests have less consumer protection than those who buy a toy, a toaster, or a plane ticket. Rarely is an important test or its use subject to formal, systematic, independent professional scrutiny or audit.

The lack of oversight makes errors difficult to detect. Individuals harmed by a flawed test may not even be aware of the harm. Although consumers who become aware of a problem with a test can contact the educational agency that commissioned it or the testing company, it is likely that many problems go unnoticed. Occasionally, consumers do notice problems with tests, and some lawsuits have ensued.

One such case was *Allen et al. v. The Alabama State Board of Education* (1999). Here, Alabama teacher candidates contended that the Alabama Initial Teacher Certification Testing Program (AITCTP) was biased against minority teacher candidates. Experts hired by the plaintiffs to determine the technical adequacy of the test needed a court order to gain access to the records of the testing contractor, National Evaluation Systems (NES). The experts found items across various subject matter tests that did not meet minimum standards for technical adequacy. They found miskeyed items in tests that had been used from 1981–1986. During one test administration, a miskeyed item resulted in at least six candidates failing who would have otherwise passed (Ludlow, 2001). Although this case was settled out of court, in a later trial Judge Myron Thompson found many irregularities in the test development and pilot testing.

Judging a more recent NES teacher test has been equally difficult. The National Academy of Sciences commissioned the Committee on Assessment and Teacher Quality to evaluate the reliability and validity of the nation's teacher tests (Mitchell et al., 2001). The committee could obtain no usable data from NES. Other researchers (Haney et al., 1999; Ludlow, 2001) have recently reported on their mostly unsuccessful struggles to access information from this company. This is highly troublesome because, as of today, NES is the nation's second-largest producer of teacher licensure tests. The committee recommended that tests not be used for making a decision of any import if the test developer refuses to release critical data for determining test adequacy.

Human Error in Testing: A Brief History

In *The Testing Trap* (1981), Andrew Strenio documented several scoring errors that occurred between 1975 and 1980. For example, in 1978 a Medical College Admissions Test mistake resulted in artificially low scores for 90 percent of the test takers on one administration and probably caused some candidates to be disqualified. A 1977 error involved changes in the difficulty level of the Law School Admission Test (LSAT). Students who took the exam before October 1977 obtained lower scores overall, and therefore were less likely to be accepted into law school, than did those who took it after October. Strenio noted that without an oversight organization, the onus for protecting consumer rights usually falls to the testing contractors themselves: *It is no slur upon the basic integrity and decency of the people working for the standardized testing industry to suggest that this is asking a lot (p. 15).*

Documenting Active Errors in Testing

In 1999, we began a systematic search for examples of testing errors. We found dozens of errors that were discovered by school officials, teachers, parents, and even students. Here we describe errors associated with three major publishers: CTB McGraw-Hill, National Computer Systems, and Harcourt Brace.

CTB McGraw-Hill In 1999, John Kline, director of planning, assessment, and learning technologies for the Fort Wayne, Indiana, community schools, reported a sharp drop in average percentile scores on the TerraNova test to Indiana's Department of Education (DOE) (King, 1999). DOE officials asked CTB McGraw-Hill to rerun the scores. McGraw-Hill found that a programming error resulted in the use of the wrong table to convert reading comprehension raw scores to percentile scores. McGraw-Hill adjusted the scores and sent out new results within two weeks (Viadero, 1999). Kline said at the time, "It's the largest glitch that we've ever seen. . . ."

Two months later, William Sandler, a statistician working for the Tennessee DOE, questioned McGraw-Hill about a score dip that affected two-thirds of Tennessee's TerraNova percentile scores. Over time, McGraw-Hill determined that a programming error caused the percentile rankings on the TerraNova to be too low at the lower end of the scale and too high at the upper end. *As a result, approximately a quarter of a million students in six states were given the wrong national percentile scores.* In addition to Tennessee and Indiana, the error also corrupted scores in New York City, Wisconsin, Nevada, and South Carolina (Viadero & Blair, 1999). Students and staff in New York City and three Nevada schools were among the most seriously affected because officials used the scores to make high-stakes decisions.

Following discovery of the error on the TerraMova, CTB McGraw-Hill posted a warning on their website: "No single test can ascertain whether all educational goals are being met."

To understand the impact of the error in New York City requires a review of decisions made in the months before the error was found. In early 1999 the TerraNova was used for the first time in New York City to measure achievement in reading and math. (Hartocollis, 1999a). News of unexpectedly low scores hit the press that May. New York State Education Commissioner Richard Mills suggested that these new lower scores accurately reflected poor student performance and recommended that low-scoring students attend summer school that year (Hartocollis, 1999b). Dr. Rudy Crew, then chancellor of New York City schools, chose the fifteenth percentile as the "cut point" below which children had to attend summer school or be retained in grade. Tens of thousands of New York City children scored below that point. Thirty-five thousand of them attended school that summer, and thousands of others were notified that they were to repeat a grade because they did not comply with the summer school attendance requirement (Hartocollis, 1999c).

On September 15, 1999, days after school started, McGraw-Hill admitted that the same error that affected Tennessee scores had also incorrectly lowered New York City students' percentile rankings at the lower end of the scale. Thus, 8,668 children whose correct scores were above the cut-off had mistakenly been compelled to go to summer school. In light of this new information, Dr. Crew announced that all the children affected by the error (many of whom had started school in a lower grade) would be allowed to advance to the next grade. Class lists were reorganized and children were rerouted to the proper classrooms in mid-September (Hartocollis, 1999c; Archibold, 1999).

In Nevada, state officials used percentile rankings on the TerraNova to identify "failing" schools, which then received state funds for improvement. Recalculation of the scores showed that three schools were erroneously cited as "failing."

Minnesota Testing Nightmare

In May of 2000, the daughter of a Minnesota lawyer learned that she had failed the math portion of Minnesota's Basic Standards Tests (BSTs), a test published by National Computer Systems (NCS). Her father contacted the Department of Children, Families and Learning (CFL), asking to see the exam. For two months CFL staffers rejected his request and "told him to have his daughter study harder for next year's exam" (Welsh, 2000, p. 1). Only when the parent threatened a lawsuit did CFL permit him to examine the test (Grow, 2000). The father, along with employees from CFL, found a series of scoring errors on Form B of the math test administered in February 2000. The errors were later traced to an NCS employee who had incorrectly programmed the answer key (Carlson, 2000). As a result, math scores for 45,739 Minnesota students in grades 8–12 were wrong. Of these, 7935 students originally told they failed the test actually passed. (Children, Families, & Learning, 2000a).

Another error involving a question with a design flaw was found on the April administration of the BSTs. NCS invalidated this item, but not before 59 students were erroneously told they had failed (Children, Families, & Learning, 2000a). Since passing the BSTs was a requirement for graduation, more than 50 Minnesota students were wrongly denied a diploma in 2000. Of this number, six or seven were not allowed to attend their high school graduation ceremonies (Draper, 2000). The State Education Commissioner expressed deep regret over the incident, saying, "I can't imagine a more horrible mistake that NCS could have made. And I can't fathom anything that NCS could have done that would have caused more harm to students. I know that NCS agrees with me" (Children, Families, & Learning, 2000b, p. 1).

CFL tried to rectify the mistakes by offering to pay each affected student $1,000 toward college tuition as well as all out-of-pocket costs, such as tutoring and mileage expenses, resulting from the error. In all, NCS paid Minnesota families $118,000 and CFL $75,000 for costs related to the error (Drew & Draper, 2001).

While NCS took full responsibility for the errors, CFL reprimanded a staff member for failing to return the father's original e-mail message. Had it been answered promptly, the error might have been caught before students were barred from graduating (Drew, Smetanka, & Shah, 2000).

In spite of the test company's attempts to remedy the situation, four parents sued NCS, claiming that the company "was aware of repeated scoring errors and quality control problems" (Corporate greed, 2002). In a court ruling in the summer of 2002, the judge denied the plaintiffs' request for punitive damages because he decided that NCS had not intentionally produced a faulty test (Welsh, 2002, p. 1). The judge reconsidered his ruling in the fall of 2002 in light of compelling evidence brought forth by the plaintiffs. He determined that the plaintiffs could seek punitive damages against NCS because they "produced prima facia evidence that [NCS] acted with deliberate disregard for the rights and safety of others" (Grant, 2002; *Kurvers et al. v. NCS, Inc.*, 2002, p. 4).

He attributed the causes of NCS's problems to managerial error instigated by a profit-seeking ethic at NCS that prevailed over other consideration for the customer. Indeed, within days of acknowledging the error, Pearson, an international distributor of educational materials, purchased NCS. Following the $2.5 billion dollar acquisition, NCS stock rose dramatically and provided the CEO with millions of dollars in profit (Wieffering, 2000). Before the case went to trial, however, NCS settled with the plaintiffs for $7 million, paying all ofthe students who missed graduation $16,000 each (Scoring settlement, 2002).

Harcourt Brace

Another error, this time by Harcourt Brace, occurred against the backdrop of California Proposition 227. Proposition 227 required California schools to educate children classified as "limited English-proficient" (LEP) in English-speaking classrooms. It also mandated other changes, including smaller class sizes and curriculum changes. Policy makers selected Harcourt's Stanford 9 Achievement Test (SAT-9) to gauge the achievement of students across the state, asserting that gains on this test would signal the success of 237 (Sahagun, 1999). Initial results reported at the end of June 1999 did show large gains for students in English immersion classes with scores of LEP students rising by as much as 20 percent in some schools (Mora, 1999).

Proponents of English immersion quickly touted these gains as an indication of the Proposition's success (Brandon, 1999; Colvin & Smith, 1999). Once these students were correctly classified, test score gains of LEP students were substantially reduced (Sahagun, 1999). LEP students' scores had risen "slightly in most grades, but still were far below the national average" (Chrismer, 1999, p. 1).

This error, like the McGraw-Hill and NCS errors, was detected by consumers and not the test publisher. However, unlike McGraw-Hill, Harcourt Brace reanalyzed the data quickly. Then Harcourt president Eugene Paslov noted, "[The error] might have been caught if the company had more than two days to analyze data from 4.3 million test forms . . . before Wednesday's deadline for posting results on the Internet" (quoted in Colvin & Groves, 1999, p. 2).

A top official from Harcourt Brace warned, "We can't check the results for each of the 1,100 districts. It's invaluable for folks at the local level . . . to check to see if there's anything that looks suspicious" (quoted in Colvin, 1999b, p. A3).

We've Made an Error . . . Errors Found by Testing Companies

In a number of instances, testing companies contacted clients to report an error. In one such case the Educational Testing Service (ETS) identified an error on a 1999 administration of the SAT that lowered the scores of 1,500 students by as much as one hundred points (Sandham, 1998; Weiss, 1998). In a similar occurrence in the United Kingdom, the Qualifications and Curriculum Authority (QCA) quickly discovered a computer programming error that resulted in over 10,000 students being misclassified on the secondary school information technology exams (Students given wrong test results, 2001). These errors were detected in the course of standard auditing procedures. Companies that regularly audit results, like ETS, are more likely to detect and correct errors both before and after results are sent out to the public.

One Question—The Difference Between Success and Failure

Errors occur when test questions are ambiguous, poorly designed, or miskeyed. On a high-stakes exam, one poorly written question can determine a student's classification as "passing" or "failing," and reversal is difficult.

Recent examples of how one question can determine passing

or failing have been found in Arizona, Virginia, Massachusetts, and Nevada. The Massachusetts error, identified by a student who had already failed the Massachusetts Comprehensive Assessment System (MCAS), involved a multiple-choice question that had more than one correct answer. Since the item was part of a retest taken by juniors and seniors who had not yet passed the high school exit exam, 449 of those who chose the alternate answer and had previously failed the test were found to be "competent" and worthy of a high school diploma—so in this case, the one question served as an arbiter of who would and would not graduate (Massachusetts Department of Education, 2002b).

In Virginia and Nevada, errors were a result of test equating—a statistical process used to make the scores of a test comparable from one year to the next. Through that process, testing contractors determine the points needed for passing the current year's test that is equivalent to the passing score on that test the year before. In both cases, the passing score was set one point (or approximately the equivalent of one question) too high (Akin, 2002; Ritter, 2002). And in Arizona, after state educators identified a miskeyed question, the scores of 12,000 high school sophomores increased and 142 students who failed the test, passed (Pearce, 2000a).

Another type of error is the faulty test question, found by test-takers or proctors during a test administration and later removed before scoring. For example, during the 2001 administration of the MCAS, two tenth-graders found one math multiple-choice item where all of the answers provided were correct (Lindsay, 2001). One of the students reported that he worked more than five minutes on an item that should have taken one or two minutes at the most. Test officials often claim that removal corrects the problem since the removed item does not affect the scores. This does not correct the disruption experienced by knowledgable test-takers who try to find a solution to a faulty question.

Something Wrong with the Rankings

As of 2002, more than two dozen states ranked school or district performance by test scores, and in twenty of these states sanctions could be levied against low-scoring schools (Meyer et al., 2002). For example, the DOE in Virginia uses scores from the Standards of Learning tests (SOLs) to assign schools to ranks, which then determine school accreditation. Schools must earn accreditation by the year 2007 (Seymour, 2001).

In October 2000, soon after SOLs results were released, administrators from the Virginia Beach school department challenged the ratings of several elementary schools, which were lower than projected. Upon investigating the complaint, the DOE admitted that an omission had produced incorrect rankings for possibly dozens of schools.

The Virginia example is not an isolated incident. As test scores are used increasingly to rank schools and award teachers' bonuses, the likelihood of making mistakes also increases. In 2002, problems with trend data emerged in Nevada, Georgia, and Virginia. In each of these states, Harcourt Educational Measurement (formerly Harcourt Brace) officials announced that errors were made in test equating so that in each state the test scores were seriously affected. In Nevada and Virginia, use of a new computer program to equate the 2002 with the 2001 scores resulted in the cut score on the 2002 test being set one point too high. In Nevada, this meant that 31,000 high school graduaton scores were incorrectly reported and 736 students were told they had failed when they had passed (Hendrie & Hurst, 2002; State despairs of getting, 2002).

In Virginia, thousands of students were erroneously told they had failed or were given test scores that were too low (King & White, 2002). And in Georgia the results were so flawed and so late that they were deemed unusable (Donsky, 2002).

All of these events and investigations counsel caution in the interpretation of changes in scores from year to year, as these could very well be the result of changes in the tests and not actual changes in achievement. Even very small modifications in tests can yield dramatic changes in results.

In Arizona, for example, the state assessment program (Arizona's Instrument to Measure Standards—AIMS) experienced a series of mishaps. Multiple errors were detected in the 2000 eleventh-grade test booklets, a tenth-grade algebra questions was adjusted because the tests were found to be too difficult (Kossan, 2000a; Pearce et al., 2001). As a result, the DOE postponed the date by which high school students must pass the state assessment to graduate (Kossan, 2000b; Flannery, 2000). Critics have asserted that the Arizona assessment program had been developed too hurriedly and that resources to support it were inadequate (Flannery, 2000; Kossan, 2000b).

One critic of the problem, *The Arizona Republic,* sued the Arizona DOE because it didn't release any of the AIMS test questions—this despite the fact that in the second test administration, 92 percent of the sophomores who had to pass it to graduate failed (Sherwood & Pearce, 2000; Pearce, 2000b). Another critic was Tom Haladyna, an expert on testing. Although he had initially helped Arizona DOE officials with test development, he quit, alleging that "the process was to hasty; [the Arizona DOE] went about it very fast, much faster than anyone in my business would want to do it" (quoted in Flannery, 2000, p. 2).

Conclusion

No company can offer flawless products. Even highly reputable testing contractors that offer customers high-quality products and services produce tests that are susceptible to error. But while a patient dissatisfied with a diagnosis or treatment may seek a second or third opinion, for a child in a New York City school (and in dozens of other states and hundreds of other cities and towns), there is only one opinion that counts—a single test score. If that is in error, a long time may elapse before the mistake is brought to light—if it ever is. Human error can be, and often is, present in all phases of the testing process. Error can creep into the development of items. It can be made in the setting of a passing score. It can occur in the establishment of norming groups, and it is sometimes found in the scoring of questions.

The decisions that underlie the formation of cut scores and passing scores are largely subjective. Glass (1977) pointed out that the idea of objectively getting cut scores that accurately differentiate between students who know and students who don't know is largely a fantasy—there is no clear distinction and no mathematical or logical support for such an idea in the realm of education testing. *The presidents of two major test developers—Harcourt Brace and CTB McGraw-Hill—(are) on record that their tests should not be used as the sole criterion for making high-stakes educational descisions (Myers, 2001; Mathews, 2000a).*

Yet more than half of the state DOEs are using test results as the basis for important decisions that, perhaps, these tests were not designed to support. In an interview with *The Cape Cod Times*, Eugene Paslov, then Harcourt Brace's president, said that standardized tests like Massachusetts' MCAS exam should not be used as the sole determinant of who graduates from high school and who does not.

With the recent passage of President Bush's No Child Left Behind Act (NCLB), the testing industry in the U.S. will become increasingly more centralized and more commercialized. An amplified demand for testing services without an appreciable increase in the number of service providers in the short term will intensify time pressures already experienced by the contractors. At the same time NCLB will heighten the reliance of state DOEs on the few contractors available, dependent on one that is more prone to error. Coupling these conditions with the lack of industry oversight creates conditions for a future that is ripe for the proliferation of undetected human error in educational testing.

SECTION SIX

The Critics Speak

RESTORING SCIENTIFIC INTEGRITY IN POLICYMAKING
Union of Concerned Scientists

On February 18, 2004, over 60 leading scientists—Nobel laureates, leading medical experts, former federal agency directors, and university chairs and presidents–voiced their concern over the misuse of science by the Bush administration. Since then, more than 1,000 have added their signatures. Here are excerpts from their statement. Everything the statement says is equally true for educational research. Committees have been stacked, reports have been condensed and misrepresented, websites have been purged, and laws written which present fiction as science.

Successful application of science has played a large part in the policies that have made the United States . . . the world's most powerful nation and its citizens increasingly prosperous and healthy. Although scientific input to the government is rarely the only factor in public policy decisions, this input should always be weighed from an objective and impartial perspective to avoid perilous consequences. Indeed, this principle has long been adhered to by presidents and administrations of both parties in forming and implementing policies. The administration of George W. Bush has, however, disregarded this principle.

When scientific knowledge has been found to be in conflict with its political goals, the administration has often manipulated the process. . . . This has been done by placing people who are professionally unqualified or who have clear conflicts of interest in official posts and on scientific advisory committees; by disbanding existing advisory committees; by censoring and suppressing reports by the government's own scientists; and by simply not seeking independent scientific advice. . . . Furthermore, in advocating policies that are not scientifically sound, the administration has sometimes misrepresented scientific knowledge and misled the public about the implications of its policies. . . .

The behavior of the White House on these issues is part of a pattern that has led Russell Train, the EPA administrator under Presidents Nixon and Ford, to observe, "How radically we have moved away from regulation based on independent findings and professional analysis of scientific, health and economic data by the responsible agency to regulation controlled by the White House and driven primarily by political considerations."

Across a broad range of policy areas, the administration has undermined the quality and independence of the scientific advisory system and the morale of the government's outstanding scientific personnel:

- Highly qualified scientists have been dropped from advisory committees dealing with childhood lead poisoning, environmental and reproductive health, and drug abuse, while individuals associated with or working for industries subject to regulation have been appointed to these bodies.
- Censorship and political oversight of government scientists is not restricted to the EPA, but has also occurred at the Departments of Health and Human Services, Agriculture, and Interior, when scientific findings are in conflict with the administration's policies or with the views of its political supporters.
- . . . The distortion of scientific knowledge for partisan political ends must cease if the public is to be properly informed about issues central to its well being, and the nation is to benefit fully from its heavy investment in scientific research and education. . . .

WHERE NO CHILD LEFT BEHIND
IS NOT THE LAW OF THE LAND

Roger Rapoport

Here's a question you won't find on any test or exam mandated by any federal, state, or local government agency:

How many American schools are exempt from No Child Left Behind?

If you guessed 58, congratulations. You go to the head of the class.

Now, here's the tough one. What federal agency runs these schools? The answer, surprise, is the Department of Defense. It runs schools for 30,000 children of military staff at bases scattered across Alabama, Georgia, Kentucky, New York, North Carolina, and South Carolina.

Not only are these schools exempt from the rigid criteria of NCLB, they are, you guessed it, fully funded by the federal government. There are no unfunded mandates here.

Sound too good to be true?

Robert Felton, a lobbyist for the National School Boards Association, told Eric Kelderman of Stateline.org, "We feel very strongly that it's a double standard. If you accept federal dollars, you ought to be governed by (No Child Left Behind). It is supposed to build accountability for federal investments. Why not this federal investment?

Good question. Look for the answers on a multiple-choice test coming to your school soon.

SCOTTSDALE'S "FAILING" SCHOOLS

Roger Rapoport

What does it take to become a failing school under "No Child Left Behind"? It's actually easier than you might think. Just have a few kids miss a key test or fail to show improved reading scores in a strong school district ahd, sure enough, you can turn a top school into a loser.

That's what happened in the Scottsdale school district, which has traditionally had some of the best test scores in Arizona. According to Ovelia Madrid, writing in the *Arizona Republic*, this upset parents in Scottsdale and Paradise Valley who are used to sending their kids to high-performing schools.

The district's English-language learners missed the (NCLB required) attendance mark by 1 percent. The feds required 95 percent attendance, and the district had 94 percent.

Ironically, in October, just a few months before the test, the Arizona Department of education found that 75 percent of the Scottsdale schools were officially designated "excelling."

NCLB CONQUISTADORES FROM UTAH SHOW UP IN PUERTO RICO

Ruth J. Sáez Vega

> Editor's note: *This strange case of NCLB highlights the absurdities in the law. There is also a missionary aspect to this invasion of Puerto Rican education in the assumed right to impose a new pedagogy and exorcise a pre-existing one.* —KSG

Puerto Rico has had a long history of conquistadores, from the early conquest by Juan Ponce de León to the American invasion in 1898 as a result of the Spanish American War. However, these obvious invasions in which foreigners take over and impose their language, culture, and ideologies haven't been the only ones. During the past century, Puerto Rico has had multiple threats to our language and culture. Education has been one of the most powerful instruments used by the conquistadores to impose a language, a culture, and a world view.

The most evident example of the intent to conquer through education has to do with language. Since 1902, many attempts have been made to impose English as the language of instruction, despite Spanish being the language of the people. It wasn't until 1949 that Spanish became the language of instruction, which is the current linguistic policy in all public schools in Puerto Rico.

As at the time of Juan Ponce de León in the early 16th century and that of the Americans at the end of the 19th century, a new group of conquistadores has arrived. Carrying the missionary flag of NCLB and its Reading First mandates, they come to impose their views, their practices, and their language on our children, our teachers, our schools, and our universities. Like the original conquistadores, they assume that nothing of worth has existed in Puerto Rico prior to their arrival.

Meeting the Conquistadores

One afternoon in 2002, the dean asked me to attend a meeting in the faculty lounge of the College of Education. The topic of the meeting was unannounced. To my surprise, five tall white men, clearly not from Puerto Rico, arrived for the meeting. Why were they here, and why was I invited to meet them? Also present were the dean, an officer from the Puerto Rico Department of Education, and two of my colleagues.

After a quick welcome, the five tall white men began to speak about a proposal they were writing for the Puerto Rico Department of Education under the No Child Left Behind Act. I interrupted to ask that we all introduce ourselves, so we did. Three of the five tall white men let us know that they were from Utah State University and that one was knowledgeable in early childhood education, another in elementary education, and the third was there "to ensure that the Reading First grant for Puerto Rico is based on scientifically-based reading research." The other two were from Spectrum Consulting, a private firm in Utah, which would work on the evaluation of the grant.

During the meeting, it was obvious that they knew very little about Puerto Rico, about our schools and their history, about our children, about our communities, and about our universities and programs. It was also clear that they were not seeking much input from us.

A few weeks later, we received a draft of the proposal from the Puerto Rico Department of Education and were asked to respond to it. Three colleagues and I read it carefully and met to discuss it and make recommendations. In an extensive letter to the Puerto Rico Secretary of Education, we expressed our concerns and warned him of the negative effects the proposal would have on our children and their education. We made very specific recommendations and asked to meet with him. After many attempts, we finally met on December 30, 2002. At the meeting we were very honest in sharing our thoughts and concerns regarding the proposal.

Months later, we had access to a new draft which, despite our multiple responses and critiques, remained essentially the same. However, according to the proposal writers: "Education faculty from the University of Puerto Rico provided feedback."

What's Wrong with the Utah Proposal?

NCLB is a federal imposition on American education, and the flaws inherent in it are the subject of this book. But the "Puerto Rico Reading First" proposal written by the professors from Utah contains many more flaws.

Our main concern with the proposal is that it has been written by people who are foreign to and have unexamined misconceptions about the culture, the language, and the social realities of Puerto Rican children, their families, their communities, their schools, and their teachers.

These misconceptions become both the basis for the proposal and its justification. The authors assume a series of problems or gaps in Puerto Rican education from kindergarten through third grade that are then to be solved by the program they are proposing.

The most significant "problems" identified by the Utah authors are: 1) poverty of Puerto Rican children and families; 2) language deficit of teachers; 3) the influence of whole language; and 4) lack of reading professionals.

Poverty

The Utah authors identify poverty as a problem, and they show an assumed deficit view of our students:

> There are limited opportunities for conceptual development and knowledge among the general student population. In many of these low-income Puerto Rican families . . . little opportunity is available . . . for children to experience anything beyond their home or neighborhood.

Many Puerto Ricans are poor. Some, of course, are not. The Utah professors have equated Puerto Rico poverty with limited experiences and lack of conceptual knowledge. However they do not offer "scientifically-based research" to support this elitist and overgeneralized assumption.

Language

The second problem identified by the Utah proposal authors is our language. One sentence reads: "However, Spanish is the mother tongue of a large majority of Puerto Ricans."

Spanish is the language of Puerto Ricans. It is also the language of instruction in our schools, and there is no "however" to that. After many previous attempts to impose English on Puerto Rico and its schools, Spanish continues to be the language of Puerto Ricans. The professors from Utah seem to assume that NCLB is a Congressional mandate to reimpose English on Puerto Rico. They write:

> In PR, aiding children in developing literacy skills in English as a second language is a challenge since many of the elementary teachers are fluent only in Spanish. This language deficit in teachers is in conflict with the Puerto Rico Department of Education (PRDE) goals related to literacy and language learning.

English teachers in Puerto Rico are certified as such, which requires them to earn a BA in English as a Second Language (ESL). Kindergarten through third-grade teachers, on the other hand, hold a BA in K–3 or elementary education, not ESL. They are not expected to speak or teach English. The Puerto Rico Department of Education has not identified any language and literacy goals which are in conflict with Puerto Rican teachers being "fluent only in Spanish," their native language. Spanish has been the official language of instruction since 1949. English has been taught as a second language.

Whole Language

The third problem identified in the Utah proposal is the influence of whole language in the K–3 curriculum. The proposal reads:

> Aggravating this dilemma—language deficit of teachers—is the potential limitation of the current literacy curriculum in Puerto Rico. The core standards in both Spanish and English have been heavily influenced by the whole language philosophy.

There is an unsupported assumption that such an influence on "core standards" is bad. Furthermore, no evidence is offered that the statement is true. While it is true that the research and the work of many educators in preschool, elementary, and university classrooms are holistic, the literacy curriculum in Puerto Rico is quite traditional. The proposal writers made no attempt to go into the schools to confirm their judgment.

Lack of Reading Professionals

The fourth problem identified by the proposal authors is the lack of reading professionals. The proposal reads:

> There is a lack of certified reading specialists available to work with teachers and children in schools. There is currently no place to train reading specialists to fill this gap. There are currently no graduate programs offering specializations in reading. There are very few education professionals who currently possess reading certificates but, in any case, these certificates were earned outside of Puerto Rico.

As a professor at the University of Puerto Rico Graduate Faculty of Education, I teach in the masters program in reading, a graduate program. Our graduates are reading professionals with mas-

ters degrees in reading. There are also masters and doctoral programs in Spanish and in ESL. All of this takes place at the
University of Puerto Rico. This information was provided to the
proposal authors, both in person and in writing. Either they have
ignored this information in the proposal or they have chosen to
treat our programs as non-programs.

What's Wrong with the Solutions the Utah Authors Propose for Each of the "Problems"?

Poverty, Limited Experience, and Lack of Conceptual Knowledge
In order to solve the "limited experience and lack of conceptual
knowledge" of poor children, the proposed Puerto Rico Reading
First program will:

- Educate parents about resources available in the community for children, such as community libraries, public zoo,
  museums, cultural events . . .
- Integrate reading across content
- Create classroom libraries with emphasis on informational
  texts.

There is an assumption that parents in Puerto Rico are oblivious to
the fact that there is a public zoo, that there are museums, and that
cultural events take place. Had the Utah authors asked, we could
have told them that public libraries are very scarce.

Interestingly, educators throughout Puerto Rico who have
been influenced by constructivist and holistic pedagogies (which
the proposal writers would oppose) have been integrating reading
across content and creating classroom libraries for years.
However, the emphasis of such libraries is not only on informational texts but rather on a variety of genres, topics, authors, and
illustrators.

Language Deficit of Teachers

In order to solve the "language deficit of Puerto Rican teachers," Puerto Rico Reading First proposes:

> The establishment of an English Language Institute developed by the University of Puerto Rico and Utah State University. Undergraduate Education students from several universities in the USA (including Utah State University) will spend a semester teaching English in Puerto Rico.

Why would we need an English Language Institute developed with Utah State University? We already have excellent programs in ESL, as well as in English, at different universities throughout Puerto Rico, with highly qualified faculty. On the other hand, as I have said earlier, there are credentialing requirements for ESL teachers in Puerto Rico. We don't permit undergraduate students from our universities to teach English regardless of their linguistic competency in that language. Why would we allow undergraduate students from Utah or any other state to do so?

Whole Language Influence

In order to counteract the "whole language influence", PPRF proposes:

- Increased coordination of university scientifically-based reading research
- (SBRR) programs with elementary school reading instruction
- Creation of certification and graduate programs
- Professor study groups led by Utah State University
- Review of standards and alignment with SBRR

Certification programs are the responsibility of the Puerto Rico Department of Education and Puerto Rican universities. There is no need for Utah State University professors to be involved in the certification programs of Puerto Rican teachers. Graduate programs already exist, and university professors in Puerto Rico do not need Utah State University professors to tell us what should or shouldn't be included in our programs, what we should or shouldn't be teaching our students, or how we should go about teaching.

Utah State University is taking control not only of the primary reading program but also teacher education, certification, and reprogramming of college faculty. In other words, Utah State University professors will control all levels of Puerto Rican education.

Lack of Reading Professionals

To work on the "lack of reading professionals", PRRF proposes the creation of programs by "highly qualified staff from the University of PR and other PR universities, Utah State University, and Emma Ecckles Jones Center for Early Childhood Education . . ." The proposed programs include the following:

- Plan and implement graduate reading programs through Puerto Rican universities
- Create a Reading Teacher Certificate for primary grade teachers and school leaders
- Create a reading specialist certificate

Even more than before, the intended control of the Utah professors is made evident. All the programs proposed in PRRF have a common denominator: Utah State University professors are at the center of the process, in control of the process.

The PRRF proposal of the Utah conquistadores negates the social, cultural, and linguistic realities of Puerto Rican children, families, teachers, schools, and communities. This should not surprise us since it was written by people who have limited experience, who lack conceptual knowledge, and who are language deficient. They have limited experience and lack conceptual knowledge of Puerto Rico. In addition, they are language-deficient, because they cannot speak Spanish, the language of Puerto Rican children, teachers, and schools.

NCLB can be seen as a seizure of educational authority by the federal government. When imposed on Puerto Rico, NCLB becomes obviously absurd. The only thing that could make it even more surreal is to put its enforcement in the hands of five tall white men from Utah.

TEACHER ABUSE

Jill Kerper Mora

Being an educator in this day and age is like being a child in a huge dysfunctional family, headed by a pair of abusive parents. The father is the federal government, a stern, unyielding bully. When questioned, he says, "I never hurt the children, their mother makes that decision." The mother is the state government, dependent on the father for resources. She remembers when once she was independent before the father decided to take charge.

These "parents" have set up a series of unrealistic, unreasonable and impossible expectations: They want every child above average—every child in America up to "proficiency" in reading and math by the year 2014! Never mind that this is a statistical impossibility, this is the expectation. If we do not comply and meet these expectations, we will be shamed and punished. It is just because we are "bad children"—lazy, mean-spirited, self-serving, and stubborn—that we haven't already cured the ills of society through the public schools.

They say we're just making excuses when we say that it is not within our means and power as educators to overcome the effects of poverty, racism, joblessness, family disintegration, migration, public apathy and disengagement, and corporate greed.

Not only are the long-term expectations unreasonable and impossible to accomplish, but we are also subjected to shaming and punishment along the way (under the guise of "accountability") if we are not making Adequate Yearly Progress toward the impossible, as measured by the abusive parents' own criteria.

Furthermore, we will not be given adequate or appropriate resources to do the job, nor the freedom to use our best judgment as to how to accomplish it. In any normal human family, parents who treated their children this way would be investigated by Child Protective Services, and probably have the children removed from the home. But as national education policy, is this just fine with everyone? Any educators who complain are further shamed and embarrassed for resisting this abusive treatment. As national education policy, is this just fine with everyone?

Let's call for an end to teacher abuse!

TEACHERS LEAVING TESTING BEHIND

Wendy Goodman

In a March 15, 2004, press release entitled *New, Flexible Policies Help Teachers Become Highly Qualified,* Rod Paige asserts:

"We know that effective teachers are one of the most crucial factors in student achievement and are needed in every school in America, regardless of state line or city boundary. That's why No Child Left Behind puts such emphasis on giving every student in our great nation an expert teacher. We are committed to the goal of a world-class teaching force and recognize the real challenges states and educators face."

At the surface, NCLB appears to work toward that goal. Title II of the act is called "Preparing, Training, and Recruiting High Quality Teachers and Principals." The focus of this section defines "highly-qualified" teachers. It encourages a range of alternative routes to teacher and principal certification. There is even an online document for teachers that advertises "support for teachers." Upon close inspection, the document is aimed at telling current teachers why they must become highly qualified.

The message current practitioners receive across the country is that experience doesn't count. Knowledge, professionalism, documented success, advanced-degree work—none of that counts. Teachers are demoralized and disenfranchised. In teachers' lounges across the country one hears a common lament, "In the past, no matter what was happening outside, no matter what was mandated, I could close the door and teach. Now they won't even let me teach any more."

During the writing of this book an unending stream of e-mails and newspaper clippings arrived on the editors' desks. Each tells the story of a dedicated teacher who is faced with disagreeable options. This section shares two of those stories.

The stories are not limited to young or novice teachers.

Individuals who, under any definition of "highly-qualified" teacher (other than NCLB's), rank among the highest, are affected, too.

I Want to Teach Not Test *by Sara Zadorozny*
Sara Zadorozny, graduate of Evergreen College in Washington, took a leave from her teaching position prior to testing season.

I leave the public education system after only four years or so. I think of my tiny four years as a teacher as a learning experience. I've learned many things about children, many things about adults, many things about teaching, learning, testing, working, playing, testing, studying, testing and testing and testing.

At the beginning of the year, I spent several hours of my professional development time planning when and how we were going to assess each student monthly in math, writing, and reading. Why monthly testing? To get ready for annual testing.

As Spring approaches, instead of the literature block I want to do, we are spending our class days writing, editing, and proofreading a piece of persuasive writing in response to a quarterly district-wide prompt. Instead of genuine reading instruction, I have to "Dibel" my 29 students to see how many words they read in a minute (as part of the DIBELS test). Another teacher regularly uses other reading tests on children pulled out of the classroom. The last two weeks of my teaching career I am spending teaching the test, for the test, about the test, and to the test. In math, I'm quickly going through several different areas in order to introduce students to things that they will be tested on in two weeks.

When do we get a chance to teach? I graduated with a BA and went back to school for my teaching credential. I wanted to be creative and feel as if I was doing something for my community. I liked the idea of teaching children all the things that I learned, and, more importantly, used on a daily basis. Now I find myself reading scripts and babysitting young America, all to find out they will end up a number on a spreadsheet, based on things that they are not learning hands-on, and in some cases, not learning at all.

Why I Can't Stay ("Not Everything That Counts Can Be Counted")
by Grace Vento-Zogby

After 32 years of teaching, I have reached a crossroad. Over these many years I have seen a number of programs, theories, and philosophies come and go. Although difficult at times, I've been able to be steadfast in my whole language beliefs. However, I am about to make a most difficult, life-altering decision. I am considering leaving the teaching profession.

I love children. I believe I was destined to be a teacher. But I cannot give support to those compromises and demands the system requires just to prove I am a competent instructor. No Child Left Behind has had a major effect on classroom practices. Unfortunately, not in a positive way. Many districts, in an effort to raise student achievement, have adopted a "one-size-fits-all" curriculum. Many wonderful teachers—as well as administrators—have been forced to compromise their beliefs in order to comply with NCLB.

I become frustrated when I see:

- First- and second-grade children who have difficulty learning, but who are working to their ability, retained because they will not meet the grade level standards, and inevitably, in fourth grade, will not be able to pass the state test.
- Fourth-grade teachers who spend the first semester getting ready for "the test."
- Remedial staff required to spend countless hours helping students "get ready for the test." I've always believed I should never ask of children what I am not willing to do

myself. I often find the tasks asked of students in preparing for the test to be meaningless and without integrity.

- Scripted reading/language arts programs adopted by districts. Programs that "provide consistency" within a building or across a school district. These same programs are robbing teachers of valuable time needed to share literature with children in meaningful, authentic ways.
- Programs that are purchased with the idea that incompetent, weak, or new teachers must have guidelines to follow. This reduces teachers to technicians, rather than professionals. The money would be better spent providing teachers with ongoing support and quality trade books.
- A middle-school principal who tells a group of elementary teachers, "I strongly suggest to my teachers they not read novels with their students. They take too much time. I require them to read short poems, short stories, and maybe a short novel. This way they will be introduced to a wide variety of genres and be better prepared to take the eighth-grade state test."

The decision to leave teaching is a very difficult and painful one to make. I know that no matter what the future holds, I will continue to be an advocate for dedicated teachers who are committed to children, and the noble goal of instilling a passion for learning.

Recently, I came across a quote by Albert Einstein, who could not talk until the age of four. He did not learn to read until he was nine. His teachers considered him to be mentally slow, unsociable, and a dreamer. He failed the entrance examination for college. He probably would not have fared well on our state tests. After he developed the theory of relativity he suggested that "Not everything that can be counted counts. Not everything that counts can be counted."

A District Sues

Roger Rapoport

Dr. Melissa Jamula, Reading, Pennsylvania, Superintendent of Schools oversees the fifth-largest school district in Pennnsylvania. But if the No Child Left Behind bureaucracy has its way, the system may soon be shrinking. The mere fact that one of the state's fastest growing districts could suddenly find itself with shuttered schools and be forced to bus its students to other communities is certainly one way to reshuffle the schoolyard deck. But this approach is certainly not what the people of Reading, one of the poorest communities in the state, have in mind. Six of the district's schools have been sent to the NCLB woodshed because they "failed to make adequate yearly progress." The district has been forced to send parents of children attending these "underperforming" schools a letter explaining that they are in year one of a federally mandated "school improvement" program. If parents request, the district is forced to bus children from these six schools to schools that have met the NCLB criteria. And seven other schools have been placed on the NCLB warning list.

If these schools don't pass NCLB muster, the federal government will require a state or private takeover, replacement of administrators and staff, and, in the worst case scenario, actually close the schools altogether.

Why Did NCLB Hit Reading So Hard?

To understand the problem and appreciate why the Reading School District has been the first in the country to file suit to have portions of the No Child Left Behind Act set aside, it's important to understand both the law and how it has been implemented. First, NCLB explicitly states that no district is required to comply with the legislation unless the new program is fully funded. Second, the federal government insists that the crucial tests administered to students under NCLB must be made available to children from non-English speaking families in their native language.

In the case of Reading, neither of these conditions have been met. "To date," says Dr. Jamula, "we have not received one cent to pay for the very expensive and cumbersome testing and special teaching requirements of NCLB." Why did the government break its promise to pay for NCLB?

"You have to understand how the money is allocated," Dr. Jamula explains. "There is some money flowing, but it isn't going to districts like ours to pay for the testing, the curriculum changes, the very complex statistical analysis, the information sent to parents, or the busing to other schools."

Districts like Reading that can't afford to bus students to their own schools are suddenly being compelled to pay the considerable cost of sending them across town. And this does not even begin to count the state funding lost when students are transferred out of district or quit to go to private schools because parents are frightened by the failure letters.

"Even worse," says Dr. Jamula, "the money that we desperately need to comply with the program is going to outside contractors on the theory that we don't have the ability to teach our own students. The government is paying for outside tutors and non-district employees to help us pass the NCLB tests."

Why won't the government give the money to the Reading School District? The answer to this question requires a look at the fuzzy new math of NCLB. First all districts are not created equally. "For example," says Dr. Jamula, "if I were running a small school district all my students would be tested and scored together in one group. This is a tremendous advantage. But in large heterogeneous districts students are split into subgroups. This process is called disaggregation, a big word that basically means breaking the student population down by race, economic background, disabilities, everything except the gifted."

For example, there are subgroups for Latinos, blacks, and kids from low-income families. Some of these students are double-counted because they cross over into two subgroups such as low-income/Latino. There is a separate group for the multiple-handicapped. The kicker is that any school with more than 40 students that fall into one of these subgroups must meet federal performance improvement standards year by year. If one subgroup fails, the entire school fails.

Dr. Jamula says "that is clearly discriminatory against schools serving the poor or diverse student bodies. The irony is that we have a very strong focus on teaching to Pennsylvania standards and benchmarks. But one of the problems for us is that the Pennsylvania test is not in compliance with NCLB law. The act says that non-English language speakers who have been in this country for less than three years have to be given the test in their native language. The problem is that the Pennsylvania Department of Education only provides English language examinations to determine 'adequate yearly progress.' Without a Spanish test we can't fairly test the 11 percent of our students who are in our English language acquisition program. And many of these kids are new. Many of these children are non-English speakers at or below the poverty line. They arrive in September and by March they have to pass a test competing with native English speakers.

"We have asked in our petition that none of our schools be sanctioned until we get technical and financial assistance for schools that are sanctioned.

"By setting these subgroups at a minimum of 40," says the superintendent, "only the large urban districts have to disaggregate. This is clearly discriminatory. And if your students pass the tests you have to have a 95 percent attendance rate. What if there is a flu epidemic or chicken pox, or a flood, not to mention the fact that we have the highest transiency rate in the state. Due in part to our substantial migrant population, more than two-thirds of our students change schools during the year.

"If this country cares about underserved children it should care about pockets of students who aren't part of any subgroup. Just because there aren't 40 similar children in the school, doesn't mean an individual child's needs should be ignored.

"The extra costs we have incurred because of NCLB are just the tip of the iceberg. We need to offer supplemental services but this money can't go to our staff, it has to go to outside tutorial services. In other words, when the funding finally flows, our district won't get any of it. And the money will go to teach kids because their subgroup failed, not because they have the highest priority or the greatest need within the student body. One kid could be doing terribly in a subgroup that passes and that child would not necessarily get any of the NCLB special resource funding. And in any case we won't be able to determine which kids receive the extra help, even if we think they really need it.

"In my view there should be accountability. We've done that in Pennsylvania. Our test is tough. Who knows what would happen to scores in Texas if they had to take a hard test like ours.

"The government should assess us with a fair evaluation system. Schools should be funded fairly and adequately. In this country the kids who have the greatest need have the least amount spent on their education."

MINORITY STUDENTS MOST AFFECTED BY CURRICULUM CHANGES, STUDY REVEALS

Council for Basic Education

Editor's Note: *CBE is a conservative organization that advocates for traditional curriculum in schools. The following excerpts are taken from a CBE news release.*

WASHINGTON—March 8, 2004—The first significant study of how the No Child Left Behind Act is influencing instructional time and professional development in key subject areas reveals that schools are spending more time on reading, math, and science, but squeezing out social studies, civics, geography, languages, and the arts.

The report, conducted by the Council for Basic Education (CBE) and funded by the Carnegie Corporation of New York, says that the shift away from these liberal arts subjects is most pronounced in elementary schools and schools with large minority populations.

The overall curriculum is becoming narrower, the report reveals. For example, elementary school principals reported decreases in instructional time for social studies, civics, and geography. Nearly three in ten principals (29 percent) overall reported decreases in time for social studies, compared to 21 percent who reported increases.

One of the areas subject to the largest cutbacks is the arts. One-quarter (25 percent) of all principals reported decreased instructional time for the arts, with only 8 percent reporting an increase in this area. One-third (33 percent) of all principals anticipate further decreases in arts instructional time, while just 7 percent anticipate increases. . . .

"The narrowing of the curriculum is worrisome because students need exposure to history, social studies, geography, and foreign languages to be fully prepared for citizenship, work, and learning in a rapidly changing world," says Raymond "Buzz" Bartlett, president of the Council for Basic Education. "Truly high expectations cannot begin and end with math, science, and reading."

The most troubling evidence of curricular narrowing occurred in schools with large minority populations, the very populations whose access to a full liberal arts curriculum has been historically most limited. Nearly half (47 percent) of principals at high-minority schools reported decreases in elementary social studies; four in ten (42 percent) anticipated decreases in instructional time for the arts; and three in ten (29 percent) of high-minority school principals foresaw decreases in instructional time for foreign language.

"These findings raise the specter of a new opportunity gap between white and minority students," says Bartlett. "We're seeing that low-income minority students are being denied the liberal arts curriculum that their more privileged counterparts receive as a matter of course. In our effort to close achievement gaps in literacy and math, we risk substituting one form of educational inequity for another, denying our most vulnerable students the kind of curriculum available to the wealthy."

"No Child Left Behind may turn out to be a Pyrrhic victory if we define its vision for achievement too narrowly and thus institutionalize long-term academic mediocrity and inequity," says the report's author, Claus von Zastrow, Director of Institutional Development at CBE.

Full report at <u>cvonzastrow@c-b-e.org</u>

From the State of Lake Wobegon:
A Report of NCLB's Likely Impact on Minnesota.
Office of the Legislative Auditor, State of Minnesota

Editor's Note: The following excerpts are taken from the No Child Left Behind evaluation report Summary #04-04a published in February 2004.

Major Findings

The federal No Child Left Behind (NCLB) Act imposes rigorous new requirements on Minnesota's education accountability system.

- While most education officials in Minnesota embrace the underlying goals of NCLB, many school district superintendents believe that NCLB is costly, unrealistic, and punitive. Local officials have particular concerns about holding students with disabilities and limited English skills to the same standards as other students.

- Even if Minnesota students' math and reading test scores improve significantly in coming years, there will likely be large increases in the number of schools failing to make "adequate yearly progress" (AYP), as defined by NCLB. More than 80 percent of Minnesota elementary schools would not make AYP by 2014, according to a simulation conducted for our office, and many of these schools would face the prospect of restructuring or other serious sanctions prescribed by NCLB.

- NCLB has had limited state and local fiscal impacts so far, but many school districts will likely bear significant new costs in future years for student assessments, sanctions for low-performing schools, and compliance with stricter requirements for staff qualifications. These costs cannot be estimated with precision, but it is quite possible that NCLB's new costs will exceed the increase in NCLB revenues.

- However, Minnesota could lose the majority of its projected $216 million in federal funding for state fiscal year 2005 if it "opts out" of the accountability provisions of NCLB. While federal NCLB funding is less than 4 percent of school districts' operating budgets, relatively few school district superintendents favor opting out.

Recommendations

Changes in the federal NCLB law may be necessary for states to have a realistic chance of complying with the law's goals for student achievement.

SECTION SEVEN

Fighting Back

SECTION SEVEN

Getting Back

FROM OZ TO HOME

Dorothy Watson

Editor's note: *In this brief allegory, presented in San Francisco, November 2003, at the National Council of Teachers of English, Dorothy Watson, Emeritus Professor of the University of Missouri, presents the sad alternatives American teachers are facing in dealing with NCLB.*

It occurred to me that if Hollywood could change the color of Dorothy's magic shoes from silver to red, and Broadway in *The Wiz* and in *Wicked* could put Frank Baum's story to dance and music, I could take a few liberties with the characters in *The Wizard of Oz*. So, here is my considerably altered version of a beloved story.

Mine is a rather short story about a teacher. We'll call her *Teacher-Dorothy*, or *TD* as she is known by her friends. TD found her life disrupted by a tornado—a political NCLB tornado that wrenched her from her happy classroom filled with students enjoying their learning, and deposited her into the terrifying land of Educational Oz. This was an Oz she had never experienced before, an Oz of mandated curriculum and methods, multiple tests, budget deficits, state and federal controls, overwhelming class size, curtailed bilingual programs, teacher bashing, and more than a few flying monkeys.

Finding herself in this sickening dilemma, TD had a fundamental decision to make. Should she stay in Oz, take the medicine doled out for psycho-educational ailments, or should she battle her way back home? Four roads lay before her. Teacher-Dorothy stood at the center of the tangle of roads.

She could take an ordinary-looking path that led her to the village of Mediocrity, where she wouldn't be called on to be particularly good at anything—not even her teaching. She could become a Mediocre Munchkin, never asked to raise a hand or her voice against increasing control and subjugation. Like the easygoing Munchkins, she might even be pleased if *someone else* got rid of the Wicked Witch ruling Mediocrity, but don't ask her to take part in any uprising. No political action for her.

OR . . .

Teacher-Dorothy's second choice wasn't a road at all, but rather an alluring meadow of beautiful, bright red flowers—a meadow that lay at the foot of McCrawl's Hill, a scraggly place with Bushes that appeared on the surface to be glossy and lustrous—Bushes that hid treacherous thorns. Just breathe in the scent of the enticing bouquet coming from this "Leave Your Teachers Behind Poppy Field." A few whiffs of the promises of the poppies and something happens to the brain; notions of being an informed professional slowly slip away. All TD needs to do is lie down, close her eyes, turn off her brain, slumber like a zombie, and wake up just in time for retirement.

OR . . .

TD could take a third road. This beautiful boulevard was glitzy with the promise of making her a star—perhaps a Paradigm Performer in the district's newly adopted controlled literacy program. Like Baum's Dorothy, TD would be Openly Courted to live in this Dainty China Country where she could become a flying monkey herself, after just a few indoctrinating Direct Destruction training sessions. Her Palm Pilot would provide her with a direct link to the wizard in the Emerald City of Oregon. *Everyone* would ask her scientific, replicable opinion and seek her approval. But rather than be tempted with gorgeous frocks of silver and gold, as Dorothy was, TD could have the great satisfaction of ensuring Success for All teachers, helping them become *aware*, with basics of literacy awareness, political-correctness awareness, testing awareness, and, most importantly, phonemic awareness. A publishing company was sure to catch her talents. TD might even star in a series of how to paint the curriculum by numbers. Videotapes (named after her—Dot to Dot) could be made and included in her professional envelopment program. Endless possibilities of rising to the top. Oz does have its enchantments.

OR . . .

Teacher-Dorothy could take the Yellow Brick road. Uprooted by the unexpected, and disrupted by things out of her control, she could make the hard decision to get out of Oz. To do so, she must pass through the "it's good enough" crowd, the "don't rock the boat" mob, and the "it's way harder than I want to work" throng.

The Yellow Brick Road would lead her through the land of Administrivia—the grim country surrounded by razor-pointed high stakes! There, if caught trying to slip through, she would be mandated to preside over the inflicting of "Stan-dardized Assessments for Non-Standardizable Kids" to the wide-eyed wonderful Winkie children. Her curriculum would be called "High Stakes Test Preparation in the Hope to Produce Look-Alike Widget after Widget after Widget."

The Yellow Brick Road also goes right through the land of No Money for Education. There she must free the innocent field mice babies held captive in decaying widget-producing school-factories with peeling lead paint, trailers either too hot or too cold; littered, dangerous, and shrinking playgrounds; and smelly, unsanitary gas station restrooms.

And then before her comes the Hill of the Quadlings. Remember them? The people with big top-nots, whose heads shot forward to smack you flat, as reprisal for speaking against the status quo? Their mantra: "Just say 'Yes'; do as you're told."

* * *

Despite all its frightening obstacles, Teacher-Dorothy chose the Yellow Brick Road. Teaching was a passion to TD, and only on this road would she find the help she needed from friends and colleagues who shared her dedication and commitment to children. Here, she would find others willing to use their brains, their hearts, and their courage to face the course that could be even crueler than the first Dorothy's locked-on green spectacles, deadly poppy fields, vicious lions and tigers and bears, and even the Great Humbug himself.

Teacher-Dorothy took the Yellow Brick Road—because she was a teacher—and there she found her partnership. She found colleagues who were brave, and smart, and always, always were guided by their hearts.

GREAT TEACHERS AND WHAT THEY KNOW

Yetta Goodman

No amount of subsidies from self-interested corporations, think tanks, or special-interest groups trying to demean public education can hide the truth. For better or worse, the American public school system teaches 90 percent of our nation's K-12 children (source U.S. Census Bureau, Internet Release date: January, 2004). Without strong, free public schools, there would be no education in America; just a nightmare where most children have no school to go to while the children of the well- to-do are pampered at elite academies. Our schools are dynamic places where teachers are always developing new curriculum and evaluation techniques that meet all students' needs. America's success reflects the success of great teachers.

Our schools are most successful when they are communities: a partnership of parents, teachers, students, administrators, scholars, and researchers who come together for the sake of learners. Their variety of experiences is brought together to continuously build and develop a learning environment that is safe for learners and awakens their curiosity of the world and their passion for asking important questions.

At the same time that the attempted "deskilling" of educational professionals is taking place, there is a general and growing consensus from within these communities that this kind of partnership is the best way to improve our schools, to make sure that they do a better job of helping students from poor families as we build on their funds of knowledge to enrich our curricula, and that the most important component of creating rich learning opportunities and high achievement for students is a well-qualified teacher. Federal intimidation will not turn competent professionals into technicians who willingly train learners for low-level jobs or who deliver sets of facts as their students turn the pages of dumbed-down textbooks.

We need to build on what we already know about outstanding teachers and the ways to organize enriched learning contexts for all students. Even the NCLB law calls for quality teachers in the classroom, although the bureaucrats naively believe paper and pencil tests are sufficient to measure quality.

What Professional Teachers Know and Do

In a review of a range of teacher research reports, published by the Economic Policy Institute in 2003, Jennifer Rice concludes that teacher quality is the most important school-related factor influencing student achievement. Characteristics that have a positive effect on student achievement include teacher experience and teacher knowledge, with course work in both pedagogy and subject-matter areas.

Wonderful stories about knowledgeable and experienced teachers and their positive influences on lives of learners have been collected over many years by researchers interested in discovering the characteristics of great teachers. In the 1980s Ken Macrorie collected stories of twenty teachers whose "students did good works" and as a result extended their "already considerable powers" (Macrorie, 1984, p. xi). He calls such teachers "enablers," disseminates their stories, and summarizes their principles, methods, and attitudes. He argues that they work in startlingly similar ways and share many attitudes and principles.

"They hold high expectations for learners. They arrange the learning place so that people draw fully on their present powers and begin to do good works. They support and encourage rather then punish. They ask learners to take chances that sometimes result in failure, and to use their mistakes productively. They nurture an environment of truth-telling that puts learners at ease when they are experiencing the excitement and unease of challenge (p. 229)."

These teachers make sure their students are knowledgeable about "the accepted word and discoveries of the authorities" and "the best that has been thought and said in the world, but the experience and thought of the learners also count a great deal" (p. 235).

These teachers know their students well. They help learners to see their errors as opportunities, to exercise their imagination, to make choices and develop responsibility, to cultivate humor, spontaneity, and joy in the classroom, to cultivate rigor, to make practice always an act with meaning. They help learners respond to the world of their peers in helpful rather than damaging ways and find ways of making public the good works of learners (pp. 231–232).

In the 1990s, Mike Rose (Rose, 1995) traveled throughout the U.S. for four years, going to urban, inner-city, and rural areas to study quality classrooms. He documents the good work of teachers and describes the kinds of schools that are possible in America. Rose shows the powerful learning that can take place for students, many of whom are members of the very groups often defined as inferior. These classrooms "represent a dynamic, at times compromised and contested, strain in American educational history; a faith in the capacity of a people, a drive toward equality and opportunity, a belief in the intimate link between mass education and a free society.

"These rooms were embodiments of the democratic ideal. . . . The teachers were working within a tradition realized by a long history of educators working both within the mainstream and outside it, challenging it through working men's organizations and women's groups. Black schools appropriated the ideal, often against political and economic resistance."

"These teachers were using the power of the institution to realize democratic goals for the learners in their charge. . . . They were creating the conditions for children to develop lives of possibility" (p. 412). Similar to Macrorie's enablers, Rose's teachers created a sense of safety and related to this is respect. In these classrooms Rose observed fair treatment, decency, an absence of intimidation, and a respect for the history, the language, and the culture of the peoples represented in the classroom (p. 414). The authority of the teacher came from multiple sources—"knowledge, care, the construction of safe and respectful space, solidarity with student's background." But the students also shared authority as they contributed to "the flow of events, shaped the direction of discussion" and as a result became authorities on their own experience and the work they were doing. The students were the agents of their own development.

Also in the 1990s, Nanci Atwell and colleagues edited a group of books collectively called Workshop (referenced below) written "by and for teachers" to learn more about the teaching of reading and writing. In these monographs, the teachers demonstrate qualities of teaching similar to those found by both Macrorie and Rose. Atwell describes the authors in the monographs as teachers who "understand development is a process of refinement, from meaningful wholes to parts, that children's reading interests are idiosyncratic, that children's reading abilities are based largely on their diverse prior experiences with text." These teachers establish "genuine literacy conversation . . . informal, authentic, open-ended, opinionated, and respectful of others." The teachers' goals are to create lifelong readers and to become the kinds of "teachers to whom children wish to apprentice themselves" (Atwell, 1989 pp. 5-7).

My own observations in many classrooms and from my discussions with many teachers lead me to advocate for Macrorie's, Rose's, and Atwell's discoveries about the characteristics of great teachers and teaching. Given the support of a caring educational community and a belief in their own knowledge and experience, teachers develop opportunities in their classrooms that provide endless possibilities for learning.

Valuing Teacher Knowledge and Experience
Most of the teachers discussed in the research studies above and the millions like them across the country are still hard at work in their classrooms supporting their students, helping them learn

and develop as democratic citizens. Hundreds of thousands of new teachers with similar passion and commitment join them each year. This great teaching force knows how to involve students in exploration of their ideas in respectful ways. They expand students' worlds to new ideas by organizing environments; they provide a respectful, democratic climate where students participate in decision-making about their own problems as well as the problems of the world. They challenge their students and as a result they extend students' interests and motivations.

In a democratic society, it is necessary to support the empowerment of teachers who are capable of unleashing the power of their students to discover their own strengths and abilities, to take responsibility for their own learning, to care for the rights of others and for social justice in our society. Empowered students collaborate with others and at the same time take on leadership roles where they live and work. In such classrooms, teachers have flexible times to respond to the ways in which the students are learning and what they are interested in. Students learn to ask significant questions and their teachers join them in a learning collaborative to find answers, to select a range of reading materials as well as materials from a range of media, to explore their own ideas for writing, and to expand on the knowledge each learner already brings to school supported by the funds of knowledge in their homes and communities. Within such learning environments, evaluation is continuous and includes self-evaluation and reflections as well as occasional tests to permit others to know what and how well they are learning.

I've recently moved into a new house. I have experienced carpenters, upholsterers, wood finishers, landscapers, and rug washers who are enthusiastic about the materials they use, who are able to talk about why they do what they do—I sense their confidence, passion, and caring. I chose them not because of their scores on tests of their fields but rather because each is knowledgeable. I admired the work of these professional artists. What I see in great teachers is similar: a confidence, passion, and caring for their profession. For teachers this means the creative organization of a rich environment and supportive community in which students flourish. We need to move from the time of the pedagogy of the absurd to the pedagogy of the liberated; the pedagogy of possibility.

The research that Atwell, Macrory and Rose report (referenced below) and my own wide range of experience with teachers highlight the importance of recognizing and honoring teachers' knowledge and experience. There are some in the field of educational research who have such narrow views about how to judge teachers and teaching that they ignore and dismiss this kind of research. Such research, known as action research or teacher research, involves a long-standing research tradition that values the stories of classrooms and schools based on carefully documented observations and in-depth analysis of the work of students. Their growth and development through their actual classroom experiences are clearly demonstrated.

I, therefore, end this plea for the public to acknowledge the importance of great teaching by making available a list of books selected from hundreds more, written mostly by classroom teachers, that include not only the voices of knowledgeable and experienced teachers and principals but also the voices of their students. I highlight teachers and principals who not only engage students in rich learning opportunities but take the time and energy to write about their research, their classrooms, and their students in order to share their results with others. I have selected books that are accessible not only to teachers and researchers but which speak to parents and the general public about the possibilities in our public school classrooms. From these research narratives, we learn important lessons about learning and teaching.

Teachers and Principals Publish

Allen, J., Michalove, B., & Schockley, B. (1993). *Engaging Children: Community and Chaos in the Lives of Young Learners.* Portsmouth, NH: Heinemann.

Atwell, N. (1998/2nd). *In the middle: New understandings about writing, reading, and learning* (2nd ed.). Portsmouth, NH: Boynton/Cook.

Atwell, N. (Ed). (1989, 1990, 1991). *Workshops 1–3 by and for teachers: Writing and literature.* Portsmouth, NH: Heinemann.

Avery, C. (2002). *And with a light touch: Learning about reading, writing, and teaching with first graders* (2nd ed.). Portsmouth, NH: Heinemann.

Berger, Ron. (2003). *An Ethic of Excellence. Building a Culture of Craftsmanship With Students.* Portsmouth, NH: Heinemann.

Bird, L. Bridges. (Ed.) (1989). *Becoming a whole language school: The Fair Oaks story.* Katonah, NY: Richard C. Owen.

Bomer, R. (1995). *Time for meaning: Crafting literate lives in middle and high school.* Portsmouth, NH: Heinemann.

Brady, S. & Jacobs, S. (1994). *Mindful of others: Teaching children to teach.* Portsmouth, NH: Heinemann.

Carr, Janine Chapell. (1999). *A Child Went Forth: Reflective Teaching With Young Readers and Writers.* Portsmouth, NH: Heinemann.

Chandler, K. (and the Mapleton Teacher-Research Group) (1999). *Spelling inquiry: How one elementary school caught the mnemonic plague.* York, ME: Stenhouse.

Christensen, L. (2000). *Reading, writing, and rising up: Teaching about social justice and the power of the written word.* Milwaulkee, WI: A Rethinking Schools Publication.

Clyde, J.; Condon, M. (2000). *Get real: Bringing kids' learning lives into the classroom.* York, MN: Stenhouse.

Cordeiro, P. (1992). *Whole learning: Whole language and content in the upper elementary grades.* NY: Richard C. Owen Publishers, Inc.

Dragan, Pat Barrett. (2003). *Everything You Need to Know to Teach First Grade*. Portsmouth, NH. Heinemann.

Draper, S. (2000). *Teaching from the heart: Reflections, encouragement, and inspiration*. Portsmouth, NH: Heinemann.

Draper, S. (2001). *Not quite burned out but crispy around the edges: Inspiration, laughter, and encouragement for teachers*. Portsmouth, NH: Heinemann.

Duthie, C. (1996). *True Stories*. York, ME: Stenhouse Publishers.

Ehrenworth, M. (2003). *Looking to write: Students writing through the visual arts*. Portsmouth, NH: Heinemann.

Fisher, B. (1995). *Thinking and learning together: Curriculum and community in a primary classroom*. Portsmouth, NH: Heinemann.

Fisher, B. (1998). *Joyful learning in kindergarten* (Revised Ed.). Portsmouth, NH: Heinemann.

Fraser, J. & Skolnick, D. (1994). *On their way: Celebrating second graders as they read and write*. Portsmouth, NH: Heinemann.

Gallas, K. (1994). *The language of learning: How children talk, write, dance, draw, and sing their understanding of the world*. New York: Teachers College Press.

Gallas, K. (1995). *Talking their way into science: Hearing children's questions and theories, responding with curricula*. New York: Teachers College Press.

Glover, M. (1993). *Two years: A teacher's memoir*. Portsmouth, NH: Heinemann.

Glover, M. & Sheppard, L. (1989). *Not on your own: The power of learning together*. New York: Scholastic.

Graf, M. (2000). *The world's best places: Classroom explorations in geography and environmental science*. Portsmouth, NH: Heinemann.

Gust, J. (1999). *Round peg, square hole: A teacher lives and learns in Watts*. Portsmouth, NH: Heinemann.

Harwayne, S. (1999). *Going public: Priorities and practice at The Manhattan New School*. Portsmouth, NH: Heinemann.

Harwayne, S. (2000). *Lifetime guarantees: Toward ambitious literacy teaching.* Portsmouth, NH: Heinemann.

Hindley, J. (1996). *In the company of children.* Portland, ME: StenhousePublishers

Jorgensen, K. (1993). *History workshop: Reconstructing the past with elementary students.* Portsmouth, NH: Heinemann.

Jorgensen, K. (2001). *The whole story: Crafting fiction in the upper elementary grades.* Portsmouth, NH: Heinemann.

Kittle, P. (2003). *Public teaching: One kid at a time.* Portsmouth, NH: Heinemann.

Kohl, H. (1967). *36 Children.* New York: New American Library.

Lensmire, T. (1994). *When children write: Critical re-visions of the writing workshop.* New York: Teachers College Press.

Lensmire, T. (2000). *Powerful writing: Responsible teaching.* New York: Teachers College Press.

Levy, S. (1996). *Starting from scratch: One classroom builds its own curriculum.* Portsmouth, NH: Heinemann.

Macrorie, K. (1944) *Twenty Teachers.* New York: Oxford University Press.

Madigan, D. & Koivu-Rybicki, V. (1997). *The writing lives of children.* York, ME: Stenhouse.

Meier, D. (1995). *The power of their ideas: lessons for America from a small school in Harlem.* Boston: Beacon Press.

Meier, D. (2000). *Scribble scrabble: Learning to read and write (Success with diverse teachers, children, and families).* New York: Teachers College Press.

Miller, D. (2002) *Reading with meaning.* Portsmouth, ME: Stenhouse Publishers.

Newkirk, T. (Ed). (1994). *Workshop 5 by and for teachers: The writing process revisited.* Portsmouth, NH: Heinemann.

Ostrow, J. (1995). *A room with a different view: First through third graders build community and create curriculum.* York, ME: Stenhouse Publishers.

Paley, V. (1992). *You can't say you can't play.* Cambridge, MA: Harvard University Press.

Paley, V. (1997). *The girl with the brown crayon.* Cambridge, MA: Harvard University Press.

Rief, L. (1992). *Seeking diversity: Language arts with adolescents.* Portsmouth, NH: Heinemann.

Rief, L. (1998). *Vision and voice: Extending the literacy spectrum* (multimedia CD included). Portsmouth, NH: Heinemann.

Rogovin, P. (1998). *Classroom Interviews: A world of learning.* Portsmouth, NH: Heinemann.

Rogovin, P. (2001). *The research workshop: Bringing the world into your classroom.* Portsmouth, NH: Heinemann.

Romano, T. (1987). *Clearing the way: Working with teenage writers.* Portsmouth, NH: Heinemann.

Romano, T.(1995). *Writing with passion: Life stories, multiple genres.* Portsmouth, NH: Boynton/Cook–Heinemann.

Rose, M. (1995). *Possible Lives: The Promise of Public Education in America.* Boston: Houghton Mifflin Company.

Tovini, C. (2000). *I read it but I don't get it.* Portsmouth, ME: Stenhouse Publishers.

Tovini, C. (2004). *Do I Really Have to Teach Reading?* Portsmouth, ME: Stenhouse Publishers.

Whitmore, K. & Crowell, C. (1994). *Inventing a classroom: Life in a bilingual, whole language learning community.* York, ME: Stenhouse Publishers.

Wilde, J. (1993). *A Door Opens: Writing in the fifth grade.* Portsmouth, ME: Stenhouse Publishers.

Wormeli, R. (2001). *Meet me in the middle.* Portsmouth, ME: Stenhouse Publishers.

Wormeli, R. (2003). *Day One and Beyond.* Portsmouth, ME: Stenhouse Publishers.

If You Want to Know More About No Child Left Behind
compiled by Yetta Goodman and the authors

Annotated Bibliography

Allington, Richard L. (2002). *Big brother and the national reading curriculum: How ideology trumped evidence.* Portsmouth, NH: Heinemann. 0-325-00513-3
The author argues that no research supports the sort of federal intrusion on local decision-making that characterizes NCLB mandates. Further, the "corrective actions" for schools that fail to meet the federal standards likewise have no research base. The NCLB is driven more by ideology than by evidence.

Berliner, David C.; Biddle, Bruce J. (1995). *The manufactured crisis: Myths, fraud, and the attack on America's public schools.* Reading, MA: Addison-Wesley. 0-201-44196-9
The underlying assumption that America's schools have failed is challenged by the authors, who demonstrate, with credible data, that public schools are performing well for many American citizens. The myth of overall public school failure, on which NCLB is based, appears to be unsupportable. On the other hand, the authors also document why public schools rarely succeed in poor communities and suggests that nothing in NCLB addresses the issues that keep these schools from succeeding.

Bracey, Gerald W. (2004). *On the death of childhood and the destruction of public schools: The folly of today's education policies and practices.* Portsmouth, NH: Heinemann.
Gerald Bracey is public schools' best defender. With authority, sensitivity, and a good sense of humor, he dis-

mantles the negative PR our public education system has endured and does it with hardcore data, not phony "science." Bracey delivers the statistics and skilled analysis that prove public schools are doing much better than critics claim.

Coles, Gerald. (2002). *Reading the naked truth: Literacy, legislation, and lies.* Portsmouth, NH: Heinemann.

In clear, straight-forward prose, the author examines the research used in the National Reading Panel (NRP) Report, the document used to justify the Reading First instructional mandates in No Child Left Behind legislation. Through a close appraisal of the actual studies, the book reveals how the NRP misrepresented the actual research findings and explains why there is no scientific basis for mandating the pre-packaged, skills-heavy, one-size-fits-all beginning reading instruction in the NCLB. The author also discusses the political context of Reading First/NCLB within the Bush administration's wider policy agenda.

Edelsky, C. (1999). *Making justice our project.* Urbana, IL: NCTE.

The author shows many examples of education aimed at creating thoughtful citizens. Unlike the education promoted under NCLB, these examples inculcate a "civic attitude" and are what Jefferson intended when he argued that for a democracy, the citizens must be educated.

Emery, Kathy and Susan Ohanian. (2004) *Why is corporate America bashing public schools?* Portsmouth, NH: Heinemann.

The authors address the question, Where exactly did high-stakes testing come from anyway? Neither parents, teachers, administrators, nor school boards demanded it, and now many communities feel powerless to stanch its appalling effect. Hot on the scent of the testing masterminds and peeling back layer upon layer of documentation, Emery and Ohanian found a familiar scent at the end of the paper trail. Corporate money, CEOs, and American big business have blanketed U.S. public education officials with their influence and their drive to un-democratize public education. The result is a many-tentacled private-public monster.

Garan, Elaine. (2003). *Resisting Reading Mandates: How to Triumph with the Truth.* Portsmouth, NH: Heinemann.
The author helps teachers dejargonize the "scientific research" and the glut of mandates that are strangling schools, hurting kids, and diminishing the roles of teachers in their own profession. It uses the very words of the National Reading Panel to empower teachers to talk back to the "research says" claims by providing easy-to-understand facts about scripted commercial programs and phonics. Many teachers have used this book to actually change education policy, and to make wise decisions in the selection of curriculum and teaching methods.

Garan, Elaine. (2004). *In Defense of Our Children: When Politics, Profit and Education Collide.* Portsmouth, NH: Heinemann.
This easy-to-read, user-friendly book guides parents and teachers through all the hot-button issues in education. In it, the author cuts through the jargon and the buzzwords to help readers ask questions and find answers to what school "reform," reading methods, high-stakes testing and "back to basics" teaching methods really mean for our children. Garan also pulls back the curtain and shows the financial conflicts of interest that coincidentally profit many of the researchers who are pushing government-favored programs *and* reforms. She helps parents and teachers to discover how to help their children become leaders, thinkers, and doers instead of blind followers destined for low-level jobs and dim futures.

Goodman, Kenneth S. (Ed.) (1998). *In defense of good teaching: What teachers need to know about the "Reading Wars"* York, ME: Stenhouse. 1-57110-086-5

The author collected these articles at the height of what the press was calling the reading wars. They refute, with data from the National Assessment of Educational Progress, the unwarranted charge that whole-language teachers had created a literacy crisis. The authors document the campaign that coordinated the attack on whole language and on the hard-working teachers who had created the movement.

Kohn, Alfie and Shannon, Patrick (Eds.) (2002) *Education, inc.* Portsmouth, NH: Heinemann.

The authors collect an eclectic set of articles which describe, discuss, and critique the business insurgence into American public schools. The book builds a convincing case against those who see students as customers or workers.

Krashen, Stephen. (1999). *Three arguments against whole language and why they are wrong.* Portsmouth, NH: Heinemann 032500119-7

NCLB rests firmly on a view of reading that says that good readers ignore context, that they process each letter of each word individually and that "skills-based" instruction is better than meaning-based instruction. These arguments have appeared in the popular as well as the professional press. The author argues that all three of these arguments are wrong and that the scientific case for "whole language" remains very strong.

Lent, ReLeah C. and Gloria Pipkin. (2003). *Silent no more: Voices of courage in American schools.* Portsmouth, NH: Heinemann.

Among the first-person narratives of teachers who've taken costly, principled stands on critical issues in education are those of Joanne Yatvin, who wrote the minority report to the National Reading Panel's findings; Steve Orel, who was fired from his position as an adult education instructor after he advocated for 522 students pushed out of Birmingham city schools a few weeks before state tests were given; and James Hope, who underwent a three-year ordeal that threatened him with loss of his Georgia teaching license for posting a few bad test items to a web site maintained by parent activists.

Ohanian, Susan. (1999). *One size fits few: The folly of educational standards.* Portsmouth, NH: Heinemann.
Filled with anecdotes and analysis, the author introduces the word "Standardisto." She provides educators and parents with ammunition to fight the corporate-politico agenda that infects schools today.

Ohanian, Susan (Foreword by Alfie Kohn) (2002). *What happened to recess and why are our children struggling in kindergarten?* New York: McGraw-Hill. 0-07-138326-3
Schools under pressure to meet NCLB test score requirements put ugly pressures on children. Starting with the issues raised in the book's title, the author documents these pressures.

Shannon, Patrick. (1989). *Reading poverty.* Heinemann.
Poverty has everything to do with schooling—how it is theorized, how it is organized, and how it runs. The author presents a detailed analysis of the different political representations of poverty and its causes, and demonstrates how each offers America a different direction for schooling and the future.

Shannon, Patrick. (2001). *iSHOP/You shop.* Heinemann
Shopping is a metaphor for asking questions about things, ideas, and consequences, and buying is a metaphor for making decisions about our lives. The author asks us to answer

the question, "What do you really want for our schools and children." He suggests that we better shop around.

Smith, Frank. (2004). *Unspeakable acts, unnatural practices: Flaws and fallacies in "scientific" reading instruction.* Portsmouth, NH: Heinemann.

The title of this book is to be taken literally. Direct reading instruction that is claimed to be "scientific" is founded on phonic activities that are unspeakable and instructional practices that are unnatural. The mandated approach to literacy instruction through phonics and phonemic awareness is a linguistic impossibility.

Taylor, Denny. (1998). *Beginning to read and the spin doctors of science: The political campaign to change America's mind about how children learn to read.* Urbana, IL: NCTE 0-8141-0275-1

This is the first of the whistle-blower books on the faulty science of President Bush and his leave-no-child-behind-no-teacher-standing educational policies. The author undermines the Texas Miracle and the California catastrophe, and exposes the ties between Washington and Big Business.

Websites to Find More About NCLB
compiled by Yetta Goodman and Georgia Hedrick

Connect For Kids – Connect For Kids Weekly
OneWorld.net
http://www.oneworld.net/link/gotolink/addhit/29036

NCLB: conspiracy, compliance, or creativity
The Hayes Mizell reader Remarks of Hayes Mizell on April 25, 2003, to the spring conference of the Maryland Council of Staff Developers
http://www.middleweb.com/HMnclb.html

V.84 No. 9 Pages 67-9–686/May 2003: Mathis
NO CHILD LEFT BEHIND Costs and Benefits
http://www.pdkintl.org/kappan/k0305mat.htm

IEA - Illinois Education Association
Millions Rev Up for Read Across America - NEA.org (2/20/2004).
More States Joining Rebellion Against NCLB - NEA.org
(2/20/2004). In the news archive.
http://www.jeanea.org

FairTest
The National Center for Fair & Open Testing
http://www.fairtest.org/

Rouge Forum
The Rouge Forum is a group of educators, students, and parents
seeking a democratic society. They learn about equality and social
justice, and adapt what they learn to teaching practice. The group
unites people across union boundaries, across community lines,
and across the fences of race and gender.
http://www.rougeforum.org

http://www.rethinkingschools.org/special_reports/bushplan/
nclb181.shtml

http://www.susanohanian.org/show_nclb_news.html

http://www.ed.gov/nclb/landing/jhtml

http://nochildleft.com/links.html

http://www.journalnet.com/articles/2003/12/12/news/local/
news11.txt

http://www.thecourier.com/opinion/columns/CM12904.htm

http://www.ceopa.org

http://www.edweek.com

An Afterword:
What Needs to Be Done to Save and Improve Our Schools
Ken Goodman

Nothing in this book was intended to suggest that our schools are perfect or do not need improvement. But we need to start with a reality base. Our public schools are among the best the world has yet achieved. We reached a point until the mean-spirited test-driven attack on our public schools began to kick in where we had some remarkable achievements to be proud of:

- Our schools were becoming truly inclusive. We had opened free access to education through high school to all economic levels of society and to even the most severely handicapped of our young people.
- An increasingly high percentage of our youth were finishing secondary schools.
- We had the highest rate of young people reaching and completing some level of higher education of any nation in the world.
- Our teaching staff was increasingly professional. Our requirements for certification at both elementary and secondary levels were high. In some states the majority of teachers held masters degrees.
- Educational research and theory had provided the base for effective, positive curricula and methods that were making it possible for a wider range of pupils to succeed and be motivated to stay in schools.

Nevertheless, our schools are not all they could be. There are a number of reasons for this but they all come from a single root: a low priority placed on education which denied our school system the resources necessary to be fully successful. Ours is a rich country with the means to conduct expensive space programs and military interventions. It is absurd that, in the 21st century, rebuilding the schools of Iraq has a higher priority than full support of our own schools.

Lack of adequate support for education has led to the following conditions:

Decaying school facilities. As a nation we care more about the condition of our sports facilities than we do about the condition of our school buildings.

A shortage of professional teachers. Inadequate salaries for teachers is a major factor in not attracting enough young people to become teachers. Even so, many young people choose teaching as a career because they want a socially useful occupation. Many choose to teach in rural or inner city schools because they see a need to be fulfilled. These heroic teachers find themselves blamed for the failures of the system. Disrespect for teachers by our politicians and media is making teaching a less and less attractive professional choice And the negative attack on teachers built into NCLB and regressive state laws is driving the most dedicated out of teaching.

Unequal Support. The amount of funding available for any child's education is very much a function of where he or she lives. Children growing up in rural areas or slums are far less well supported than those in middle-class or upper-income communities. They are more likely to have uncertified teachers, dilapidated and unsafe school rooms, outdated materials and insufficient supplies. NCLB claims to address this problem—but it does so by demanding the same test performance for all children regardless of this unequal support. The law punishes diversity and rewards schools that push low achievers out of their classrooms. NCLB punishes the teachers and the local communities for society's failure. And it accelerates the drop out rate among those least favored in our society.

What Needs to Be Done

Repealing NCLB is certainly necessary. But it is only the most recent act in a sustained attack on our public schools. Laws in many states are equally absurd—trying to bring increased educational achievement through unreasonable demands and punishments for schools, teachers and pupils.

The Bush administration is trying to institutionalize the anti-public schools agenda, from restrictions on what counts and may be funded as research to how the federal bureaucracy controls curriculum, methodology, testing, teacher certification and teacher education. All this needs to be undone. The slogans and unachievable promises of a law that claimed to leave no child behind are a clever cover for the systematic destruction of our hard won universal free public education system.

Here are some essentials that must happen to save our schools:

- The American people must come to the defense of their neighborhood schools. Its not enough to get the full funding the administration promised. Parents must demand the state and federal politicians and bureaucrats get out of their kids classrooms.
- This must be part of a national recognition that education is the highest priority for our nation and that there are no cheap quick fixes. We can find a cure for cancer but not by punishing the patients and professionals for not achieving one, We can have highly effective schools but not by punishing kids and teachers for not getting there yet.
- The education profession needs to unite with parents to defend and improve neighborhood schools. Their unions and professional organizations need to develop a strong positive agenda built around safe strongly supported neighborhood schools that serve all pupils well .
- The press and the media must shine a light on the absurdi-

ties masquerading as school reform. NCLB and the attack on public schools were sold to the American people through expensive and highly sophisticated public relations campaigns that misled communities around the nation. Partly that's because many major media outlets are controlled by multinational corporations whose aims are the same as those of the National Business Roundtable and the neoconservative think tanks that have funded and managed the campaign. Fortunately some enterprising journalists have seen through this fraud. It's important to encourage them in their efforts to save our schools.

- The attack on public education is shifting to an attack on professional teacher education. In mid 2004, funding for an investigation of education colleges was hidden in a unrelated appropriations bill and passed by Congress without debate. It will look at whether the colleges are teaching the federally mandated "evidence based" methodology in reading and math. NCLB and other laws seek to put controls in the hands of the same bureaucrats in Washington who've taken control of the public elementary and secondary schools. Alternate certification programs are being promoted to bypass professional teacher education entirely. In Idaho, reading educators in the state's universities and colleges are being forced to adopt a methodology developed and promoted by Albertson's super markets.

- University faculty and their professional organizations need to see the attack on professional education as an attack on the autonomy of the university in America.

To reverse the damage done by the campaign to discredit and destroy our public schools, there are some actions that need to happen:

Immediately the parents, leaders and professionals in every community need to organize to defend their neighborhood ele-

mentary and secondary schools. They need to reject the labels, the high-stakes tests, and the outside interventions. If necessary they need to opt out and reject the money NCLB promises- it's an illusion anyway.

Local school boards need to reject the pressures to conform to federal mandates. Parents need to become active in local school board elections and demand the welfare of children and young people become the key criterion for local decision-making. School boards need to show respect for their professional staff and their students and to create a positive atmosphere of mutual trust and respect.

State legislators, state school boards and the professionals in the state departments of education need to take back their constitutional authority to make policy for their state's schools. They must reject the federal government's shift from supporting state and local education to controlling them. In doing so they need to involve all those with a stake in the state's education programs in a calm and informed reconsideration of the condition of their state's schools and what they need to serve all pupils well.

And at the national level a similar effort needs to go into bringing together all groups in American society to consider, calmly and without finger pointing, a long-range plan for achieving what has always been the mission of our system of free, universal, public education. This plan should be given the high priority that education at all levels deserves. American education does not exist in a vacuum. It is a part of American life and culture and any changes need to be done with a sense of the history and traditions that have made it what it is.

Neither can we consider our education apart from that of the rest of world. Many of the same forces that have created this critical situation in the U.S. are also present in other developed and developing nations. The children in the shoe factories and sweat shops of Asia and the cocoa farms of Africa are victims of the same multinational companies seeking to control American education. Just as American prosperity required that we get our children out of the factories, mills and fields and into school, we need to help other nations to get all of their children into schools. The policies of the World Bank and International Monetary Fund have often forced developing nations to reduce their spending on schools and social service to qualify for aid.

Developing nations don't need us to tell them how to run their schools. There are in fact in many parts of the world, a rising level of teacher professionalism and a growing access to schooling. Through international organizations like UNICEF and UNESCO we can not only help the children of the world but we can regain some of the respect that our military and economic adventures have lost for the United States.

A Final Hope
Elsewhere in this book I said I've come to regard this period in education as the Pedagogy of the Absurd. NCLB is an absurd law. Its mandates, procedures, implementations and evaluations are webs of absurdity including the ultimate absurdity—that in 14 years—or any period for that matter, all students could achieve test scores expressly set to be achieved by only 20 percent of test takers. Even more absurd is that politicians, journalists, professional educators and the public are treating this absurdity seriously. I know that at some time in the future people will look back at this period and see the absurdities for what they are. They will say—as we do about the holocaust—how could people not only have not seen the absurdity but actually participated in attempting to carry it out. I have no doubt that sanity will return; in fact, as this book goes to press, polls are showing a major trend toward public awareness and rejection of NCLB.

I cannot believe that those who planned and executed this attempt to privatize American education will succeed in destroying our public schools. But I shudder to think of the price that will have been paid by the victims: children deprived of joyful childhood in kindergartens without recess, or overage pupils repeating grades because of failed high-stakes tests, and tedious skill and drill classrooms in the hands of harassed and unhappy teachers forced to teach with methods and materials they abhor. How many adolescents will drop out or be pushed out of secondary schools that have no place for them? How many of the best teachers will quit rather than participate in the absurdity?

The hope of the editors and contributors to this book is that sanity will come sooner rather than later and American schools will be set back on the road to accept and educate all of our young people.

CONTRIBUTORS

Book Editors

Kenneth S. Goodman is Professor Emeritus, University of Arizona, College of Education, Department of Language, Reading and Culture, Tucson. His research and theory about the reading process has earned respect among language arts educators everywhere. He offers scientific information and evidence to support his beliefs about the misinformation that has contributed to the current confusion about testing and how children read and write.

Patrick Shannon is Professor of Education, Pennsylvania State University, Dept. Of Curriculum and Instruction, University Park. He is a former preschool and primary grade teacher who studies the politics that surround reading policies, programs, and practices. His current project is an investigation of adolescents' construction of the purposes of history through film and fiction.

Yetta M. Goodman is Regents Professor of Education, University of Arizona, College of Education, Tucson. In addition to her research in early literacy, miscue analysis and reading and writing processes, she has popularized the term kidwatching and advocates for public acknowledgment of professional educators' knowledge and experience.

Roger Rapoport is an investigative reporter and editor. He has written about higher education, the nuclear weapons industry, California politics, technology and medicine. His previous books include, *Hillsdale: Greek Tragedy in America's Heartland*, *The Great American Bomb Machine*, *California Dreaming: The Political Odyssey of Pat and Jerry Brown*, and *The Superdoctors*. He lives in Michigan and California.

Authors of Articles

John C. Aerni is a high school teacher in the Kwethluk Community School in the lower Kuskokwim School District in rural Alaska.

Jo Beth Allen is a researcher and professor at the Department of Language Education, College of Education, The University of Georgia, Athens, Georgia. She often collaborates with classroom teachers to study literacy learning and instructional practices.

Richard L. Allington is a researcher and professor at the University of Florida, College of Education, Gainesville, Florida. He is incoming president of the International Reading Association. He studies and writes extensively about special education and literacy issues.

David Berliner is a researcher and Regents Professor in the Department of Educational Leadership and Policy Studies at the Arizona State University, Tempe. He has published landmark books and articles about testing and cross cultural comparisons.

Mary L. Fahrenbruck is a doctoral student at the University of Arizona, College of Education, Department of Language, Reading and Culture, Tucson

Bruce Fuller is a Professor of Education and Public Policy at the University of California, Berkeley. He is a director of Policy Analysis for California Education, a cooperative venture between U.C. Berkeley, U.C. Davis and Stanford University.

Wendy Goodman is a bilingual classroom teacher in the Tucson Unified School District, Tucson, Arizona who publishes articles and books on literacy and social studies learning.

James V. Hoffman, researcher and professor at the University of Texas, College of Education, Department of Curriculum and Instruction, Austin, consults in many countries on teacher education, reading instruction and reading research.

Farin Houk-Cerna, a kindergarten teacher at the Lister School in Tacoma, Washington writes a monthly column for the *Tacoma News Tribune.*

George Madaus is a professor and researcher at the Lynch School of Education at Boston College. He studies and writes about testing, measurement and public policy issues.

Richard J. Meyer is a researcher and professor at the University of New Mexico, College of Education, in the department of Language, Literacy and Sociocultural Studies, Albuquerque. He works collaboratively with teachers in their classrooms.

Jill Mora researches, teaches and writes about language minority students in the School of Teacher Education at San Diego State University. She is presently directing a cross cultural teacher education program in Mexico.

John Novack, an assistant director of research and evaluation in the Long Beach Unified School District, also lectures at the University of Southern California.

Jerry Parks is the retired principal of Corse Elementary School in Burlington, Iowa.

Kathleen Rhoades is a doctoral candidate at the Lynch School of Educationis a PhD candidate in the Lynch School of Education at Boston College.

Ruth Sáez Vega researches and teaches in the Facultad de

Educacion, Universidad de Puerto Rico, San Juan, Puerto, Rico. She consults and does teacher workshops in many countries throughout Latin America.

Misty Sailors teaches in the Department of Interdisciplinary Studies, Curriculum and Instruction, in the College of Education and Human Development, University of Texas in San Antonio.

Steve Strauss is a neurologist in the Department of Medicine, Division of Clinical Neurophysiology, Franklin Square Hospital, Baltimore, Maryland. He also has a doctorate in linguistics

Thomas G. Sticht, an International Consultant in Adult Education recently received the Ghandi Medal for his work. He lives in El Cajon, CA.

Dorothy Watson, Professor Emerita at the University of Missouri, College of Education, Columbia, Missouri consults with schools and teachers about the teaching of reading.

INDEX

WE WELCOME YOUR COMMENTS

The publisher of *Saving Our Schools: The Case For Public Education In America* welcomes your comments and suggestions. If you have a No Child Left Behind story that you would like us to consider for our website or a future edition of this book, please e-mail it to KGoodman@u.arizona.edu or mail it to RDR Books 2415 Woolsey Street, Berkeley, CA 94705, or you can fax us at (510) 228-0300. We'd also like to hear how you've used this book in furthering the fight against No Child Left Behind.